Lincoln Christian College

592

632

D1206969

CHARLES II AND THE
CAVALIER HOUSE OF COMMONS
1663-1674

Author and Publishers are
indebted to the trustees
of
THE TAIT FUND
for a contribution towards
the cost of publication

CHARLES II
AND THE CAVALIER
HOUSE OF COMMONS
1663–1674

by

D. T. WITCOMBE
B.Litt., M.A. Oxford, Ph.D. Manchester

MANCHESTER UNIVERSITY PRESS
BARNES & NOBLE, INC., NEW YORK

© 1966 D. T. WITCOMBE

All Rights Reserved

MANCHESTER UNIVERSITY PRESS
316–324 OXFORD ROAD
MANCHESTER 13, ENGLAND

First published
in the United States
1966
BARNES & NOBLE, INC.
105 Fifth Avenue, New York 3

for

PAT

Printed in Great Britain by Butler and Tanner Ltd
Frome and London

942.066
W81
c.1.

FOREWORD

THE Parliaments of Charles II have attracted the attention of numerous historians in recent years. Two major contributions have been made, one by an American scholar, Mary W. Helms, in her intensive examination of the 1660 House of Commons in an as-yet-unpublished Bryn Mawr dissertation, and the other by J. R. Jones, *The First Whigs*, a careful study of the three Exclusion Parliaments. But until the appearance of Dr Witcombe's work about all we had on the Long Parliament of Charles II was W. C. Abbott's article, published almost sixty years ago.

To understand why parliamentary monarchy, restored with such high hopes in 1660, failed to work, it is necessary to ask how and why Charles could not find a *modus vivendi* with the 'Cavalier' House of Commons elected in 1661. To these questions Dr Witcombe has provided some provocative answers.

This book is primarily (and correctly) based on a meticulous study of the *Journals* and the published debates. But along with these, the author has made extensive use of certain important manuscript collections, especially the Carte and Tanner MSS. in the Bodleian, the Verney MSS. at Claydon, and the Coventry papers at Longleat. From these and many other sources he has been able to construct a clear and detailed narrative of what went on in the Lower House during the eleven crucial years before the emergence of Danby as chief minister.

Dr Witcombe has demolished the idea, so attractive and convenient, of a neat two-party system. In place of disciplined 'court' and 'country' parties logically and inevitably opposed to one another, he presents a picture of complicated grouping, shifting allegiances, and confused motives. He also points up the fact that, given the evidence presently available to us, we cannot ascertain the actual affiliations of the vast central mass of silent back-benchers whose actions were recorded only in anonymous divisions. 26560

This work has had many readers in its dissertation form. News of its completion evoked numerous requests to see it, and copies have been passed from hand to hand on both sides of the

v

Atlantic. It is thus a pleasure to see it, in revised form, in print so that it may reach the larger audience it deserves.

BASIL D. HENNING

Saybrook College
  Yale.

PREFACE

I am surprised that my ancestors should ever have permitted such an institution to come into existence. I am a
stranger, and found it here when I arrived, so that I am
obliged to put up with what I cannot get rid of.

James I on Parliament

JAMES' gloomy acceptance of an irritating, yet not intolerable,
partnership echoed Elizabeth and anticipated William. To
have a 'company of fellows' looking into all your actions must
always be an irritation to any head of state, but the annoyance
could only be increased when the critics were frequently im-
practical and ignorant, and the head of state no mere representative of the people but the elect of God. Yet the existence
of a Parliament need not necessarily destroy the effectiveness or
independence of the executive. In the sixteenth, and again in the
eighteenth century flattery, organization, and, where necessary,
a bribe won for the executive the grants of money which made
possible the continuance of government, just as the discipline
of political parties secures these grants today. Parliament was,
after all, no monolithic institution. Its decisions were those of
some three to four hundred individuals—of those in other words
who troubled to attend debates—and if two hundred and fifty
members could be persuaded to support the sovereign's ministers, then that was all that was required. Nevertheless, in the
seventeenth century these two hundred and fifty votes proved
elusive, and, despairing of winning them, three kings and a
military dictator came to feel that their authority could not be
maintained without the abolition, temporary or permanent, of
parliamentary institutions.

One of those who came to this conclusion was Charles II.
Within ten years of his ecstatic reception by a parliamentary
assembly Charles' exasperation had become so great that he
was ready to embark on the most hare-brained of plots to find a
substitute for parliamentary supply. Whether the breakdown
of the constitution which followed his attempt was inevitable
remains an open question, nor can those who believe that it was
avoidable agree upon whom to blame. The following detailed

study of eleven sessions of Charles' longest Parliament may perhaps shed some light on these questions, and on the wider issue of how far parliamentary monarchy was a practical possibility in the seventeenth century.

It may of course be objected that this is not new ground. The politics of Charles II's reign have attracted the attention of many previous historians, and it might be thought that there can be little to add to their accounts. Here the word 'detailed' in the previous paragraph may serve for explanation. Despite the many studies already completed there has been no previous attempt to take the day-to-day record of the Journals, and of the parliamentary diaries, and to make this, rather than the commentary provided by letters, diaries and memoirs the centre of a narrative. Relying on the latter type of source previous writers have often offered interpretations without fully describing the events which have to be explained; by concentrating on the duller routine account of how the House of Commons spent its time I hope to have provided not only a new interpretation, which must be subject to revision, but also a foundation on which future interpretations can be based.

Once we turn to commentary we at once face a major difficulty. Although the *decisions* of the House of Commons are on record in the form of Acts, rejected bills, and resolutions, there is a marked lack of evidence to explain how these decisions were reached. Usually there would have been a division, and often, though by no means always, the division figures survive. What does not survive is any record of how individual members voted, or even of which members were present when the debate and divisions took place. Of the five hundred and nine members entitled to attend some sixty have frequent speeches recorded in the parliamentary diaries. Letters, or other sources, shed some light on the views of perhaps another forty: for the remainder it is impossible to say whether they bothered to make the journey to Westminster at all. The question of party lists will be discussed later; at this point it is only necessary to say that they do not materially extend our understanding of debates. On most issues we are left with a limited number of expressed views—which may not always be a representative sample—and with a final decision reached by the votes of an anonymous silent, majority.

Having recognized this difficulty it is possible to make some deductions. Members of the 'court', that is of the group, or more frequently groups, who tried to advance the interests of the king's ministers, wrote frequently to other royal servants, notably those in Ireland, giving what they believed to be the official 'party line'. Members of the 'opposition' were more cautious, but if they kept their thoughts off paper a comparison of speeches made in the house makes an alternative 'line' quite frequently discernible. To write of debates without using some kind of label would be impossible, and thus 'court' and 'country', or 'opposition', groups will be referred to frequently. Nevertheless, since continuous repetition of inverted commas would become wearisome, it should be understood that these terms seldom mean more than a particular group adopting a particular line in a particular debate.

Another point requiring explanation is the limitation of this study to eleven sessions, from 1663 to 1674. Professor Henning has referred to recent investigation of the Convention and Exclusion Parliaments. Within the period of the Cavalier Parliament the first session, though of the greatest interest, went almost unrecorded by contemporaries; there are many questions to be asked about it, but little material from which to construct answers. As for the period from 1674 to 1678, this has not only been covered by a number of political biographies but may also be considered one in which co-operation between King and Commons had already become impossible. Brief sketches of the missing sessions have in fact been given, and it may be possible for me to return to them at some later date. In the meantime I hope that the years I have chosen may be found to have a unity of their own.

One final difficulty must be mentioned with regret. In a debate the most carefully phrased oration may count for less than an impromptu shaft of wit. Tones of voice, gestures, timing are of the greatest importance, especially when many of the audience have arrived uncommitted. In the records however such details are usually passed over and we are left to wonder why the plausible arguments of Temple, or of Birkenhead were so often 'laughed at', whilst the clumsy truculence of Henry Coventry commanded affection and respect. Yet again we are brought back to the impossibility of providing a full explanation for the decisions taken by three hundred individuals—it would be no easy task to provide such an explanation for the decisions taken by parliament today. It can only be hoped that this account may shed some light on corners previously obscure, may rescue some ghosts from oblivion, and may provide fresh ammunition for the controversialists in the endless argument over consultative and authoritarian forms of government.

DENNIS WITCOMBE

The Manchester Grammar School
1966

ACKNOWLEDGEMENTS

IN writing this account of the Cavalier House of Commons I have benefited greatly from the advice and criticism of others. Among these I must mention first Dr Anne Whiteman, who guided my first steps in research; Mr D. H. Pennington, under whose supervision I wrote the greater part of this study; Mr R. C. Latham, at whose seminar I received constant advice and encouragement; and Professor B. D. Henning, who not only provided the stimulus for publication but found time to write a foreword. I have learnt much from conversations with Professor Caroline Robbins, Dr Clayton Roberts, and Dr H. G. Rose-veare, and from correspondence with Dr G. R. Abernathy. I have profited from criticism by Professor Mark Thomson and Mr David Ogg, who examined my B.Litt. thesis, and by Mr Ivor Roots who acted, with Mr Pennington, as examiner for my Ph.D. Finally, as a schoolmaster, I have gained very greatly from the comments of several generations of sixth-formers at Emanuel School and, latterly, at the Manchester Grammar School.

In gathering material I have been helped by the courtesy and efficiency of a number of librarians. In particular the staffs of the Bodleian Library and of the John Rylands Library made it possible for me to cover much ground in a limited time, whilst I have had continual cause to be grateful to the Librarian and staff of the Institute of Historical Research. By kind permission of Professor Henning, and of Mr E. L. C. Mullins, and through the industry of those working on the seventeenth-century sections of the History of Parliament, I have been able to provide a limited biographical guide to members, which it would otherwise have been quite impossible for me to complete in time for publication. For permission to quote MSS. I must thank the Most Honourable the Marquess of Bath, the Right Honourable the Earl of Spencer, and Sir Harry Verney, Bart. Professor Robbins, Professor C. D. Chandaman, Dr E. S. de Beer and Dr Roseveare have allowed me to read and quote from past theses, and I must also acknowledge the permission granted for such quotation by Goldsmiths Librarian at the University of London.

The main part of my research was carried out as a research scholar of St John's College, Oxford, and as a research student of the University of Manchester. This was followed by ten years of part time work, based partly on the University of Manchester and partly on the Institute of Historical Research. My thanks are due to the President of St Johns, the Director of the Institute and in particular to the Ph.D. committee of Manchester University, who bore patiently with my repeated appeals for postponement of my submission date. In the final stages of publication I have received helpful advice from Mr T. L. Jones of the Manchester University Press. The fact that I was able to present an orderly typescript in place of an unintelligible scrawl is due to the labours of Mrs M. Turner, who was at times required to show psychic rather than secretarial ability. No manuscript of any kind could have been completed without ten years of patient encouragement and advice from my wife, to whom in gratitude I dedicate this book.

D. T. W.

CONTENTS

ABBREVIATIONS

B.M.	British Museum.
Cal. S.P. Dom.	*Calendar of State Papers Domestic.*
Cal. S.P. Ven.	*Calendar of State Papers Venetian.*
C.J.	*Journals of the House of Commons.*
Chandaman	C. D. Chandaman, London Ph.D. thesis, 1954, 'The English Public Revenue 1660–1688'.
Clarendon, *Life*	*The Life of Edward, Earl of Clarendon*, 1827.
Dering	*The Parliamentary Diary of Sir Edward Dering 1670–1673.*
Econ. Hist. Rev.	*Economic History Review.*
Eng. Hist. Rev.	*English Historical Review.*
Grey	*Debates of the House of Commons 1667–1694.*
H.M.C.	*Historical Manuscripts Commission.*
Hunt. Lib. Quart.	*Huntingdon Library Quarterly.*
L.J.	*Journals of the House of Lords.*
Marvell	*Letters and Poems of A. Marvell*, ed. H. Margoliouth, 2 vols., 1952.
Milward	*The Diary of John Milward 1666–1668.*
Pepys	*The Diary of Samuel Pepys*, ed. H. B. Wheatley 1904–5.
Parliamentary History	*The Parliamentary History of England . . . to the reign of Charles II*, 1740–3.
PRO	Public Record Office.
Roseveare	H. G. Roseveare, Cambridge Ph.D. thesis, 1962, 'The Advancement of the King's Credit 1660–1672'.
	(Dr Roseveare was kind enough to let me see a slightly revised draft of this thesis and there may possibly be slight differences in pagination between this and the copy in the Cambridge University Library.)

NOTE

QUOTATIONS
> In quotations the spelling and punctuation have been modernized.

DATES
> Since this study is concerned only with English history all dates are given in Old Style, though with the year taken to begin on January 1st. In a few cases, notably when the reports of foreign ambassadors have been cited, this has produced a discrepancy between the date given in my footnote and that on the original document.

CHAPTER I

THE CONVENTION AND THE FIRST SESSION OF THE CAVALIER PARLIAMENT

ON February 4, 1658, Cromwell dismissed his last Parliament having failed, as completely as Charles I, to find a way of reconciling effective power with Parliamentary criticism and advice. Seven months later Cromwell was dead and two years of constitutional anarchy had begun. At last in 1659 General Monck led the largest of the contending military forces south into England and, securing the financial support of the City Presbyterians, required the survivors of the Long Parliament to dissolve. There followed, in March 1660, elections to a parliamentary 'Convention', the members of which took their seats on April 25, 1660.[1] On May 1 this Convention passed a resolution that the government of the Kingdom ought to be in the hands of the King, Lords and Commons, and to remove an obvious discrepancy between what was and what ought to be the political situation, ordered the dispatch of a fleet to bring Charles Stuart back from exile.[2] In the year 1297 King Edward I, secure in his authority, had deigned to call his lords, knights and burgesses to attend a parliament; now the lords, knights and burgesses, secure in the support of Monck's guards, agreed, in the most respectful terms, to allow their rightful King to return to the land over which he was supposed to exercise sovereign power.

Considering the circumstances under which Charles met his first parliamentary assembly,[3] their relationship was remarkably free of strain. The royal title was confirmed, money was provided

[1] The elections to and conduct of the Convention have recently been made the subject of two theses: T. W. Evans, 'Hyde and the Convention Parliament of 1660', London M.A. 1964, and Mary E. W. Helms, 'The Convention Parliament of 1660', Bryn Mawr Ph.D., 1963.

[2] *C.J.* viii. 8, 20, May 1, 10.

[3] The Convention was not a Parliament, since no King had summoned it. Charles gave his assent to an act declaring it to be one, 12 Car. II, cap. 1, but the Cavalier Parliament, by ostentatiously confirming certain of its acts, put on record the fact that they had been passed by an unlawful assembly, 13 Car. II, cap. 7.

to pay off the army, a land settlement was hammered out, an act of indemnity was passed.[1] True, this did not take place quite as quickly as the King might have hoped—the failure to disband the army for ten months, or to provide for the immediate expenses of government, helped to increase an already large standing debt[2]—but on the whole it was managed very well. Only two points remained: religion, and the revenue. On these the outcome, partly through the court's own mistakes, was far less satisfactory.

As far as religion was concerned, the Convention's attitude was not at first very clearly defined. In June the anglicans made an advance; in July the presbyterians counter-attacked, helped by the persistent cavalier weakness of absenteeism.[3] Despite considerable argument nothing had been settled when the House adjourned for the autumn recess. During that recess Charles published a Declaration expressing support for a modified episcopacy, and for changes which might have made it possible for most presbyterians to remain within the establishment.[4] On their first day back the Commons ordered a bill to be drafted with this Declaration as its basis, but on November 28, by the narrow majority of 183 to 157, this bill was indefinitely postponed.[5] Thus ended Charles' best chance for twelve years to secure parliamentary support for some form of toleration. No further action was taken and it was left for the next Parliament to provide a settlement.

The second court lapse was over Charles' revenue. The actual sum agreed upon, £1,200,000, was adequate, indeed rather more than adequate, for the peace-time needs of the administration,[6] but in reckoning up the various bills, the court allowed one of them, worth £200,000, to be reckoned twice.[7] In addition to this they failed to make clear how much debt had

---

[1] D. Ogg, *England in the Reign of Charles II*, i, 153–6, 161–4.

[2] Chandaman, ii. 522–7, gives a less gloomy picture than W. A. Shaw, *Cal. Treasury Books 1660–67*, pp. i–xii.

[3] R. S. Bosher, *The Making of the Restoration Settlement*, pp. 146–50.

[4] Bosher, op. cit., pp. 184–9; K. G. Feiling, *History of the Tory Party*, pp. 128–9; Ogg, op. cit., i. 165.

[5] Bosher, op. cit., pp. 195–9; *C.J.* viii. 191, 194, Nov. 27, 28; *Parliamentary History* (1760, 1763) xxiii. 27–31, Nov. 28; *Cal. S.P. Dom. 1660–61*, pp. 354, 406, letters of Sir Edward Nicholas, Nov. 8, Dec. 7.

[6] Chandaman ii. 646–52.

[7] Ibid., ii. 532; *Parliamentary History*, xxiii. 25, Nov. 27.

accumulated since the King's return. This debt, the double reckoning of the Excise, and delay in establishing an effective method of collecting the money, combined to produce what was, by 1664, a formidable deficit at the Treasury.[1]

Records of the Convention's debates are sparse but it appears that for most of the time leadership was in the hands of men connected with the court. Arthur Annesley and Ashley Cooper, both lost to the Lords before the Cavalier Parliament met, Heneage Finch, long to labour as a mainstay of the court group in the Commons, Alan Broderick and Job Charlton, loyal cavaliers, and Prynne, outdoing even these in his new devotion to monarchy, all figure prominently in debates.[2] Some of these may have become members of the Chancellor's committee—a small group, formed either now or at the beginning of the next Parliament, which met daily, learnt the King's wishes, and attempted to guide the Commons into the chosen path.[3] If Clarendon was already 'managing' parliament, then he could congratulate himself on the general tone of debates.[4] It remained to be seen how the next Parliament would deal with religion and supply.

The Convention was dissolved on December 29, 1660. Writs for the new Parliament went out early in the spring. The election that followed would be worthy of a detailed study: royalist sentiment must have played a part but local interests were important also, whilst the new House of Commons did contain, in addition to its cavalier majority, nearly a hundred members of the Long Parliament, and perhaps half of the Convention.[5]

---

[1] Chandaman, ii. 539–41 again presents a more cheerful reckoning than W. A. Shaw, *Cal. Treasury Books 1660–67*, pp. xxviii-xxxiii.

[2] *Parliamentary History*, xxii. 374–6, 385–8, 412–21, 428–30, 463, 470–7, xxiii. 1–5, 10–11, 16–18, 21–2, 24–31, 35–7, July 9, 16, Aug. 1, 4, 6, 9, 14, 17, 30, Sept. 4, 5, 12, Nov. 6, 12, 17, 19, 21, 27, 28, Dec. 3; *C.J.* viii. 4, 11, 18–19, 41, 97, 104, 149, May 1, 4, 9, 22, July 21, 27, Sept. 4. The future opposition were however also represented, by Meres, Temple, Swinfen, Littleton, Birch, Holland, Tomkins, Boscowen and Clarges, *Parliamentary History*, xxii. 365–71, 376–9, 385–8, 405–14, 421, 428, 473–7, xxiii. 1–5, 7, 10–11, 24–31, 35–7, July 2, 4, 11, 16, 27, 30, Aug. 1, 14, 17, 18, 22, Sept. 5, 12, Nov. 6, 8, 12, 27, 28, Dec. 3.

[3] Infra, Chapter II.

[4] One example of this is the refusal to put grievances before supply, *C.J.* viii. 104, July 27. Contrast later sessions, infra, Chapters VIII, X–XIII.

[5] W. C. Abbott, 'The Long Parliament of Charles II', *Eng. Hist. Rev.* xxi (1906), p. 21; H. N. Muckerjee, 'Elections for the Convention and

The technique of challenging unwelcome elections had not yet been developed—it was the opposition who were to pioneer it later in the reign—but if Clarendon could have looked into the future there would have been several among those chosen whose entry he might have been glad enough to block.[1] Nevertheless, the King was pleased with the new House; he complimented them handsomely, whilst in return the Speaker became quite incoherent with devotion.[2]

Apart from a long exchange of compliments, the most important features of the opening were requests made by the King and Chancellor for Parliament to confirm the Act of Indemnity, to improve the revenue, and to settle religion. Particular stress was laid on the need to concentrate on public business, and not waste too much time on private bills.[3] Brought down to earth the Commons showed themselves zealous enough, but something less than perfect. On religion they made their position clear by ordering, within ten days, that the Covenant should be burnt by the public hangman, and that all their members should take the sacrament according to the usage of the Anglican church.[4] Whether they got all their members to comply is not clear; they certainly had considerable difficulty with Alder-

---

Cavalier Parliaments', *Notes and Queries*, clxvi (1934), pp. 417–21. One example of how local interests could be concealed is given in my thesis on 'The Parliamentary Career of Sir William and Mr. Henry Coventry', Oxford B. Litt., 1954, pp. 23–4, where I try to show how William Coventry's selection for Yarmouth was less the product of the Duke of York's nomination than of long rivalry between the Corporation and the Freemen, each of whom claimed to control the franchise. There is still room for a full investigation of this 1661 election.

[1] Among such members were Howard, Tomkins, Whorwood, Lee, Meres, Temple, Garraway, Hampden, Cavendish, Vaughan, Seymour, Boscowen, Littleton, Swinfen, Wheeler and Birch. None of these was to show the bitterness of the extreme whigs but they do provide more than half of the entire opposition leadership for this Parliament. This makes it difficult to accept without reservation claims that growing opposition to Charles within the Parliament showed the influence of 'public opinion' as reflected in by-elections, W. C. Abbott, the 'Long Parliament of Charles II', *Eng. Hist. Rev.* xxi (1906), pp. 31, 45, 257–8, 262–3, 282.

[2] 'The presence of this glory, and the glory of this presence do transport me', *L.J.* xi. 240–6, May 10, and compare *Cal. S.P. Ven. 1661–4*, p. 32, Aug. 21, 1661.

[3] *L.J.* xi. 240–4, May 8.

[4] *C.J.* viii. 247, 254, May 13, 17; B. M. Egerton MSS. 2043, f. 8, diary of Col. Bullen Reymes, May 17; Bosher, op. cit., pp. 221–2.

man Love, member for London, whilst on the vote for burning the Covenant a division of 228 to 103 showed that moderate nonconformists were by no means without friends in the House.[1] For the time, however, persecuting Anglicanism remained triumphant; on July 19 a new Act of Uniformity passed its third reading and was sent off to the more tolerant Upper House.[2]

So far as supply went the Commons were sympathetic but slow. On June 18 they agreed that the revenue was falling short by £265,000 a year, and accepted responsibility for remedying this, but they then spent so much time arguing over the Act of Indemnity, to say nothing of better ways of packing butter or paving the streets, that no progress had been made when they adjourned for the summer recess.[3] When they returned in November Charles made them a rousing speech[4] and they were stirred to great activity. Within a month they carried a bill to provide £1,200,000 for relief of immediate debts;[5] after some further argument they added, in the following March, a tax on hearths, which should, by their reckoning, have brought the ordinary revenue to very near the figure previously agreed.[6]

Whilst these, and many other bills were passing, Charles was making the first of many efforts to improve the lot of all outside the Anglican church. Using Clarendon as his emissary he appealed, not without success, to the compassion of the Upper House.[7] At this, for the first time, the Commons dug in their

---

[1] *C.J.* viii. 254, 289, May 17, July 3, and compare *C.J.* viii. 444, March 5, 1663.

[2] *C.J.* viii. 296, July 9, Bosher, op. cit., 223–4.

[3] *C.J.* viii. 273, 275–316, July 18, 19–30, and especially 313, July 26.

[4] *L.J.* xi. 332–3, Nov. 20. This included a promise that they should be free to inspect his accounts, a promise which the House did not entirely neglect, B.M. Egerton MSS. 2043, f. 21, Reymes, Nov. 28.

[5] *C.J.* viii. 317, 333, Nov. 21, Dec. 16. This supply was to be raised by the Cromwellian method of assessment, a notable sacrifice of sentiment to efficiency, though the preamble stated that this was to be the last time that this method was used, 13 Car. II, Stat. 2, cap. 3, and see infra, pp. 19, 32.

[6] *C.J.* viii. 376, 385, March 1, 12; 14 Car. II, cap. 10; Lydia M. Marshall, 'The levying of the Hearth Tax, 1662–88', *Eng. Hist. Rev.* li (1936), p. 628; Chandaman, i. 237–40. In 1666 the Commons were prepared to buy out the tax for £200,000 a year, infra, Chapter V, although its true yield between 1662–4 was only £115,000, Chandaman, i. 303.

[7] *L.J.* xi. 409, March 17; *Cal. S.P. Ven. 1661–4*, pp. 124–5, March 31; *Cal. S.P. Dom. 1661–2*, p. 324, March 31; Bosher, op. cit., 241–3, but contrast pp. 249–50.

heels. Despite strong opposition from their own tolerant minority they rejected amendment after amendment sent down by
the Lords, and eventually, since some settlement was necessary,
both Lords and King were forced to give way.[1]

Debates of the Convention are badly reported; those of the
first session of the Cavalier Parliament are not reported at all.
Scanning the Journal for evidence of efficient management, we
find on the credit side two supply bills and confirmation for
many of the Convention's Acts;[2] against this we have to set long
delays caused by private bills[3] and the failure to gain any concessions over religion. One further point of interest in the
Journal is that certain men appear with particular frequency
as tellers in divisions. If this evidence is combined with that in
records of the Convention, it will suggest that Edward Seymour,
Sir Richard Temple, Sir Thomas Littleton, Edward Vaughan,
Sir Robert Howard, and Sir Thomas Meres, were already
deliberate, if not particularly successful, opponents of the court.[4]

The first session ended on May 19, 1662. Actual sittings had
occupied one hundred and sixty-five days, a far higher number
than in any later session, and the product took the form of forty-
eight public and sixty-two private Acts.[5] Most of these Acts
were welcome to both court and country; of those which might
have led to a struggle the supply bills seem to have passed with
little opposition, whilst the divisions produced by the Act of
Uniformity had cut right across the court and country party
lines.[6] All that should have remained for the future was an

[1] *C.J.* viii. 404–17, April 12–30; Bosher, op. cit. 253–4.

[2] 13 Car. II, caps. 7, 11, 14. The most important of the acts confirmed
was that of Indemnity.

[3] The court's original request to avoid this, supra, p. 4, was disregarded,
and Charles spoke on the matter again on March 3, 1662, *C.J.* viii. 377–8.
The total number of private bills passed in the session was 62.

[4] *C.J.* viii. 264, 269, 272, 306, 310, 315, 334, 340, 367, 373, 383, 389,
393, 406, 421, 423, 427, 431, 433, June 5, 13, 15, July 19, 24, 29, Dec. 17,
19, 1661, Feb. 18, 26, March 10, 18, 24, April 15, 29, May 5, 7, 12, 1662;
B.M. Egerton MSS. 2043, ff. 11, 18, 22, 24, 26, 30, 33, 37, 43–5. May
28, Nov. 22, 29, Dec. 4, 13, 19, 1661, Jan. 10, 14, 27, Feb. 3, 1662. Also
active in this session were Whorwood, Tomkins, Birch, Lee and Boscowen,
C.J. viii. 288, 291, 298, 344, 367, 386, 428, 433, 435, July 3, 5, 1661, Jan.
13, Feb. 18, March 13, May 14, 19, 1662.

[5] The public acts were divided into 13 Car II, caps. 1–15; 13 Car. II,
Stat. 2, caps. 1–4, and 14 Car. II, caps. 1–33.

[6] *C.J.* viii. 276, 291, 334, 407, 409, 410, May 17, June 20, July 5, Dec. 16,

occasional review of finance, an obligation which the Commons seemed quite prepared to accept, and the granting of extra-ordinary supply in time of national emergency. Doubtless the country backbenchers would still have their grumbles: even during the Convention they had showed concern over falling rents, declining trade, leniency towards catholics, the billeting of troops, and possible incompetence or dishonesty on the part of the administration.[1] If, however, they pursued these griev-ances too seriously, Charles could always prorogue or dissolve them. The future seemed promising enough, provided only that Charles would be content to let the religious settlement alone.

1661, April 16, 17, 26, 1662. At times the cavalier majority seems to have been barely 20, and 103 members were found to vote against the burning of the Covenant. For a clearer indication of the failure of court and country grouping, to correspond with tolerant or persecuting principles, see the debates of 1673, infra, Chapter X.

[1] *C.J.* viii. 48, 97, 102, 110, 120–1, 199, May 29, July 21, Aug. 3, 15, Dec. 6, 1660; *Cal. S.P. Dom. 1660–1661*, pp. 255, 357, Sept. 4, Nov. 15, 1660; 12 Car. II, caps. 20, 27, 28.

CHAPTER II

COURT FACTION AND THE RISE OF OPPOSITION

HOWEVER much Charles may have tried, in later years, to free himself from parliament, it cannot be denied that he gave it every chance to serve him at the beginning of his reign. Barely six months after the first session had ended he announced his intention of calling a new one, and of asking parliament to help him 'exercise, with a more general satisfaction, that power of dispensing which we conceive to be inherent in us'.[1] In making this proposal he seems to have been prompted less by his official parliamentary manager, Clarendon, than by the latter's rival, the new Secretary, Henry Bennet. Whilst the Chancellor, without having abandoned his earlier desire to see some form of toleration introduced, now doubted if an attempt at this time was practicable, Bennet saw in his hesitations a chance to outbid him for the favour of the King.[2]

Charles made his announcement in December 1662. At once the bishops began to mobilize a parliamentary opposition.[3] Clarendon took to his bed, writing doubtfully that the plan might prove a very 'ticklish' commodity[4] whilst at least two of the court members whom Bennet recalled to strengthen the King's party proved to be violent enemies of any form of toleration.[5] Undeterred, Charles opened the new session on February 18, defending stoutly his proposal of indulgence.[6] The Lords voted him thanks for his speech, endorsed its publication, and within a few days were discussing a bill which offered him at

[1] Charles' proclamation, dated Dec. 26, is printed in W. Cobbett, *Parliamentary History*, iv. 257–8. Catholics were especially included.

[2] For a brief comment on the difficulty of establishing Clarendon's position on religion see Appendix 2.

[3] *Cal. S.P. Dom. 1663–4*, p. 64, March 2.

[4] Lister, *Clarendon*, iii. 233, letter of Clarendon to Ormonde, Jan. 31.

[5] Carte MSS. 221, ff. 19–20, Bennet's letter of Jan. 13, recalling Henry Coventry and Sir Winston Churchill, two strong Clarendonians who consistently opposed toleration.

[6] *L.J.* xi. 478.

least a part of what he asked.[1] The Commons voted no thanks, set up a committee to investigate the recent release of a prominent dissenting minister, and then dropped the whole subject for a week.[2]

The fact that Thomas Clifford and Sir Solomon Swale, both later revealed as catholics, opposed a debate suggests that its conclusion was already foreseen.[3] Charles had couched his original proposals in the form of an answer to certain calumnies—that he was opposed to the Act of Indemnity, to parliamentary government, and to the established Church. Playing a game they were to perfect over two decades the Commons thanked him for his gracious reassurance, which they affected to see as the main part of his announcement. Then, almost as a footnote, they turned to the proposal for indulgence, rejected an adjournment by 161 to 119 and agreed *nem. con.* that the King should be sent an address denying both the wisdom and the legality of any such measure. Lest there should be any remaining doubt about their views they asked the same committee to suggest remedies against the growth of popery.

Not for the last time Clarendon had judged the temper of the Commons better than his rivals. The Chairman of the drafting committee was Heneage Finch, Solicitor General and one of the most prominent members of the court; several others on the committee were normally considered courtiers, yet the address was as uncompromising as if drafted by the most violent opponents of the Crown.[4] The ancient prerogative of dispensing, conceded by most modern commentators,[5] was firmly rejected, and the King's royal word made subordinate to a parliamentary statute. The Declaration of Breda, so the address declared,

---

[1] *L.J.* xi. 479, 482–91, Feb. 18–March 12. Their draft bill is summarized in *H.M.C. 7th Rep.*, House of Lords MSS., app., p. 167; it gave relief to protestants but not to catholics.

[2] *C.J.* viii. 436–9. The preacher was Dr Calamy, whose arrest and subsequent release had aroused much comment, *Cal. S.P. Dom. 1663–4*, pp. 8, 10, Jan. 10, 13 and *Cal. S.P. Ven. 1661–4*, pp. 228–9, Feb. 1.

[3] *C.J.* viii. 439–440. For Clifford's views on religion see C. H. Hartman, *Clifford of the Cabal*, pp. 29, 282–4. Swale was expelled from the house as a catholic on June 19, 1678, *C.J.* ix. 501.

[4] *C.J.* viii. 441–3, Feb. 27.

[5] For a full discussion of the dispensing power see the articles by E. F. Churchill, *Law Quarterly Review* xxxviii (1922) pp. 420–34.

contained only a promise to discuss the problem of religion with parliament.

nor could it be otherwise understood, because there were laws of uniformity then in being, which could not be dispensed with but by Act of Parliament. They who do pretend a right to that supposed promise put their right into the hands of their representatives, whom they chose to serve for them in this Parliament . . .

If any shall presume to say that a right to the benefit of this declaration doth still remain, after this Act of Uniformity passed, it tends to dissolve the very bonds of government, and to suppose a disability in your Majesty and your Houses of Parliament to make a law contrary to any part of your Majesty's Declaration, though both Houses should advise your Majesty to it. . . .

It will in no way become the gravity or wisdom of a Parliament to pass a law at one session for uniformity and at the next session (the reasons for uniformity continuing still the same) to pass another law to frustrate or weaken the execution of it . . .

and finally

It is a thing altogether without precedent and will take away all means of convicting recusants, and be inconsistent with the methods and proceedings of the Laws of England.

This combination of bad history and bad law recalled the arguments which had proved so effective in the days of Hampden and Pym.

Charles' comment on receiving the address was that its length demanded consideration at more leisure.[1] He did, it would seem, commission Clarendon to draw up a defence of his proposals and the latter, with what feelings we cannot be certain carried out this task, but the defence remained undelivered.[2] Instead Charles swung round and, on April 1, put out a new proclamation against priests and jesuits. When the Commons added bills against both recusants and dissenters he made no objection;[3] the third of five attempts to overcome the religious intolerance of the cavaliers had ended in failure.[4]

---

[1] *C.J.* viii. 444, Feb. 28. He added that he remained as convinced as ever of the loyalty and affection of the house.

[2] G. R. Abernathy, *Journal of Ecclesiastical History*, xi. 1960, pp. 71–3.

[3] *C.J.* viii. 445–6, 461–2, 488–9. The Bill against popery was reported on March 6, the bill against conventicles was first read on May 21.

[4] Earlier attempts had been made in 1660 and 1662; later ones took place in 1668 and 1672.

Disappointed as he must have been, Charles did not bring the session to an end. In their address rejecting toleration the Commons had inserted a promise that, if its abandonment should lead to insurrection, they would gladly place their 'lives and fortunes' at the service of the King.[1] Twisting this slightly out of context Charles asked them, on March 16, to turn their attention to the deficiencies of his revenue. Three days later the Commons appointed a committee for this purpose.[2]

In the previous session Charles had received both a lump sum, of £1,200,000, and an annual levy on hearths expected, albeit somewhat optimistically, to produce some £300,000 a year.[3] Not surprisingly the Commons showed a certain reluctance to consider yet another grant; a cavalier courtier noted how 'the constant fountain of supply' seemed 'stopped', whilst a supporter of the indulgence remarked sourly that at least the House might have backed persecution with money.[4] Yet for all this the revenue committee did meet regularly: twenty-two sessions are recorded between March 18 and June 4,[5] and there may well have been others in a less official form. Many members of this committee held office or could be classed as courtiers;[6] if they seemed anxious to discover methods of avoiding waste, rather than of providing fresh revenue, this should not be taken to imply any deliberate opposition to the Crown.

What the revenue committee's slowness did provide was time for any grievances, public or private, to be aired. As early as February 25 a committee had been set up to prevent encroachments on our trade, and on April 7, having rather widened their terms of reference, they produced a report, of which the most important recommendation concerned the

---

[1] *C.J.* viii. 443.

[2] Ibid., 450–4.

[3] Chandaman, i. 234, 239, note 23. The true yield of the hearth tax, in the first year of its collection, was £88,000, ibid., ii. 700.

[4] Carte MSS. 47, f. 403, Henry Coventry, April 18; 46, ff. 51–2, Bennet, May 15.

[5] *C.J.* viii. 452–492, passim.

[6] *C.J.* viii. 454. These included Sir Philip Warwick, Sir John Duncombe, Sir Allen Apsely and Solicitor-General Finch, whilst the chairman was Sir Charles Harbord, Surveyor General of Crown Lands. Also included were some country stalwarts, amongst them Birch and Tomkins.

import of cattle from Ireland.[1] At this time it was widely
believed that land values were falling.[2] Among explanations
offered was competition from Irish livestock, and even in the
Convention there had been some attempt to limit the trade.[3]
To learn how strongly the ordinary cavalier member might
feel about this it is only necessary to look ahead to comments
by John Milward or Sir Ralph Verney.[4] Proposers of an
embargo could feel confident of being well received.

Yet if the trade in Irish Cattle was a genuine country
grievance it could easily become something more. An embargo
would, so the Lord Lieutenant, Ormonde, believed, cripple
Ireland's already shaky economy.[5] He was firmly opposed
to any such ban, and so too was his friend the Chancellor.
Enemies of Clarendon, or of Ormonde—notably Buckingham,
who hated them both—had in Irish Cattle Bills a perfect way
in which to ingratiate themselves with the country gentlemen and at the same time irritate and alarm the ministers.[6]
In a later session such a proposal was certainly used for a
political end. For this one the evidence is inconclusive, but at
least one of the bill's opponents believed resentment against
the trade to be so widespread that members needed no outside
encouragement to support the bill.[7]

[1] *C.J.* viii. 440–1, 467–8. The committee's somewhat xenophobic instructions had been to 'prevent encroachment in trade by the Jews, the
French or any other foreigner'.

[2] Ogg, op. cit., i. 53–4. A good contemporary statement of this view can
be found in William Coventry's 'Essay on the Decay of Rents' of which
there is a copy in B.M. Add. MSS. 32,095, ff. 243–5.

[3] *C.J.* viii. 97, 102, July 21, 25, 1660.

[4] Infra, Chapter V.

[5] His views are expressed in many letters. Two typical ones are: Carte
MSS. 51, ff. 219–20, Sept. 12, 1666, and 49, f. 361, Oct. 13, 1666. See also
T. Carte, *Life of James, Duke of Ormonde* (1851), iv. 234–42.

[6] For Buckingham's attitude see Clarendon, *Life*, iii. 135–42, 145–57, and
T. Carte, *Ormonde*, iv. 263–4.

[7] 'It was not to be avoided. The complaint of the fall of rents from all
gentlemen whose estates lie in pastures was so great, and so many even in
the house concerned that there was no opposing it.' Henry Coventry, May
8, *H.M.C. Ormonde MSS.*, new series, iii. 58. The Norfolk members reduced
the period during which the ban was applied, as their county made a profit
out of fattening lean Irish cattle for the London market. See Sir John
Holland's speech in Tanner MSS., Bodleian Library, 239, f. 40v, and compare *The Diary of John Milward*, ed. Robbins (1938), p. 9, for a similar attempt in 1666.

More irritating at this time was an early demonstration
of the trouble-making capacity of Sir Richard Temple, member
for Buckingham, who, having inherited debts of over £20,000
from his father, was already a suitor for the post of parliamentary manager.[1] At some point in this session he seems to have
approached the King offering to advance the Crown's business
in the Commons more effectively than Clarendon,[2] and he
continued his attempt to win some lucrative employment
until eventual success, in the form of a commissionership of
customs, enabled him to clear the bulk of his debts within
three years.[3] In 1663, however, his offer was refused and he
was soon able to show how easily one disgruntled member
could embarrass the Crown.

At this time, and indeed throughout the reign, even the
most loyal cavalier backbenchers seem to have viewed office
holders with considerable suspicion. Inefficiency and corruption were believed, probably with some justification, to
be widespread, and a demand for an enquiry was always
well supported. On April 13, the day before the House was
due to rise for Easter, Temple proposed that a committee
should be appointed to investigate the sale of offices.[4] The
court opposed this, at first with some success, but after others,
of a 'more cunning and less zealous temper', had lent their
support, it was agreed that a committee should be set up with
instructions to examine the relevant statute, V Edward VI,
and see if it could be made more effective. Temple became
chairman of this committee, which in due course recommended

---

[1] I have based my comments on Temple largely on articles by G. Davies,
E. F. Gay and C. Roberts in *Huntingdon Library Quarterly*, iv, vi, and xx
(1940–41, 1944, 1956–7). Dr G. R. Abernathy, of Charlotte College, North
Carolina, has recently been investigating Temple's career more closely and
believes that the extent both of his debts and of his connection with the Duke
of Buckingham have been exaggerated. His conclusions will be published
shortly and my own comments should be taken as subject to some possible
revision.

[2] Infra.

[3] Temple's career recalls the comments of H. R. Trevor-Roper, *The
Gentry 1540–1640*, supplement to the *Econ. Hist. Rev.* (1953), pp. 52–3, though
in view of the warning given by G. E. Aylmer, 'Office Holding in English
History', *History*, xliv (1959), pp. 236–7, many more examples of such behaviour would be required to justify generalization about the economic
problems of office-seeking backbenchers.

[4] *C.J.* viii. 471; Carte MSS. 47, f. 403, Henry Coventry, April 18.

an enquiry into all appointments made since June 1660: any who bought places would be offered free pardon and the retention of their posts if they would denounce the sellers. Again the court opposed the suggestion, and had some success, but the weight of 'some great person'—possibly the Duke of Buckingham—was thrown into the scale, and on May 2 Temple and another ambitious would-be courtier, Thomas Clifford, told for a majority of 120 to 85. The court challenged the retrospective clause when the bill was given its second reading, but they were again defeated and it went forward to committee.[1]

Temple was not the only man with such ideas. On May 5 Lord Bruce, making his only recorded contribution during the four years he spent in the Commons, proposed a bill to place all offices, military and civil, into the hands of 'such persons as have been loyal persons, and conformable to the Church of England'.[2] This combined prejudice against office holders with prejudice against dissenters, and seems to have been accepted without a division. Albemarle and Sandwich, to say nothing of half the captains in the fleet, now stood in danger of losing their positions.

By these proposals Bruce and Temple placed the court in an extremely difficult position. If office was limited to loyal members of the Church of England the navy at least would lose much of its efficiency.[3] The sale of offices was obviously hard to defend yet, in the navy at least, it was an old practice, justified by precedents going back at least half way to the much quoted act of Edward VI.[4] Whilst Henry Coventry deplored the enquiry as an invasion of the prerogative[5] his brother William prepared a lengthy justification of his own share in

[1] *C.J.* viii. 472–4, April 13, 30; Carte MSS. 47, ff. 403–4, Henry Coventry, April 18. Coventry does not name the 'great person' but within a few years the connection between Buckingham and Temple was well established. The Earl of Bristol is another possible claimant for the role.

[2] *C.J.* viii. 475–6; *Cal. S.P. Dom.* 1663–4, p. 132, May 8.

[3] *Pepys*, iii. 105–7, 145, 167, May 6, 7, June 2, 24. In fact Albemarle and Sandwich were later excepted by a proviso, ibid., iii, 114, May 15.

[4] For a useful comment on this see G. E. Aylmer, 'Office Holding as a Factor in English History 1625–42', *History*, xliv (1959), pp. 230–1.

[5] 'Which way particular men intend their own advancement and their adversary's destruction was never more visible, but which way the King's preservation and his enemies' destruction is intended was never less visible', Carte MSS. 47, ff. 403–4. April 18, and compare the same writer on May 12, *H.M.C. Ormonde MSS.*, new series, ii. 52.

such transactions—a justification which, five years later an even angrier House of Commons accepted without question.[1] Meanwhile the bills could only be checked by a prorogation which would also remove any hope of a supply.

Even the supply committee itself produced proposals to trouble the court. The alienation of crown lands was to be enquired into;[2] the Post Office, designed to supplement the income of the Duke of York, was to be sold to the highest bidder;[3] most serious of all, the whole revenue was to be appropriated to meet specific charges.[4] Appropriation had much to commend it—two years later it was to become part of a court bill, though one to which both Chancellor and Treasurer were much opposed. On the other hand it made the satisfaction of day-to-day needs less simple, it might lead to embarrassing enquiries by parliamentary committees and, to Clarendon and Southampton the most damaging objection, it was more or less a new idea.[5] Behind all these proposals was the suggestion, repeated over and over during the reign, that the existing revenue was adequate, and that economies rather than new grants should provide for all the King's needs. Such a belief was, at this time at least, unfounded; on the other hand it appears less unreasonable if we remember the improvements that had already been made in the two previous years.[6]

Bills against catholics and dissenters, against faults in the administration, in favour of appropriation, these were enough to disturb the court, but scarcely less exasperating were the

---

[1] William Coventry's defence is in Coventry MSS. Longleat, ci. ff. 225–34. See also V. Vale, *Cambridge Hist. Journal*, xii (1956), especially pp. 114–26. Coventry later surrendered his right to make such sales in exchange for an additional salary of £500, *Cal. S.P. Dom. 1613–4*, p. 674, Aug. 26, 1664.

[2] *C.J.* viii. 455, March 23.

[3] Ibid., viii. 468, 480, April 8, May 12. See also Chandaman, i. 340–1.

[4] *C.J.* viii. 478, May 8; *H.M.C. Ormonde MSS.*, new series, iii. 52–3, Henry Coventry, May 12.

[5] Clarendon, *Life*, iii. 15–20; Roseveare, pp. 46–7, and compare infra, Chapter IV. There had been appropriation clauses in previous bills, for example 12 Car. II, cap. 9, clause 7, but these had been for extraordinary grants. For much earlier precedents see also J. S. Roskell, 'Perspectives in English Parliamentary History', *Bulletin of the John Rylands Library*, xlvi, 1963–4, 450, 472.

[6] Although Charles' average revenue for the first ten years was only £960,000, his income between Michaelmas 1662 and Michaelmas 1663 had been nearly £1,500,000, Chandaman, ii. 506–7.

many innocent but time-wasting minor measures. Widow Ramage wanted permission to sell certain lands, the Marquess of Worcester wanted some reward for his 'water commanding' engine, fish spawn was being destroyed in the rivers, hackney coachmen were proving obstreperous, the plumbers wanted to prevent the adulteration of lead.[1] All this took time and still Charles waited for his supply.

An interesting commentary on the reliability of sources for this session is provided by comparing letters sent, on the one hand to our ambassadors, Fanshaw and Winchelsea, and on the other to Ormonde in Ireland. To the first two the Secretaries wrote of Parliament's evident desire to serve the King, mentioning only in passing certain 'peevish' votes.[2] To Ormonde, however, Bennet and his fellow courtier O'Neill wrote bitterly that loyal cavaliers were now behaving like the men of '41.[3] Whilst Bennet, mourning the loss of the proposed toleration, exchanged recriminations with the Chancellor,[4] Charles was reported 'sunk in luxury and pleasure', prepared apparently to let the session drift.[5] This report was soon to be disproved. By a series of personal messages Charles showed that he was still ready to appeal to the latent loyalty of the cavaliers.

Charles' first intervention came on May 16 when he rejected sharply an address containing three country requests.[6] He would not necessarily give the Post Office to the highest bidder, reliability was a factor also to be considered. He would not allow the export of geldings, and finally he would not give up his right to appoint consuls in foreign ports. The Commons swallowed this in silence, they voted him no thanks but the topics were allowed to lapse. Ten days later Charles sent

[1] *C.J.* viii. 455, 460, 464, 465, March 21, 30, April 4.

[2] *H.M.C. Finch MSS.* i. 254–5, letters of Morrice to Winchelsea, April 10, 21; *H.M.C. Heathcote MSS.*, pp. 76–7, 80, 83, 87, letters of Morrice, Warwick, Bennet and William Coventry to Fanshaw, March 31, April 12, 20, May 7, 14.

[3] Carte MSS. 46, f. 52; 221, f. 52, letters of Bennet, May 15, June 6; Carte MSS. 32, ff. 357–8, 390–1, 405–6, 597–9, letters of O'Neill, April 14, May 5, 15, June 20.

[4] Carte MSS. 32, f. 477, O'Neill, May 26.

[5] Carte MSS. 32, ff. 368, 405–6, O'Neill, April 28, May 15, and compare *Pepys*, iii. 115, May 15.

[6] *C.J.* viii. 484–5.

Bennet to urge haste in providing a supply. As in the previous session he professed complete willingness that they should inspect his accounts,[1] a point of some importance in the future, but stressed the need for at least an interim grant. On June 4 Harbord at last produced a report.[2]

So much has been written of the Commons' blindness over finance, of their refusal to admit deficiencies in the revenue, that it seems necessary to emphasize how again, as in 1661, their own committee agreed that Charles was receiving nearly £200,000 short of what had originally been promised. The House accepted this report and agreed to provide at least a further £120,000, hoping to make up the remainder by improved methods of collection. Having given the court grounds for hope they adjourned for the Whitsun recess, and when they reassembled Charles called them to Whitehall, where he made them a really vigorous speech.[3]

I have sent for you this day to communicate with you, as good friends ought to do when they discover the least jealousy growing which may lessen their confidence in each other. It is a freedom very necessary to be used between me and you, and you may all remember that when there was lately a little jealousy amongst you, upon somewhat I had said or done, I made all the haste I could to give you satisfaction: for which you all returned me your hearty thanks and were, I think, really satisfied.

He went on to assure them of his confidence in their loyalty:

You are the very same men who, at your first coming together, gave such signal testimonies of your affection and friendship to my person, of your zeal for the honour and dignity of the Crown and liberal support of the government, and of your horror and detestation of those men whose principles, you discerned, keep them awake to take all occasions to disturb the peace of the kingdom and to embroil us all in a new civil war: which is as much their endeavour now as ever.

The House, by their cheerful vote of supplies, had given him a great reputation abroad and made his enemies despair. Was

---

[1] Ibid., viii. 492-3. Compare 461-2, April 1, and *Cal. S.P. Ven. 1661-4*, p. 243, April 26. These offers contrast sharply with his attitude in 1666, infra, Chapter V.

[2] *C.J.* viii. 497-9. For further comment see Chandaman, i. 535-8.

[3] *C.J.* viii. 499-500, June 12; *Cal. S.P. Ven. 1661-4*, p. 251. Clarendon was consulted before this move, Carte MSS. 47, f. 52, his own letter of July 6.

it possible that they could now be changed in their affections? Charles believed that it was not.

> And yet I must tell you, the reputation I had from your concurrence and tenderness towards me is not at all improved since the beginning of this session, indeed it is much lessened. And I am sure I never stood more in need of that reputation than at present, to carry me through many difficulties in which the public is at least as much concerned as myself. Let me and you think never so well of ourselves, if all the world knows, or believes, that we are poor . . . if our friends think we can do them no good and our enemies believe we can do them no harm, our condition is far from being prosperous. You cannot take it amiss (you shall use as much freedom with me when you please) that I tell you there hath not appeared that warmth in you of late, in the consideration of my revenue, as I expected, as well from some of your messages as from my own confidence in your care and kindness.
>
> It hath been said to myself that it is usual for Parliaments to give the Crown extraordinary supplies upon emergent occasions but not to improve the constant revenue of the Crown. I wish, and so do you, that nothing had been lately done in and by Parliaments but what was usual. But if ill Parliaments contrive the ruin and disinherison of the Crown, God forbid but good Parliaments should repair it. . . .

He repeated yet again his offer that they should inspect his treasury's accounts, but pointed out that such an inspection could hardly be completed before the summer recess. Meanwhile an immediate grant was essential—an Irish plot was only one of several recent occasions for expense—and he urged them to provide a speedy vote.

> I do pray you heartily that the effect of this day's conversation may be the renewing our confidence in each other and raising our joint reputation; which will be the strongest security, with God's blessing, the Kingdom can have for its peace, plenty and full prosperity. And upon my word you will all have great comfort in what you shall do for me, upon this my very earnest and hearty recommendation.

With its mixture of flattery and scolding, reproof and exhortation, this speech can bear comparison with those of Elizabeth at her best. Possibly its delivery was poor, on other occasions Charles stumbled over his words or read them badly.[1] Certainly the response was a good deal less enthusiastic than the court

---

[1] At the end of this session, *Pepys*, iii. 213, July 27, and in 1664 and 1674, infra.

might have hoped. By a majority of only 159 to 111 the Commons agreed to an immediate grant. Four days later they fixed on the method, not the efficient but unpopular Cromwellian 'assessment' but the 'ancient' and very far from efficient way of subsidy.[1] Four lay subsidies were granted, the clergy added four more, and with this and bills to improve the collection of the excise and hearth tax, the King had to be content.[2]

It took over a month to complete these bills, time for further troublemaking, or at least for the completion of bills already under way. However, the bills for checking faults in the administration were allowed to lapse, the bill for appropriation was not even drafted, the bill against catholics stuck in the upper house. As for the bill against conventicles, the tolerant party first proposed something like an occasional conformity clause, which only failed by 94 to 89, after which the bill went to the Lords where it was delayed until the session was over.[3]

Meanwhile, angry perhaps at the poor response to his long speech, Charles had decided to hit back at Sir Richard Temple. Henry Coventry was sent with a message to the Commons informing them that Temple had offered, if preferred as parliamentary adviser, to see the King's business through the Lower House.[4] In view of later protests against 'undertaking' we would have expected an outburst of rage. None came, however: Temple denied the charge, the House asked for verification; the Earl of Bristol was named as the go-between and eventually, in a long 'comedian like' address, persuaded the House that

[1] *C.J.* viii. 503, June 16. On the ineffectiveness of subsidies see Sir Philip Warwick's comment to *Pepys*, Nov. 22, 1664, iv. 274, and also Chandaman, i. 401–10.

[2] 15 Car. II, caps. 11, 13. The usefulness of these bills is made clear by Lydia M. Marshall, 'The Levying of the Hearth Tax', *Eng. Hist. Rev.* li (1936), p. 629, and Chandaman, i. 141.

[3] *C.J.* viii. 513–14, June 30. The clause would have excused those who attended 'frequent' church services and took the Sacrament three times a year. See also Carte MSS. 81, ff. 191–2, 240–1 for notes by Lord Wharton on these proposals. Hints of attempts to distinguish peaceful nonconformists from potential rebels can be found in a speech by Sir John Holland, Tanner MSS. 239, ff. 45v–46v, and in a letter from O'Neill, Carte MSS. 32, f. 390, May 5. It is not clear whether the Lords' delays were deliberate or due merely to Bristol's 'impeachment' of Clarendon. Some of the Commons suspected the former, Carte MSS. 32, f. 732, O'Neill, July 25.

[4] *C.J.* viii. 501–2, June 13.

neither he nor Temple had done anything to merit blame.[1] In Bristol's later attempt to 'impeach' Clarendon before the Upper House the Commons showed no interest whatsoever.[2] Neither the attack nor its failure produced a resolution, or even a debate, and on July 27 the session came to an end.

On the final day the Speaker presented the Subsidy bill as an 'extraordinary' supply, to provide defence against the unsettled state of the nation.[3] Persecution *had* been 'backed with money', but the deficit revealed by the revenue committee remained unrepaired. That committee's report was ignored not only by the Speaker but, strangely, by the King, though the latter did cast some doubt on whether the yield of the subsidy would be a full one. Charles also expressed 'regret' that the bills penalizing catholics and dissenters had remained unfinished, promised to take action himself, and exhorted members to quieten their 'countries' and damp down malicious rumours. With that he prorogued Parliament to the following March.

During this rather disappointing session two types of opposition had appeared. The first, backed by an overwhelming majority in the Commons, was to the King's own declared aim of toleration. The second, shared by many independent members, but stimulated by careerist politicians, was directed against the King's servants and advisers, and particularly against their handling of the revenue and their failure to defend the landed interest. Clarendon seems to have given up hope of quieting the first type of opposition; he made no further gesture in support of toleration whilst a number of his followers came out strongly against it. The second kind however he considered impertinent and was prepared to ignore. His rival, Bennet, reversed this view, being prepared to make concessions over many minor grievances and hoping that by this means opposition to both supply and toleration might be overcome.

The clash of views, more marked in later sessions, did reveal itself at this time in a fierce struggle for the post of Parliamentary manager. This post was held, as it had been since the

---

[1] *C.J.* viii. 503-4, 507, 511-15, June 16, 26, 27, July 1; *Pepys*, iii. 177-8, July 1; Dorothea Townsend, *George Digby, Second Earl of Bristol*, pp. 223-6.

[2] This can be followed in *L.J.* xi. 555-560, July 10-14, passim. Clarendon's own account is in *Life*, ii. 256-63 and see Dorothea Townsend, *Bristol*, pp. 227-32.

[3] The closing speeches are in *L.J.* xi. 578, July 27.

beginning of the reign, by Clarendon, who met each day a committee of loyal members and attempted through them to make clear the King's wishes to the House.[1] During the session of 1663 Sir Richard Temple had questioned the effectiveness of this committee and had offered to provide a more effective service, only to be rebuffed contemptuously by the King. A second challenge, which cannot be dated precisely, came later in this year, and enjoyed far more success.

According to Clarendon, who is our only informant for the whole affair, Secretary Bennet approached Charles with the complaint that the old system of management was proving ineffective.[2] The Chancellor was summoned and at once denied that this was true, adding however that his task as controller of that system was made considerably more difficult by young courtiers, lacking proper respect for age and dignity, who put forward their own ideas as though they spoke for the King. This was a clear reference to the proposal for toleration, now implicitly repudiated by Charles, and could also have been applied to such a man as Clifford, Bennet's follower, who had joined Temple in one of the latter's more irritating moves.[3] Charles found the Chancellor's reply unconvincing, and ordered him to add to his advisory committee this very Clifford, together with, so Clarendon says, Sir Winston Churchill. The latter was, however, linked with Ormonde, with Henry Coventry, and thus with Clarendon himself, whilst he seems to have taken no part in any management discussions. Very possibly his name is given in error for William Coventry who was at this time a close ally of Bennet, a friend of toleration, and as active in discussing parliamentary tactics as Churchill was inert.[4]

At first glance this reorganization appears a very sensible

---

[1] Clarendon, *Life*, i. 361, ii. 208.

[2] Ibid., ii. 206–11; Barbour, *Arlington*, pp. 78–9.

[3] By supporting the bill against selling offices, supra, p. 14; Clifford was already a Gentleman of the Privy Chamber and held a reversion for a Teller's place in the Exchequer, Hartmann, op. cit., pp. 25, 30.

[4] Clarendon names Coventry as supporting Bennet's original complaint, *Life*, ii. 206–7, and by 1664 he was being consulted on parliamentary policy, infra, Chapter III, whilst Churchill's only parliamentary activity seems to have been to oppose the Irish Cattle Bill of which Bennet and Coventry half approved, infra Chapter IV. A. L. Rowse, *The Early Churchills*, pp. 39, 43–4, accepts Churchill as an active member, largely on the evidence of committee lists. The reliability of such lists is, however, open to doubt.

move.[1] The grievances scorned by Clarendon were not trivial—he was to learn within three years how deep-rooted was the hostility to Irish Cattle—and as for the efficiency of his committee, at least one of them was found complaining, at a critical stage of the debates, that he knew neither 'what the House intends, nor what we at Whitehall wish that they should.'[2] On the other hand the resolute anglicanism of the Commons was to prove perhaps the most permanent feature of this Parliament, and here Clarendon had gauged more truly than his rivals the feeling of a majority in the House. Allowing for all the Chancellor's irritating ways, and his blindness on many issues, it seems that in deciding against him Charles was preferring, as he was to do in 1670, advisers who told him what he would like to believe to those who pointed out unwelcome probabilities. Worst of all, if Clarendon *was* to be overruled, was the latter's retention in a position of ostensible authority. For the next four years there were to be at least two parties of the court—three if the Buckingham faction is included[3]—and the loyal country member, anxious to please the King, might well be in doubt as to which course he should pursue.

A really strong anglican policy might have caused members to forget their discontents; concessions and gratifications of the kind advocated by both Temple and the Arlington–Coventry faction might have smoothed the way for at least limited toleration. The alternation of concessions with sharpness, as Charles first veered away from Clarendon and then came back to acceptance of his advice, produced a complete breakdown of parliamentary relations. That this was staved off for five years is itself a high tribute to the continuing loyalty of the cavalier commons.

[1] A view expressed in an article which I contributed to *The Bulletin of the Institute of Historical Research*, xxxii (1959), pp. 190–1. This was written before I had looked in detail at later sessions of this parliament.

[2] *H.M.C. Ormonde MSS*, new series, iii. 52, Henry Coventry, May 12.

[3] Buckingham was in favour at court but his followers were encouraged to make themselves a nuisance to the Chancellor, A. Browning, *Thomas, Earl of Danby* (1951), i. 32–3, 42.

CHAPTER III

CAVALIER POLICY AND SUPPLY

WE said earlier that Charles would never summon Parliament unless he had some definite end in view. Usually it would be money, sometimes religious toleration, but in 1664 he specified only one thing; the repeal of the Long Parliament's Triennial Act. By that act, if a King should ever allow three years to pass without calling a session, the Lord Chancellor should, on his own authority, issue writs for a new parliament. To Charles, with his strong feeling for the dignity of kingship, his irritation at the need to tolerate this 'company of fellows',[1] such a provision was a source of keen annoyance. Already in 1662 the act's repeal had been proposed, to be thwarted by shortness of time and the opposition of Mr Vaughan.[2] In 1663 repeal had again been considered, but nothing had been done.[3] Charles now told the Commons plainly that he considered the act a stimulus towards rebellion, that he would never allow any parliament to meet under its terms and that he required its immediate removal from the book of statutes.[4]

Typical of the divisions still troubling the court had been the need to postpone this opening address for five days, whilst the area around Wimbledon was combed for the elusive Earl of Bristol who was rumoured to be preparing yet another attack on the Chancellor.[5] Neither the Earl nor the attack materialized, however, and when the session did get under way the King had good cause to be pleased with its course. On the day

[1] For Charles' view of Parliament as an irritating collection of busybodies see G. Burnet, *History of my Own Time*, ed. O. Airey (1897), ii. 3.

[2] *C.J.* viii. 395, April 3, 1662; *Cal. S.P. Dom. 1661–2*, p. 330, April 3.

[3] *Cal. S.P. Ven. 1661–4*, p. 249, June 12.

[4] For his speech see *L.J.* xi. 582, March 21.

[5] *C.J.* viii. 534, *L.J.* xi. 581, March 16; *Cal. S.P. Dom. 1663–4*, pp. 353, Nov. 27, 515, March 14; *H.M.C. Finch MSS.* i. 297–8, 302, letters of Secretary Morrice, Dec. 23, 1663, March 24, 1664. *Cal. S.P. Ven. 1661–4*, pp. 273, 276, 285, 288, Dec. 1663–March 1664, and *Cal. S.P. Ven. 1664–6*, pp. 1, 6, April 1664 provide further evidence of the anxiety Bristol could still arouse. Henry Coventry's interesting letter on this subject in Carte MSS. 47, f. 420 is dated Feb. 13, 1665, but was in fact almost certainly written a year earlier.

following the royal speech William Prynne moved the repeal of
the 1641 act, which he denounced in a somewhat puritan meta-
phor as an idol 'whose head was of gold but whose body was of
base metal'. To bandy precedents with so venerable an anti-
quary might have unnerved any member, but it did not deter
Sir Richard Temple from rising in the original act's defence.
Taking the war into the enemy camp he declared roundly that
this act itself had fallen short of what was due, for by a law of
Edward III annual, rather than triennial, parliaments had been
decreed.[1] Next day Temple, supported by the veteran Edmund
Waller, and by Sir Thomas Littleton, attempted to postpone
further discussion. Against them Sir John Holland, who had
approved the 1641 act when it had first been proposed, declared
that having seen the harm caused by such measures he could
never believe good could come from any parliament which met
without the King's consent. The attempt to adjourn failed by
129 to 42—many members seem still to have been absent—and
the repealing bill was sent to a Committee of the whole House.[2]

Measures rushed through a thin house were to become a
bugbear of the country opposition.[3] In response perhaps to
urgent letters, opponents of repeal hastened to London, fore-
most among them Mr Vaughan, and on Monday the latter
spoke for an hour, outshining Temple even as the latter had
outshone Prynne.[4] To answer him the King called on Heneage
Finch, the opponent of Indulgence in 1663, but a formidable
debater much respected by the cavaliers. With 'reason and
rhetoric' Finch secured the passage of the act—though by a
diminished majority of 134 to 88,[5] and on April 5 the King in
another halting speech, thanked the House and gave his royal
consent.[6]

[1] *C.J.* viii. 534–5, March 21, 22; B.M. Add. MSS. 35, 865, f. 212, note
by Arthur Capel on these debates; Verney MSS., Claydon, Dr. Denton to
Sir Ralph Verney, 25 March, 1664, printed in part in *H.M.C. 7th Rep.*,
p. 484; *Pepys*, iv. 78, 82, March 21, 26.

[2] *C.J.* viii. 536–7, March 23, 24; Holland's speech is in Tanner MSS,
Bodleian Library, 239, ff. 49–51.

[3] *Infra*, pp. 53–5, 97 note 6.

[4] *H.M.C. 7th Rep.* p. 484, Denton to Verney, March 31; Verney MSS,
Claydon, Denton to Verney, April 3, 1664; *Pepys*, iv. 86, March 28. The
latter part of Vaughan's speech is in B.M. Stowe MSS. 304, ff. 77–8.

[5] *C.J.* viii. 538, March 28. The opposition, it will be noted, has doubled its
strength.

[6] *L.J.* xi. 593; *Pepys*, iv. 93, April 5.

'Farewell Magna Charta', wrote Sir Ralph Verney's friend from London.[1] Certainly the latter years of the reign were to show the ineffectiveness of the remaining sanctions against non-parliamentary rule. On the other hand it is hard to believe that a Chancellor would ever have issued writs without the King's consent. For him to have done so would have been to start a new civil war, and Parliament would have met, or failed to meet, according to which side triumphed in the field. In the long run the best guarantee of frequent parliaments was not a statute but an empty treasury; although the trade boom and improved administration enabled Charles to carry on his government in the '80s,[2] any attempt to wage war would at once have thrown him back into dependence on parliamentary supply.

Even in 1664 money was far from plentiful. Charles had already told the Commons of his disappointment at the yield of the last subsidy.[3] Some men, he had declared, thought it no wrong to cheat the revenue—a complaint by no means peculiar to that day—and his words should have gone home more strongly since many members had helped to supervise the subsidy's collection.[4] When he thanked Parliament for repealing the Triennial act his speech contained a strong hint that a further supply would not be unacceptable,[5] but the Commons failed to respond. What they did offer this session was another bill to improve the collection of the hearth tax, allowing the crown to take over the appointment of collectors. The yield rapidly increased, as did the unpopularity of the tax,[6] and with this, a new licensing act, and an act to improve discipline in the navy, Charles had to be content.

In securing the repeal of the Triennial Act Charles had

---

[1] *H.M.C. 7th Rep.*, p. 484, March 31. For a somewhat 'whiggish' treatment of this whole affair see Caroline Robbins, 'The Repeal of the Triennial Act', *Hunt. Lib. Quart.* xii (1949).

[2] Chandaman, ii, 613–30.

[3] In his opening speech, *L.J.* xi. 583, March 21.

[4] The commissioners were named in the act, 15 Car. II, cap. 9, clause 6.

[5] *L.J.* xi. 593, April 5. Morrice later assured Winchelsea that no supply had been hoped for, *H.M.C. Finch MSS.* i, 312, May 7, but this may have been another example of putting the best face on matters when writing to an ambassador.

[6] Lydia M. Marshall, 'The Levying of the Hearth Tax, 1662–1688', *Eng. Hist. Rev.* li (1936), p. 630.

chosen to call on cavalier sentiment for support. In his opening speech he had referred directly to potential rebels, whose aim was to revive past strife.[1] Given such a lead it was not surprising that the persecuting majority should strike again at the 'fanatics'. On March 29, the day after the repealing act had been completed, a new bill was ordered 'to supply defects in former laws' for the defence of the established church.[2] If this measure was opposed in the Commons, as were most persecuting bills, no record has survived. The Lords tried to amend it, and several conferences took place between them and the Commons,[3] but in the last day of the session it passed, adding a savage emphasis to the rejection, in the previous year, of Charles' plea for indulgence.[4]

If these two bills were such as Clarendon could have approved the third main product of this session caused him dismay. Having struck a blow at Irish Cattle the Commons' committee on trade had now turned to consider the Dutch as a threat to our economy. From a committee of which Clifford was the chairman came a report demanding action against them; the House endorsed this and offered their 'lives and fortunes' in support.[5]

In later years the charge of having favoured this war was fiercely bandied to and fro. Clarendon, who certainly opposed the war himself, blamed Bennet and Coventry for its promotion, but the latter at least can be cleared by reference both to his memoranda, and to Pepys' record of his conversation at this time.[6] Various merchants favoured war and tried to influence

[1] *L.J.* xi. 582–3, March 21.

[2] *C.J.* viii. 539. For alarmist intelligence of supposed seditious meetings see *Cal. S.P. Dom. 1663–4*, pp. 279, 318, 325, 508, Sept. 25, 26, Oct. 29, Nov. 2, 1663, March 8, 1664.

[3] *Pepys* notes one of these, iv. 123–4, May 13. Others took place on April 1, 2, 28, May 12, 14, 15, 16, whilst on April 28 there seems to have been a long debate, *C.J.* vii. 541–2, 552, 562–6.

[4] 16 Car. II, cap. 4, usually known as the First Conventicle Act. No distinction was made between the preacher and any of those who attended; on a third conviction the penalty was a fine of £100 or transportation for seven years.

[5] *C.J.* viii. 537, 548, March 26, April 21. A full copy of the report, with specific allegations against the Dutch, is in PRO SP 98/35.

[6] Clarendon, *Life*, ii, 303. *Pepys*, iv. 106–7, 134, 232, April 20, May 29, Sept. 21, 1664, Coventry's memoranda are in Coventry MSS., Longleat, 101, f. 19, and 102, ff. 1–13. The second of these is referred to by V. Vale,

the Commons committee;[1] the Duke of York was also in favour, as was our resident at the Hague, Sir George Downing; the Duke of Albemarle wanted war, and so probably did Charles himself.[2] In later years Charles told the Commons that they had made the war and were responsible for supporting it with money. In view of their promise of March this seems a justified demand, yet if, as is at least possible, the original committee had been swayed by a bellicose minority, this would explain why a majority of the House were soon to become so critical of the way in which their money was being employed.[3]

The session ended on May 17, Parliament being prorogued to August. Throughout the summer rumours of war abounded, whilst Charles' ministers argued amongst themselves. Eventually Charles borrowed £200,000 from the City of London and began to arm, whilst with the despatch of Sir Robert Holmes to cruise off the African coast hostilities had virtually begun.[4] One thing at least was achieved by this decision. However much court factions disagreed about toleration, and about who should hold the chief governmental posts, for the time their parliamentary aims became united: whilst the war lasted all other matters took second place to the securing of supply. Even so agreement on ends did not extend to methods: before the next session a violent argument took place over the best way to coax money from the Lower House.

Our account of this dispute comes only from Clarendon, but it tallies closely with the events of the session which followed.

'Clarendon, Coventry, and the Sale of Offices', *Camb. Hist. Journal* xii (1956), pp. 112–14.

[1] *Pepys*, iv. 43–4, 89, 94, Feb. 19, April 1, 5. Sir Richard Ford, Deputy Governor of the African Company, was licensed to publish Mun's *England's Treasure by Foreign Trade* on March 24, *Cal. S.P. Dom. 1663–4*, pp. 310, 527.

[2] *Pepys*, iv, 87, 89, March 30, April 1; Coventry MSS., Longleat, 102, ff. 5–7.

[3] Clifford, the chairman of the committee was a fierce supporter of hostilities, Hartmann, *Clifford*, pp. 31–4. It must be admitted, however, that as early as 1660 the Convention had shown hostility towards the Dutch, *Cal. S.P. Dom. 1660–1*, p. 255, Sept. 4, 1660. Charles' challenge to the Commons was made on Oct. 10, 1665, *L.J.* xi. 684.

[4] *Cal. Treasury Books 1660–7*, pp. 608, 624, July 4, Nov. 14; K. G. Feiling, *British Foreign Policy 1660–1672*, p. 129.

He and the Treasurer, it appears, though opposed on principle to the war, thought that it would now be wise to make the most of Parliament's war fever and obtain a grant large enough to cover the entire expense.[1] Against this William Coventry and Bennet argued that the war was unlikely to be a short one: to drain dry the Commons' fund of loyalty might be to remove all hope of the second or third votes which might very well be necessary. At the same time Coventry seems to have feared that a large sum might be frittered away, whilst the Commons, taking up Charles' previous invitations, might demand a full account of all they gave.[2]

On this occasion Charles preferred Clarendon's advice and it was agreed that the largest possible sum should be obtained. There then arose the question of how best to set about this, and again the Chancellor had ready an answer.[3] It was useless, he declared, for the proposal to come from a courtier, or from a man of no great wealth who would contribute little himself. He had been in touch with three Norfolk gentlemen, one of whom was Sir Robert Paston. They were men of rank, yet not identified as courtiers; he suggested that one of them should be asked to propose the sum. This plan was accepted; the navy office prepared accounts exaggerating the amount already spent[4] and, perhaps in the hope of having more to show, the meeting of Parliament was postponed for three months. It was thus on November 24 that a new session was opened with a speech by the King.[5]

Charles explained that he had already borrowed from various sources, including the City, as much as £800,000. He asked for a quick grant of supply, and for one which would prove 'real and substantial, not imaginary as the last subsidies were'. He denied strongly the persistent rumour that such a grant might be followed by a peace, and ended by repeating his request for speed. Clarendon followed this with a long

---

[1] Clarendon, *Life*, ii. 303–4.

[2] PRO, SP 29/105, f. 141v. Coventry to Bennet, Nov. 24. The likelihood of the Commons demanding an exact account was also recognized by the French ambassador, PRO 31/3/113, f. 101, Dec. 1, 1664.

[3] Clarendon, *Life*, ii. 307–9.

[4] *Pepys*, iv. 274–5, Nov. 22, 25. This was just the conduct against which William Coventry had warned his colleagues. Within two years Pepys was to learn the hazards of deceiving the Commons, infra, Chapter V.

[5] *L.J.* xi. 624–5.

detailed narrative, contrasting the King's patience and fair dealing with the perfidy and stubbornness of the Dutch. The Commons voted thanks for both speeches and agreed to consider them on the following day.

The supply debate of November 25 became the subject of a myth, the origin of which can be found in the Chancellor's memoirs. Anxious to show how right he and the Treasurer were, in asking for the largest possible sum, Clarendon gives a long and circumstantial account of how this was agreed virtually without opposition.[1] This account, though accepted by some later writers,[2] fails to explain the entry in the Journal of a division of 172 to 102, not indeed on the motion for supply, but on the no less important motion, that 'the question be now put'.[3] Other slight indications of opposition can be found, but the whole matter can be cleared up by collating the Journal with a letter written by Thomas Clifford on the evening of the actual debate.[4]

The day it seems began with some minor business, an election petition and three bills of no importance. Then, probably by arrangement, messengers came from the House of Lords desiring the Commons' approval of two votes of thanks, the first to the King for his care of the nation's interests, and the second to the City of London for lending money to set out a fleet. This latter vote carried with it a clear implication that means would be found to repay the loan, and the opposition took alarm. Prynne and Vaughan opposed concurrence, but the court overrode their objections and both votes were approved. By now it was after ten and without further delay the main business was called. Sir John Holland, perhaps one of the three Norfolk men the Chancellor had nominated, stood up and spoke of the need to grant a supply, but did not name any sum. Next Sir Robert Paston rose to deliver the speech which was to pave his way to a viscountcy and earldom.[5] After denouncing the Dutch he declared that not

[1] Clarendon, *Life*, ii. 309–11.

[2] For example, G. Burnet, *History of my Own Time*, ed. Airey, i. 390; V. Barbour, *Arlington*, pp. 79–81; O. Airey, *Charles II*, pp. 208–9; L. von Ranke, *History of England* (1875), iii. 424.

[3] *C.J.* viii. 568, Nov. 25.

[4] This letter, to William Coventry, is in B.M. Add. MSS. 32,094, ff. 24–7; see also *Pepys*, iv. 276, Nov. 25.

[5] Paston's speech is in B.M. Add. MSS. 35,865, f. 88.

merely a speedy, but a great and certain sum was required; the machine of war needed strong hinges (*sic*), and to do the work no less than £2,500,000 was required. This motion, from a professed member of the country, stunned the House into silence. After a pause several other members rose to agree that a supply was necessary, but without commenting on the figure. Gradually feelings warmed against the Dutch and the court's hopes rose, yet there were also some objections that if a definite figure was named this would itself rule out supply by 'the old way' of subsidy, the yield of which, as the court knew only too well, was bound to be uncertain. The opposition seized on this and desired that the House might at once resolve into grand committee, to discuss methods of raising money before fixing on a sum. Sir Edward Walpole and Sir John Goodrick spoke strongly for this but the court again secured a victory, carrying a resolution that the sum should be named by the House.

Vaughan now spoke, declaring 'in the presence of God', that he would live on bread and water rather than that the reputation of the King, or the honour of the nation, should suffer, and these loyal sentiments were echoed by Temple and by another prominent backbencher, William Garraway. They did, however, also carry a proposal that the fixing of a sum should be no restriction upon the committee which would later discuss ways and means. This achieved, Vaughan rose again to execute a complete volte face and suggest that in fact a sum of £500,000 would do the present business very well; if more was required the King could come to them again. Walpole, Sir Henry North, and Littleton supported this, whilst Holland now compromised at £1,500,000, adding that if money was 'the sinews of war' it was also 'the heart blood of the people'.[1] In answering this challenge the most prominent court speaker was Trevor, a future Secretary of State, whilst Clifford was probably active as well. With much difficulty the court did at last get a vote upon the 'previous question' which, as we have already seen, was carried by a majority of seventy. The opposition conceded defeat, and to the main question there were only the four or five noes to which Clarendon proudly refers.

Well might Clifford end his letter by asking his correspond-

[1] Holland's speech is in Tanner MSS. Bodleian Library, 239, ff. 33v–34v.

ent for a narrative of the first great sea fight in exchange.
The so-called demonstration of complete harmony between
legislature and executive was in fact one of the hardest fought
political engagements of the reign. To this debate the court
had brought both strength of numbers[1] and unity of purpose.
They were soon to slacken their grip, and by that slackening
to throw away much of the advantage they had gained. In
his opening speech Charles had stressed the need for speed.
Prices were rising rapidly, the usual sources of credit had been
heavily strained, whilst if merchants were asked to accept
deferred payment they might demand not the official four,
but as much as forty per cent interest.[2] Even if the court had
exaggerated the amount laid out before November, expenses
continued throughout the winter, and it was vital that ready
money should swiftly be made available. Speed in passing a
supply bill was not an impossibility: the bill of 1662 had taken
twenty-five days to pass the Commons and that of 1665 was to
be concluded in a fortnight.[3] In this session, however, the
supply bill received its first reading on December 17, more
than three weeks after the great debate; it did not reach the
Lords until February 3, a further six weeks delay, and the
first money does not seem to have come in before Easter 1665.[4]
By that time the £800,000 of loans had been spent, and thus
a third of the new supply had already been anticipated.[5] For
all the court's efforts the war had not been put on a sound
financial basis.

To see how these delays arose we have to rely, for the most
part, on the journals. The first vote had specifically left the
method of tax for future discussion, and the next two days

[1] For the efforts made to secure a good attendance of court members see
William Coventry's letter of Nov. 25, PRO SP 29/105, f. 154; a dispatch
from the French ambassador of Nov. 22, PRO 31/3/113, f. 44; and *Hatton
Correspondence* (Camden Soc. 1878), i. 40–1, letter of Sir Charles Littleton,
Nov. 26.

[2] *Pepys*, iv. 361–2, April 1, 1665; Clifford's speech in the debate of Oct.
27, 1670, *Grey*, i. 270.

[3] *C.J.* viii. 317–33, Nov. 21–Dec. 16, 1661; ibid., viii. 614–19, Oct. 11–21,
1665.

[4] *C.J.* viii. 580, 594; Chandaman, ii. 437. The yield was however quicker,
and far larger, than was stated by the editor of the *Calendar of Treasury Books*,
on which see Chandaman, op. cit., i. 8, and note.

[5] *Pepys*, iv. 364, April 7. The French ambassador was aware of our condition, PRO 31/3/114, f. 83, Feb. 6, 1665.

were spent in wrangling over 'ways and means'.[1] Sir John
Holland and others still hankered after the old way of subsidy,
and indeed the act of 1662 had specifically banned any further
use of 'assessment'; however, since the latter was the only
method which could produce a certain sum, a new name was
found, and Charles was offered £69,000 a month for three
years as 'a Royal Aid . . . in a regulated subsidiary way'.[2]
Assessment, though far better than subsidies or a poll tax,
still left the way open for considerable delay. The proportion
to be raised from each 'country' had to be settled by a vote
and here even the courtiers thought first of their constituents.
The future Speaker, Sir Job Charlton, followed by Sir Robert
Atkins, a future Baron of the Exchequer, took the chair of the
committee, but progress was exasperatingly slow. In an effort
to speed things up Charles announced the remission of £20,000,
to ease the most severely assessed counties but this only produced further wrangling over how to share out the money.[3]
Whilst the revenue committee searched through precedents,
even looking back as far as the Ship money awards, Christmas
approached, and since to miss the holiday was unthinkable
the House adjourned for a three weeks recess.[4]

Returning, in rather limited numbers, on January 12, the
Commons showed that they were not prepared to ignore
entirely those wicked rumours against which Charles had
warned them earlier. To meet the persistent suggestions that a
peace might still be made and the money pocketed by the

---

[1] *C.J.* viii, 569, Nov. 26, 28; *Cal. S.P. Ven. 1664–6*, p. 66, Dec. 11; Bennet's
letter, undated, quoted in W. Cobbett, *Parliamentary History*, iv, 36–7, note.

[2] Holland's speech advocating a subsidy is in Tanner MSS. 239, f. 36v.
The ban on future use of assessments is in 13 Car. II, Stat. II, cap. 3, clause
32, and the euphemistic title of the new act in 16 & 17 Car. II, cap. 1,
clause 1. See also *C.J.* viii. 569, Nov. 28, and, for a good account of the
Cromwellian assessment, M. P. Ashley, *Finance and Commercial Policy under
the Cromwellian Protectorate* (1934), pp. 72–83.

[3] *C.J.* viii. 570–80, Nov. 29–Dec. 17; Carte MSS. 75, ff. 281–2, letter of
William Coventry, Dec. 11; PRO 31/3/113, f. 86, dispatch of the French
ambassador, Dec. 19; *Further Correspondence of Samuel Pepys, 1662–72*, J. R.
Tanner, p. 33, Dec. 15, 1664; Tanner MSS. 239, f. 38, for a speech of
Holland claiming rebate for Norfolk; *Calendar of Wynn Papers 1515–1690*
(1926), p. 379, letter of John Wynn, Dec. 20. See also Chandaman, op. cit.,
ii. 416–18, and compare a comment by Sir Edward Dering, *Diary*, ed. Henning, pp. 121–2, Feb. 18, 1673.

[4] *C.J.* viii. 575, 580–1, Dec. 12, 20.

King a clause was proposed for the supply 'to be applied for the righting of your Majesty and your Majesty's subjects against the Dutch'.[1] The first three words were, on a division, rejected, and the implied appropriation made less strict, but some suspicion seems to have remained, for on February 15 it was suggested that if peace should be made any outstanding monthly payments should be transferred at once to pay the many creditors of the navy.[2] This proposal was also dropped, but it was clear that Parliament would want to know how their money had been spent.

For one thing at least the court had reason to be thankful: the long delay in completing the supply bill had not been due to bills initiated by the country. No other bill of importance was in fact completed, or even discussed, during this session. The price of coal was fixed as a precaution against war profiteering,[3] bills were passed to provide a better choice of jurors and to reduce delays in legal proceedings, whilst the current emergency did not prevent the completion of twenty private acts. Yet on the whole the Commons had been co-operative. By any standard their vote of supply had been generous. Having shown such restraint and allowed their grievances to slumber they would now expect a glorious and speedy triumph over the Dutch. Anything less would give the vanquished opposition all the ammunition it required.

[1] Ibid., viii. 581, Jan. 12, 1665. For the continuance of such suspicions see *Cal. S.P. Ven. 1664–6*, p. 87, March 5.

[2] *C.J.* viii. 602. Some at least of these creditors were still seeking repayment three years later, *Cal. S.P. Dom. 1667–8*, p. 31, Nov. 19, 1667.

[3] The price of fuel was said to have trebled, *Cal. S.P. Ven. 1664–6*, p. 92, March 19, due largely to Dutch success in capturing Newcastle colliers, *Pepys*, iv. 303, Jan. 3.

CHAPTER IV

THE OPPOSITION REVIVES

IRISH CATTLE AND APPROPRIATION

IN 1664 Clarendon had urged Charles to make the most of Parliament's war fever and to obtain one large and final grant. This Charles had done but when, in October 1665, Parliament reassembled, they had to be told that still more money was required. True there had been a victory in the summer;[1] nevertheless the Dutch fleet remained 'in being', and the massive grant, only a third of which had as yet been collected, was fully anticipated or already spent.[2] Meanwhile falling rents threatened to revive complaints against Irish competition;[3] activity among the sectaries might be made the excuse for further persecution[4] and, despite the general success of our arms, there had been certain blunders by naval commanders which could be made the basis of a further attack on the administration.[5] On the credit side was the prevalence of the plague. The session was held at Oxford, but London was only sixty miles away and members had thus a powerful incentive to complete their work with all possible speed.

In his opening speech Charles dealt plainly with the need for money, adding that 'a more powerful neighbour' was showing signs of joining in the war.[6] Clarendon then explained, for the first time, how the King had been forced into debt during the

[1] On June 3, Ogg. op. cit., i. 286–8.

[2] So Charles explained in his opening speech, *L.J.* xi. 684, Oct. 10. See also *Pepys*, v. 109–10, Oct. 15.

[3] Verney MSS., Claydon, letter of Sir Ralph Verney, Feb. 16, 1665, reporting that Sir Richard Temple had been forced to sell off several of his manors.

[4] *Cal. S.P. Dom. 1664–5*, pp. 497–542, Aug. 1–30, 1665, passim, including several letters from Sir William Coventry (knighted on March 3, 1665), who was usually tolerant but at this time seems to have believed in a real threat of rebellion.

[5] The most notable of these were Sandwich's 'breaking bulk' dealt with in this session, infra, and the failure to follow up the victory of June, dealt with in the session of 1667–8, infra, Chapter VII.

[6] *L.J.* xi. 684. At this reference to France the whole house 'hummed', and further evidence of hostility to that country appeared in a later debate,

opening months of his reign, though he failed to forecast the
calamitous drop in the customs, excise, and hearth money
revenues which was to take place in the second year of the war.[1]
The House responded at once, promising a further £1,250,000
to be raised by monthly assessments. Solicitor-General Finch
was asked to prepare a bill and this he presented on October 13.[2]

So far all had gone well. On the bill's second reading, however, Sir George Downing stood up to propose some remarkable
amendments.[3] Returning from his embassy to Holland, Downing had been struck by our comparative failure to mobilize
credit in aid of the war. Seeking out Bennet, now Lord Arlington, and William Coventry, knighted earlier in the year, he had
devised with them a scheme which he hoped would encourage
men to lend more freely to the Crown. The new grant was to
be appropriated to the repayment of an entirely new loan, the
lenders to be repaid in the same order in which they had
invested, as soon as the money came in. The proposals had been
explained to Charles who had expressed his approval. No one,
however, seems to have told either Clarendon or his friend Lord
Treasurer Southampton what had been agreed.[4]

When Downing made his proposals the Commons found them
to their liking. Temple's suggestion of a subsidy was brushed
aside, and in ten days the bill, with Downing's amendments, was
ready for the Lords.[5] There, at a time when speed was vital,

---

Carte MSS. 34, ff. 427, 429, letters of Sir Robert Southwell and Broderick,
Oct. 11, 12.

[1] *L.J.* xi. 685, Oct. 10. In the financial year Michaelmas 1664–5 the
revenue from these three main funds totalled £893,000 but in the following
year it dropped to £488,000, Chandaman, ii. 700. Here, rather than in an
inadequate war supply, was the real cause of Charles' future embarrassments
but this seems never to have been understood either by the King or Commons.

[2] *C.J.* viii. 614–16, Oct. 11, 13. The figure was agreed in quarter of an
hour, Carte MSS. 34, f. 429, letter of Broderick, Oct. 12.

[3] Clarendon, *Life*, iii. 10–11. Downing had already delivered a very long
speech in justification of the war, Carte MSS. 34, ff. 429, 431, letters of
Southwell and Broderick, Oct. 12; Carte MSS. 215, f. 214, letter of Broderick,
Oct. 8.

[4] Clarendon, *Life*, iii. 10–11. Downing's proposals and the events arising
from them are described in detail by Roseveare, pp. 43–53.

[5] *C.J.* viii. 616–19, Oct. 13–21. For Temple's attempt see Carte MSS. 34,
ff. 431–2, letter of Southwell, Oct. 12. Downing's scheme was praised by the
Speaker at the end of the session, *L.J.* xi. 699, Oct. 31.

Southampton attacked the amendments, only to be warned off
by Charles himself. A violent argument then took place in
Clarendon's bedroom—the Chancellor was confined to his bed
by gout—and the two senior ministers reflected bitterly on both
the novelty and the alleged inconvenience of Downing's scheme.
Charles became angry and snubbed the Chancellor, Coventry and
Arlington were present to witness this, and although the bill was
saved the rift within the court had become wider than ever.[1]

One possible cause of Charles' rudeness to Clarendon may
have been annoyance at the concluding passages of the latter's
opening address. Having made his request for supply Clarendon
had gone on to denounce the activities of the fanatics, 'scorpions
. . . kept warm in our bosom', who might, if not crushed, 'sting
us to death'.[2] The activity to which the Chancellor referred was
not entirely imaginary—it had impressed so strong a friend of
toleration as Sir William Coventry[3]—but the Commons reaction went far beyond what circumstances might have required.
On October 19 they ordered a new bill against dissenters, the
Five Mile Act, which passed the Commons within a week.[4] One
clause of this act imposed on suspected conventiclers an oath
against attempting 'any alteration of government in either
Church or State'.[5] By a second bill, introduced on October 26,
this oath would have been imposed on all office holders, and
also on all members of the Commons.[6]

The Five Mile Act was an exaggerated response to a real
danger. The second bill was far more. It would inhibit opposition, discourage any further attempt to bring in toleration, and
thus please the most conservative in both the Commons and the
court. In 1669 a similar measure was put forward by a group
known as 'Clarendonians';[7] in 1675 a better known bill was
introduced by Danby, as a step in his defence of 'Church and
King'.[8] Ironically it was said to have been Danby, at this time

---

[1] Clarendon, *Life*, iii. 10–11, 15–26.

[2] *L.J.* xi. 688–9.

[3] Supra, p. 34, note 4.

[4] *C.J.* viii. 618–721, Oct. 19–25. For a full account of this bill's passage
through the Lords see Caroline Robbins, 'The Oxford Session of 1665',
Bulletin of the Institute of Historical Research, xxi (1948), pp. 219–23.

[5] 17 Car. II, cap. 2, clause 1.

[6] There is an account of this in 'Letter to a Person of Quality', printed by
W. Cobbett, *Parliamentary History*, iv, app. xl.

[7] Infra, Chapter VIII.   [8] Infra, Chapter XIII.

plain Sir Thomas Osborne, who as a follower of Buckingham and enemy of the Chancellor turned the scale against the 1665 bill, bringing about its defeat on the second reading by the narrow majority of 57 to 51.[1] Not only men like Temple or Marvell, but also tolerant courtiers like Arlington and William Coventry must have been glad to see it fail.

The country cavaliers had gained the Five Mile Act and lost this non-resisting oath. Their tolerant colleagues joined them in two further thrusts, to erect new barriers against Irish Cattle, and to check the misconduct of officials. The second of these aims was expressed in a bill against the embezzlement of prize goods, read on October 18 and directed against the unfortunate Earl of Sandwich.[2] Sandwich had given good service during the summer; through no fault of his own he had achieved little success, but eventually he had brought in two rich East Indiamen as prizes. Impatient of the correct procedure he had failed to wait for the prize commissioners to inspect the ships and, 'breaking bulk', had distributed a share of the plunder amongst his officers and men.[3] Unfortunately the commissioners included several members of the Commons, among them Edward Seymour, who were furious at this slight on their authority.[4] Matters were made worse when Sandwich, going down to spend a well earned leave at Clarendon's country house, failed to provide ships to keep the Dutch from harassing our coasts.[5] When he arrived in Oxford he found members bitter against him;[6] the bill of October 18 was the way in which their resentment was expressed.

[1] C.J. viii. 622, Oct. 27. For Osborne's alleged intervention see 'Letter to a Person of Quality', Cobbett, loc. cit. but this account does not quite tally with the figure in the Journal.

[2] C.J. viii, 617, Oct. 18.

[3] There is a full account of this incident based in part on MSS no longer available, in F. R. Harris, Life of Edward Montague, First Earl of Sandwich, ii. 1–12.

[4] Pepys, v. 105, Oct. 11. Some of these were members who had been given their positions as a reward for past services in debates, Clarendon, Life, ii. 334.

[5] Harris, op. cit., ii. 13–17. The Duke of York had written to Coventry on Oct. 9 urging that a fleet should be kept up, B.M. Add. MSS. 32,094, ff. 65–6.

[6] Carte MSS. 215, f. 214, letter of Sir Alan Broderick, Oct. 8. The Commons were said to have voted £10,000 to the Duke of York and 2s. 6d. to Sandwich, Pepys, v. 130, Nov. 6.

The importance of this attack is twofold. Clarendon asserts that it was instigated by Sir William Coventry, a charge repeated by Pepys who was a friend and colleague of them both.[1] If this charge is true then Coventry must be ranked with Bristol as an early exponent of that unhappy practice by which one minister would turn Parliament against a rival, often to succumb in due course to a similar attack.[2] In the second place, the fact that Sandwich was removed from his command[3] established a precedent for making Parliament the judge of who should serve the King, a precedent soon to be used against Clarendon himself.

All this had been packed into a bare three weeks and might have been thought quite sufficient to occupy the members' time. Yet taking precedence, it would seem, over all other matters, was another bill, drafted by Sir Richard Temple, and designed to protect the landed interest; this was an extension of the restrictions on the Irish Cattle trade into a complete embargo. The bill was introduced on October 18, but on the preceding day its contents had become known to Ormonde's friend Lord Conway, who hurried to inform first Clarendon, then Arlington, and finally Solicitor-General Finch.[4] Broderick was summoned from the country, Sir Winston Churchill and Sir Robert Southwell armed for battle, and so the struggle began.

Against normal custom the bill was opposed on its first reading, which it nevertheless passed by 103 to 52.[5] It then went forward to a large committee, which was ordered to hear

[1] Clarendon, *Life*, ii. 469–70; *Pepys*, v. 117–18, Oct. 25.

[2] 'Your excellencies will note that this Parliamentary machine is a contrivance devised purposely by intriguing ministers to work it against each other', *Cal. S.P. Ven.*, *1673–5*, p. 155, Oct. 27, 1673. See also the famous 'drunken' speech of the Earl of Carnarvon, W. Cobbett, *Parliamentary History*, iv. 1073, Dec. 23, 1678. In fairness to Sir William he had shown concern over the handling of the prizes before Sandwich made his blunder, *Cal. S.P. Dom. 1664–5*, p. 564, letter to Arlington, Sept. 16, and this anxiety had been echoed by Albemarle in his letter to Sandwich of Sept. 19, Carte MSS. 75, ff. 363–4.

[3] He was retired honourably to the position of ambassador at Madrid, Harris, op. cit., ii. 21–31. The bill against embezzlement was then dropped having been read only twice, *C.J.* viii. 617, 619, Oct. 18, 21.

[4] Carte MSS. 34, ff. 442–5, letters of Conway and Broderick, both of Oct. 19; 46, f. 211, letter of Arlington, Oct. 18.

[5] *C.J.* viii. 619, Oct. 18. Finch spoke 'incomparably' against the bill but 'if an angel in heaven had offered . . . the highest reason' it would have been in vain, Carte MSS. 34, ff. 442–3, Conway, Oct. 19.

evidence from any members of the Irish Privy Council who might be present at Oxford.[1] Robert Boyle, Sir William Petty, Broderick, Southwell, even the Bishop of Limerick, addressed the committee, as did the Solicitor-General.[2] A hundred members were present: the opponents of the bill were allowed neither a copy, nor even a breviate, but had to argue for four hours, having heard the bill read only once. Finch talked on until he was completely exhausted—the following day he collapsed at a meeting of the 'cabinet council' and had to be carried to his house—but his devotion was not shared by all his colleagues. At the first division the votes were tied and the chairman, Littleton, soon to be reputed one of Arlington's supporters,[3] gave his voice for the bill. After this some members of the Irish lobby began to drift away, later challenges were beaten off by 3 and 5 votes, and the bill went forward to its final reading which it passed, on October 23, by 81–68.[4]

After so much excitement came an anti-climax. The bill was delayed in the Lords and was unfinished when Parliament was prorogued.[5] Yet its opponents could find no great comfort in what they themselves regarded as a mere postponement of the issue. Its revival was considered certain,[6] but worse still, Arlington and William Coventry seemed more than half inclined to regard surrender as a fair price for supply.[7] The friends of Ormonde and Clarendon were left to pin their hope on the uncertain promise of the King, who had declared that he would never give such a measure his consent.[8]

[1] *C.J.* viii. 619, Oct. 26.

[2] Carte MSS. 34, ff. 448–53, letters of Broderick, Berkley and Southwell, Oct. 22, 23, 24.

[3] G. Burnet, *History of my own Time*, ed. Airey, i. 478.

[4] *C.J.* viii. 620, Oct. 24; Carte MSS. 34, ff. 452–5, letters of Southwell and Broderick, Oct. 24, 26.

[5] This delay had been foreseen and probably intended, Carte MSS. 46, ff. 217–19, letters of Arlington, Oct. 25, Nov. 1; 34, ff. 454–5, Broderick, Oct. 26.

[6] Carte MSS. 34, f. 413, letters of Southwell, misdated Sept. 1, ff. 463–5, letters of Sir Winston Churchill and Conway, both of Oct. 29; Carte MSS. 47, f. 462, Henry Coventry, Aug. 26, 1666. All these writers were opponents of the bill.

[7] Carte MSS. 46, ff. 209, 217, 219, letters of Arlington, Oct. 11, 18, Nov. 1, 1665, and ff. 440–1, Jan. 19, 1667; Carte MSS. 47, ff. 428, 464, letters of Sir William Coventry, Oct. 29, 1665, Sept. 22, 1666.

[8] There are many references to Charles' desire to check the proposed

The session ended on October 31, not without one last blow at the court. By an unopposed resolution Temple and Whorwood, neither of them *persona grata* at court, were instructed to attend the King with a request that, when Parliament should next meet, the officers of the navy, ordnance and stores should be nearly ready to present their accounts.[1] Charles' reply is, perhaps fortunately, unrecorded, but when the time came the Commons would not be slow to repeat their request. On a more gracious note, thanks were voted to the city of Oxford for its loyalty in the late civil war[2]—a strong hint that cavalier sentiment was very far from dead—and Charles prorogued parliament to February of the following year.[3]

Observing progress from across the channel the Venetian resident in Paris saw this session as having been dominated by the Chancellor.[4] In fact the latter's grip, re-established in 1664, was now beginning to slacken. The Supply Bill, the most important measure of all, had been removed from the control of his supporter, Heneage Finch, and its management given to Downing, a new and able member of the Arlington–Coventry group. The non-resistance test, a future shibboleth of the 'true cavalier party', had failed, whilst the success in the Lower House of the bill against Irish Cattle showed both the strength of country opposition, and the Chancellor's inability to mobilize the full strength of the court. Sandwich's removal meant not only the loss of a friend but also the establishment of a most dangerous precedent; that a minister 'not liking' to the Commons should be dismissed by the King.[5] Though Clarendon describes the session cheerfully enough in his memoirs it is difficult not to see it as heralding his fall.

Admitting this it may still be asked if Charles drew the right conclusions when, two years later, he decided that the Chan-

---

embargo. Typical are letters of Broderick, Carte MSS. 35, f. 101, Oct. 13, 1666, Arlington, 46, ff. 217, 385, Oct. 25, 1665, Oct. 13, 1666, and Anglesey, 217, ff. 336, 344, Sept. 25, Oct. 20, 1666.

[1] *C.J.* viii. 623.

[2] Ibid.

[3] *L.J.* xi. 699–701. Foreshadowing future difficulties a useful bill to provide remedies against the plague had to be abandoned because of an inter-house dispute, Carte MSS. 34, f. 468, Broderick, Nov. 2.

[4] *Cal. S.P. Ven. 1664–6*, p. 233, Dec. 15, 1665.

[5] See Sir William Coventry's comment in a debate after Clarendon had been dismissed. *Milward*, app. ii, p. 329.

cellor must go. Clarendon was coming to stand for 'Church and King' and this policy had received in the Five Mile Act a strong vote of confidence. The approval late in the session of a gift of £120,000 to the Duke of York was another gesture by the cavaliers;[1] despite occasional differences the Duke and the Chancellor were agreed on fundamentals and when it came to a crisis the latter proved his father-in-law's most loyal friend.[2] Above all if we are to employ hindsight and blame Clarendon for losing his grip on the Commons then we must also remember the subsequent failure of his rivals. The banning of Irish Cattle, the acceptance of appropriation and the inspection of accounts, the sacrifice of Clarendon himself, were none of them to produce for the King toleration or supply. When supply was obtained it was less by reason of these earlier concessions than by the relinquishing of toleration in deference to the resolute anglican-ism of the 'Clarendonians', the surest source of support in what remained a house of cavaliers.

[1] 17 Car. II, cap. 9. The proposal was made by Sir John Goodrick on Oct. 24. Although the House showed little support no one was willing to speak against the motion, which was eventually passed *nem con. C.J.* viii. 621; Carte MSS. 34, f. 433, Southwell, Oct. 24.

[2] At this period Clarendon and the Duke were in disagreement over the advancement of Sir William Coventry, and of the latter's gifted nephew Sir George Savile, later first Marquis of Halifax. In the next session, how-ever, and at the time of Clarendon's impeachment, Duke and Chancellor were closely agreed. Infra, Chapter V.

THE DOMINANCE OF THE OPPOSITION

Royal Aid	£2,450,000
More	£1,250,000
3 Months Militia money @ £70,000	£ 210,000
Customs from which the King promised £240,000 p.a.	£ 480,000
Prizes	£ 300,000
Debt owed by the Navy	£ 900,000
	£5,590,000
Charge of the Navy for two years	£3,200,000
So what has become of all this sum?	£2,390,000

READERS familiar with the standard apologies for Charles II will have little hesitation in identifying this reckoning. Clearly, they will exclaim, this must be the work of those ignorant and prejudiced Commissioners whom the Commons appointed to go through the government's accounts.[1] If they make this assumption they will be wrong: this is in fact the reckoning of Samuel Pepys, perhaps the most competent member of the whole administration, and it was entered in his diary on October 10, 1666.[2] To answer Pepys' question was one part of the task facing the court in the session of 1666. The other, and still more difficult, part lay in persuading an angry and suspicious House to grant yet a further supply.

How would Parliament respond? Whom would they attack first? Ministers seeking the best way to serve the King were never free from the fear of being themselves called to account.[3] Nevertheless money had to be found, the administration was paralysed for want of it,[4] and some kind of platform had there-

[1] See for example, W. A. Shaw, introduction to *Cal. Treasury Books 1667–8*, pp. li–lxvii; and A. Bryant, *King Charles II* (1955) p. 154, and *Samuel Pepys, The Years of Peril*, pp. 12–14, 20–3, 28–36.

[2] *Pepys*, vi. 13–14; and compare v. 417 for Sept. 23.

[3] Some seem to have divided their time between trembling for themselves and smirking over the unhappy prospects of their colleagues, *Pepys*, v. 365–6, 387, 409–11, Aug. 5, 26, Sept. 14, 15, and vi, 5–6, Oct. 5.

[4] Ibid., v. 386, 405, 413, Aug. 26, Sept. 8, 19.

fore to be agreed. Left over from the previous session were at
least two questions of importance: Irish Cattle and accounts.
Clarendon wanted to oppose a cattle bill and to deny inspection
of accounts; Arlington and William Coventry were ready to
give way on both these points if it would smooth the way to a
supply.[1] Argument there must have been, but it is not recorded.
The contest, not only between court and country, but between
the factions within the court, can only be traced by following
the progress of the session.

Charles met Parliament on September 21, after a postponement of three days.[2] Even on this delay the court had been
divided. Some had wished to wait until the members for the
'old loyal counties' of the north and west had arrived; others
had feared that those areas would send up the bitterest enemies
of Irish Cattle.[3] To wait could thus be taken as a hint that the
King would incline towards the policy backed by Arlington and
Sir William Coventry—that concessions on any matter, Irish
Cattle included, would be justified if they secured a grant of
money—though at this stage he was still assuring the Irish
lobby that he would never agree to a complete embargo on the
cattle trade.[4] Meanwhile Charles made no reference to this
dangerous topic in his speech, but explained that, notwithstand-
ing the 'success of the summer', the war was still continuing:
the enemy were insolently confident that our recent misfortunes
must have brought us to our knees, and although great efforts
would be made to prove their assumption false this would en-
tail heavy anticipation of the revenue already granted for 1667.

The Commons replied with an immediate resolution of
thanks for the King's 'great care and management of the present
war'; furthermore they would 'supply his Majesty proportion-
ately to his present occasions'. To discover what those present

---

[1] Infra, pp. 55–6, and supra, Chapter IV; Clarendon, *Life*, iii. 129–32,
136–43.

[2] *L.J.* xiii. 4. Clarendon asserts that the court hoped to push supply
through a thin House, *Life*, iii. 127, but Arlington explained to Ormonde
that the King had waited deliberately for more members to arrive, Carte
MSS, 46, f. 371, letter of Sept. 18. This second account tallies with the
Journals, *C.J.* viii. 624–5, Sept. 18, 21.

[3] Carte MSS. 72, ff. 97–8, letter of Sir Edward Massey, Sept. 22; 217, f.
336, letter of Anglesey, Sept. 29. See also *Pepys*, vi. 10–11, Oct. 8; and Feiling,
History of the Tory Party, p. 2.

[4] Carte MSS. 217, ff. 336, 342. Anglesey, Sept. 29, Oct. 16.

occasions might be, however, they added a second resolution: that 'Tuesday next be appointed for the officers of his Majesty's Navy, Ordnance, and Stores, to bring in their accounts'.[1] Having thus committed themselves to granting at least some money, and at the same time having produced a flurry of activity at the navy office,[2] they were free to see about their own concerns.

On September 22 a new bill against importing foreign cattle was read for the first time. As before Norfolk members were quick to protest, but the bill was granted a second reading without a division.[3] At this stage Clarendon, Anglesey and Finch still hoped for its rejection in the Commons, though Arlington and Sir William Coventry thought that, at best, this could only take place in the Lords.[4] At the second reading, on September 26, Finch put forth his best oratory but failed to stop the bill going to committee: still its opponents resisted, and in one of the divisions the votes were tied at 200 each side.[5] On October 5, however, Edward Seymour, by now rivalling Temple for first place among the trouble-makers, proposed the insertion of the term 'nuisance' into the bill, to prevent its circumvention by the grant of royal 'dispensations'.[6] Finch denounced this as unprecedented, Temple at once proved him wrong, and Finch then suggested that to support this clause was to invade the King's prerogative. Far from deterring members this only made them more annoyed, and though Broderick hastened from Ireland and Denham rose from his sick bed to vote against the bill, it went through its third reading by the safe majority of 165–104.[7] The burden of resistance thus passed to the Upper House.

[1] *C.J.* viii. 628, Sept. 26; *Milward*, p. 8.

[2] *Pepys*, v. 423–4, vi. 1–3, Sept. 29, 30, Oct. 1, 2.

[3] *C.J.* viii. 626, Sept. 22; *Milward*, pp. 3–4. The Norfolk interest had been stated three years earlier, supra, p. 12 note 7.

[4] Carte MSS. 35, f. 86, Finch, Sept. 29; 47, ff. 126–7, Clarendon, and f. 464, Sir William Coventry, both of Sept. 22; 217, f. 336, Anglesey, Sept. 29; 46, ff. 365, 377–8, Arlington, Sept. 11, 22.

[5] *C.J.* viii. 627, Sept. 26; *Milward*, pp. 7–9, Sept. 26, 28; Carte MSS. 217, f. 338, Oct. 6, Anglesey.

[6] *Milward*, pp. 14–15, Oct. 5, 8, 17. On the legal point see Halsbury, *Laws of England*, 2nd ed. (1937) xxiv, 25–6.

[7] *C.J.* viii. 635, Oct. 13; *Milward*, p. 22; Clarendon, *Life*, iii. 142; Carte MSS. 35, f. 101, Broderick, Oct. 13, and 46, f. 385, Arlington, Oct. 13. The second of these letters makes clear Arlington's preoccupation with supply.

With this bill out of the way the Commons were prepared to consider accounts and to debate supply. So far as accounts were concerned, and in marked contrast to most other business, the King was served by two superbly competent spokesmen: Pepys, who knew all too well the deficiencies he had to hide, kept his fears to himself and out-talked the fiercest 'hot-spurs' on the investigating committee; when it came to a debate in the house, Sir William Coventry took over, speaking from a carefully prepared brief. Against this defence the charges of incompetence were levied in vain. Colonel Birch, himself once a servant of the navy, William Garraway, a fervent royalist soured by neglect, Sir William Thomson, Edward Boscowen, and the rest of the committee, found themselves answered point for point. At last, on October 11, the committee laid its report before the House.[1]

On the whole the contents of this report were much better than the court had feared. Of the doubtful items which had worried Pepys both the prize money and the three militia assessments were omitted, though the former was referred to a separate committee. It was true that Duncombe failed in his attempt to add a supplementary estimate of £54,000 for 'necessary expenses'—he was beaten down to £34,000—whilst the House refused to accept a figure of £150,000 for 'wear and tear'.[2] The general attitude, however, of both committee and House showed that, as in earlier years, a majority could still be convinced by clear reasoning if this was backed by apparently reliable figures. Unfortunately four more years had still to pass before the main revenue debates were entrusted to spokesmen as competent as Coventry and Pepys.

It is illustrative of the contrast between the Navy Office and the main group of the court that when the supply debate began it was left to one of the opposition—Temple—to make the first definite proposal.[3] He suggested £1,600,000: the court thought this too little, and failing to make much impression did at least get an adjournment to the following day. The House was now in Grand Committee and Temple's group, abandoning their attempt to fix a sum, suggested that the committee should first agree on method, and that this should be by land tax.[4] For

---

[1] *C.J.* viii. 634, Oct. 11; *Pepys*, v. 417–19, 423–4; vi. 2–14, Sept. 22 to Oct. 10.

[2] *Milward*, pp. 20, 26–7; *C.J.* viii. 634, Oct. 11; *Pepys*, vi. 15, Oct. 15.

[3] *Milward*, p. 20, Oct. 11.   [4] Ibid., p. 21–2, Oct. 12.

reasons that will be discussed later the court objected; Temple then tried to adjourn from the Committee back to the House. At last, about two o'clock the Speaker did resume the Chair and a sum of £1,800,000 was proposed—the additional £200,000 was to cover interest charges—and on this both sides eventually agreed.

After three weeks, and a surrender on the Cattle Bill, the court had now secured a definite offer, even though this was much less than their necessities required. On the other hand they had conceded the initiative to the opposition, and they were hardly to regain their authority as leaders within the next three years. Moreover, though agreement on a figure was welcome, there still remained the question of how the money was to be raised. The court hoped to secure an additional excise: they further hoped, reasonably enough, that this might be turned into a perpetual tax which would increase the permanent revenue of the Crown.[1] For just that reason many of the country opposed excise, finding all kinds of objections to raise.[2] The very name, with its Long Parliament associations, was declared 'ungrateful to the people of England'; the officers employed to collect the tax would become 'as so many vermin and caterpillars to devour us', and would themselves consume half the yield; the high-handed methods to be expected from such officers would arouse great resentment and so prove a major threat to the country's peace. Somewhat disingenuously it was objected that the time needed to draft an excise bill would deprive the King of money which was urgently required; it is hard to believe that such a delay could have been any longer than that caused by the long search for an alternative method. Last, but no means least, was the invasion of the sacred right of property: any man's shop, warehouse, even home would be liable to intrusion by the exciseman. All these arguments, reiterated during three weeks of wearisome debate, combined to secure for the court's excise a rejection scarcely less resounding than the more famous one of 1733.

[1] Carte MSS. 35, ff. 105–6, Broderick, Oct. 20; *Pepys*, vi. 48, Nov. 5; *Milward*, pp. 21, 25, 28, Oct, 12, 16, 18.

[2] Carte MSS. 34, ff. 459–60, Conway, Oct. 27; *Milward*, app. pp. 308–10, speech of Sir John Holland. For a graphic description of the conception, parentage, and habits of 'the monster excise' see A. Marvell, 'Last Instructions to a Painter', *Poems and Letters*, i. 144.

If not excise, then what? The Presbyterians, led by Swinfen, were in favour of a land tax, the previously employed system of assessments. Others of the country favoured a forced loan from 'monied men'—rejected later as a possible device to undermine the act of indemnity—a tax upon luxuries, a tax on corn at the mill, or the selling of offices after the manner of France. Most generally approved was the proposal of a Mr Orme of Peterborough, who suggested that the Hearth Tax, highly unpopular since its collection had been made more efficient, should be bought back from the King at eight years' value, taking its yield as £200,000 a year.[1]

From October 15 to November 3 the argument continued. Marvell, writing his epic account of the excise bill's rejection, saw the court as a troop, 'for diligence renowned and discipline',[2] but in fact such diligence as there was appeared on the other side. Downing complained to Pepys that the court cut across each other's speeches and split their strength; Broderick wrote helplessly of drifting at 'the accident of wind and tide'; meanwhile the navy lacked even money to buy rum.[3] At last, after spending days discussing what compensation should be given to the King when he had surrendered the hearth tax, someone thought of asking him if he was prepared to do this. If he had agreed he would have got a good bargain, the Commons' habit of over-estimating yields would have worked against them on this occasion, but whether or not Charles realized this the monied men who would have had to find the immediate cash fought shy of the scheme, and on November 8 Secretary Morrice told the House that the proposal must be dropped.[4] Weary of conflict the court offered assurance that there would be no further talk of a home excise; Garraway then graciously

---

[1] *Milward*, pp. 21–38, Oct. 12–Nov. 8, passim; *Pepys*, vi. 22, Oct. 15; Carte MSS. 35, ff. 105–6, Broderick, Oct. 20.

[2] Marvell, i. 144.

[3] Carte MSS. 35, ff. 105, 111, 118, Broderick, Oct. 20, 27, Nov. 3; *Pepys*, vi. 26, 70–71, Oct. 19, Nov. 23.

[4] *Milward*, p. 38, Nov. 8; Carte MSS. 34, ff. 459–60, Conway, Oct. 27. Clarendon, *Life*, ii. 181, says that he and Southampton opposed the bargain. It would have meant abandoning a permanent source of revenue for a lump sum, always a bad principle; on the other hand the tax was unpopular, hard to collect, and yielded on average under £120,000 a year, Chandaman, i. 303, and Lydia M. Marshall, 'The Levying of the Hearth Tax 1662–88'. *Eng. Hist. Rev.* li (1936), 629–44.

proposed that the bulk of money should be raised by an eleven-
monthly assessment, to begin in May 1668 when the two existing levies, of 1664 and 1665, would have expired. The full sum
would be made up by a Poll Bill, by a limited excise on foreign
commodities which was in fact to be used only to meet the cost
of coining bullion, and by a tax on legal documents which was
later abandoned.[1] At no point had the court controlled these
debates.

Whilst all this was in progress four other problems were
maturing for the court. These concerned the Canary Patent, the
impeachment of Lord Mordaunt, the renewed struggle over
Irish Cattle and the establishment of some really effective
method by which the Commons could check the administration's accounts. Taking first the Canary Patent: this was a
charter passed under the great seal by Clarendon which
allowed a single group of merchants to enjoy the monopoly of
importing Canary wine.[2] The reason for granting the monopoly
had been sensible enough: to increase our bargaining power
against the islanders who had been playing off one merchant
against another and had managed to double the price within
twenty years. Naturally, those excluded from the monopoly
were resentful, and on October 1 had presented a petition to
the Commons. Irrespective of its merits this offered a chance to
strike a blow at the Chancellor. On October 29 Edward
Seymour reported that the charter was 'an illegal patent, a
monopoly, and a grievance to the subject'.[3]

The immediate reaction of the House was to consider an
impeachment against the patentees. This was later rejected, and
it was decided to ask the House of Lords to join in requesting
that the charter be annulled.[4] The Lords, however, seem at this
time to have been more than ever conscious of their dignity, and
despite two sharp reminders they ignored the Commons' message for over a month. They then summoned both the patentees
and the petitioners to attend before them, but the latter failed
to appear. At this the Lords decided that the Commons had

[1] *Milward*, pp. 38–9, Nov. 8.

[2] A full account is given by Caroline A. J. Skeel, 'The Canary Company',
Eng. Hist. Rev. xxi (1916).

[3] *C.J.* viii. 629, 643, Oct. 1, 29; *Milward*, pp. 10, 33. Several of Clarendon's friends disapproved of the patent: Carte MSS. 35, ff. 191, 195,
Broderick and Conway, Dec. 29; 48, ff. 80–1, Ormonde, Jan. 18.

[4] *Milward*, p. 33, Oct. 29; *C.J.* viii. 643, Oct. 29.

proceeded irregularly in not first discussing the matter at a conference, and declined to proceed any further.[1] The Commons made one effort to keep the affair alive but it finally lapsed, to be revived as part of the charge in Clarendon's impeachment.[2]

One probable reason why this was not pursued more vigorously was that three more serious disputes had developed between the Houses. The first of these originated with a petition presented by a Mr William Taylor, who alleged that a long series of injuries had been suffered by himself and his family at the hands of Lord Mordaunt, then Constable of Windsor.[3] Mordaunt was a sometime royalist conspirator, loyal but with many enemies even among his own cavalier associates; he was also a trusted friend of Clarendon.[4] Taylor, who claimed himself to be an 'old cavalier', had been quarrelling with Mordaunt since at least 1664, and had apparently annoyed him particularly by proposing to stand as parliamentary burgess for Windsor.[5] Whether Mordaunt had in fact assaulted Taylor's daughter, and frightened his young son into fits, was never established; his less violent actions had, however, been taken at the King's express command.[6] The importance of the Commons' reaction was that they not only proposed an impeachment, the first against any person of quality in this reign,[7] but also that by involving themselves in a long-drawn procedural struggle with the Lords, they gave the opposition a chance to delay other business, and in particular supply.

Taylor's petition was received on November 2, but was

[1] *L.J.* xii. 25–6, 35, 38, 42–3, Nov. 10, 12, 26, Dec. 3, 10; *C.J.* viii. 654, 661, Nov. 26, Dec. 21.

[2] *C.J.* viii. 677, Jan. 16, 1667; Milward, p. 64, 86, 114, Oct. 14, Nov. 6, 1667.

[3] The charge is entered in full in *C.J.* viii. 666–7, Dec. 21.

[4] Clarendon, *Life*, i. 356.

[5] Taylor's father-in-law was canvassing support against Mordaunt in Aug. 1664, B.M. Egerton MSS. 2538, f. 249, letter of William Parkhurst, Aug. 8, 1664.

[6] In Nov. 1665 the King had ordered Mordaunt to turn Taylor out of his lodgings, *Cal. S.P. Dom. 1665–6*, p. 79, Nov. 30; and compare *Cal. S.P. Dom. 1666–7*, p. 220, Oct. 26.

[7] There had been threats of impeachment against pamphleteers, for example *C.J.* viii. 393, March 24, 1662, and Bristol's 'impeachment' of Clarendon in 1663. Had Sandwich not been removed from his post by Charles he might have been impeached in 1665.

immediately stolen from the table of the House. This alleged attempt to delay proceedings merely aroused members' interest and a committee was ordered to investigate the charges.[1] Nothing was heard from this committee for some time, but on December 18, when the court were particularly anxious to press on with other business, it suddenly produced a report stating that Mordaunt was guilty of the charges and merited impeachment. Drafting the articles took time, as did the necessary searching after precedents without which no impeachment would have seemed complete. At last the papers were sent to the Lords, to whom, on January 17, Mordaunt in his turn submitted a written answer to the charge.[2] All now appeared clear for a trial, but the Commons' 'managers', who included Littleton and Seymour, found hard evidence elusive.[3] Lynch law had worked with Strafford and was virtually to be used against Clarendon, for an attack on whom some thought this to be a dress rehearsal:[4] this time, however, the Lords seemed certain to require some modicum of proof so a procedural quarrel was hastily worked up and messengers were still scampering to and fro between the Houses when it came to the adjournment.[5] Mordaunt received a royal pardon in the following summer for crimes he may or may not have committed. After Clarendon's fall he surrendered his office, and was said to have joined the ex-Chancellor in France.[6]

Third in this series of interhouse disputes came on over the bill to prohibit the trade in Irish Cattle. When this bill had reached the Lords, on October 15, many of its opponents had feared that this was the end of the struggle. So it might have been but for the rashness of Buckingham who, in his determination to inflict every possible humiliation upon both

[1] *Milward*, pp. 35–6, Nov. 2–3; *C.J.* viii. 663–5. The removal of the petition may possibly have been a device for publicizing the affair.

[2] *C.J.* viii. 665–9, Dec. 21, 22, 29; *L.J.* xii. 60–2, 70, 77–9, Jan. 5, 11, 17.

[3] Carte MSS. 35, f. 281, Broderick, Jan. 26.

[4] Ibid., 35, ff. 191–2, Broderick, Dec. 29.

[5] *C.J.* viii. 680–1, 684–90, Jan. 21–Feb. 6; *Milward*, pp. 68, 71–82, Jan. 22–Feb. 8.

[6] *Cal. S.P. Dom. 1667*, p. 277, July 8; *Cal. S.P. Dom. 1667–8*, p. 608, Sept. 29, 1668; B.M. Add. MSS. 36,916, f. 115, Starkey news letter, Oct. 10, 1668. Clarendon, *Life*, iii. 374 mentions the kindness shown him in France by Lady Mordaunt. *Pepys*, vii. 43, July 29, 1667, believed firmly in Mordaunt's guilt and was indignant at his escape.

Clarendon and Ormonde, pushed matters on with a boisterous-
ness that recoiled upon himself. After considering the bill in
committee for several weeks the Lords had finally proposed two
amendments: the first, to remove the word 'nuisance', as an
insult to the King, and the second to allow a proviso in favour
of 20,000 carcasses offered by the people of Ireland as a gift to
those unfortunates in London who had been made destitute by
the Fire. During the debates on these amendments Buckingham
had been involved in a brawl, had been sent, with Ormonde's
son Ossory, to the Tower, and had narrowly escaped a duel.
His conduct had disgusted many of the Lords and encouraged
them to follow the Chancellor's advice and stand firm against
the unreasonableness of the Lower House.[1]

The amended bill was returned to the Commons on November 24, just when the first supply bill—for a poll tax—was getting under way. Progress in the latter bill slowed up considerably whilst all the arguments about the former were gone over
once again. In the end both amendments were rejected, the one
concerning the gift of carcasses on the partly justified assumption that it was a trick to undermine the whole bill. The Lords
stood fast by their proposals, several conferences failed to secure
agreement, and the bill was deadlocked when the House came
to the winter recess.[2]

Before dealing with the fourth, and last, of the major
country challenges, we must look back for a moment at the
progress of supply. It will be remembered that whilst a grant
had been approved in principle on September 21, and the
amount fixed on October 12, no decision on method had been
reached until November 8. Then, however, the House had
passed several resolutions binding themselves to press on without
interruption, and although these had not been entirely effective
some kind of progress had been maintained throughout the next

---

[1] *L.J.* xii. 13–34. Oct. 16–Nov. 23, passim; Clarendon, *Life*, iii. 145–53;
Carte MSS. 34, ff. 459–60, Conway, Oct. 27; 35, ff. 120, 122, 124, 126, 144,
148, Conway, Nov. 10, 13, 27, Broderick, Nov. 10, 24, Burlington, Nov. 10;
46, ff. 398, 402, Arlington, Nov. 13, 20; 217, ff. 336, 342–54, 358, Anglesey,
Sept. 29, Oct. 16, 20, 23, 27, Nov. 3, 10, 20, 27. These letters are used by
T. Carte, *Ormonde* (1851) iv. 263–73.

[2] *C.J.* viii. 653–8, 660–1, Nov. 24–Dec. 12, passim; *Milward*, pp. 46–7,
54–5, Nov. 24, Dec. 5; *L.J.* xii. 48–50, Dec. 17. At one point, in December,
Anglesey hoped that the Commons might be turning against the bill, Carte
MSS. 217, f. 360, Dec. 11.

E

four weeks.[1] Meanwhile, on November 9, a new bill had been
brought into the Commons proposing that a committee should
be set up to take account of public money, and to hear witnesses on oath. This bill was abandoned, on the ground that
only the House of Lords had the right to administer an oath,
and, quite politely, the Commons asked the Lords if they would
care to form a joint committee. On November 28, the day after
the Commons had insisted on retaining the word 'nuisance' in
the Cattle Bill, the Lords sent them a message refusing to allow
commoners, even in conjunction with peers, to administer an
oath.[2] There was a ten day lull and then, on December 7,
Garraway suddenly proposed and carried a proviso to the
almost completed Poll Bill, tacking to it a clause setting up a
commission for taking account of public money.[3]

On several previous occasions Charles had not merely
allowed, but exhorted, Parliament to examine his revenue.[4] He
had already permitted examination of departmental accounts
by a Commons' committee, and it is hard to see why Garraway's proposal annoyed him so much. Nevertheless he was
furious: in a last-minute effort to stop the proviso he was said to
have sent messengers to all the playhouses and brothels, the
most likely places, he reasoned, to find members of the court.[5]
In the House there were some who felt, like John Milward, that
whilst examination of accounts would be an excellent thing, to
use a 'tack' was going too far; nevertheless the proviso passed
by 119 to 83.[6] Charles' temper cannot have been improved by
the fact that it had the backing of Seymour and, possibly, of
Sir Robert Howard, both considered to be followers of Buckingham.[7] Not for the last time the King's patience was strained to
the utmost by the 'whimsical' conduct of his friend the Duke.

---

[1] *C.J.* viii. 548–51, 653–8, Nov. 10, 12–17, 23–4, 26, 29, 30, Dec. 1, 3;
Milward, pp. 41–3, 45–7, 49–53.
[2] *C.J.* viii. 647–8, 655, Nov. 9, 10, 27; *L.J.* xii. 24–30, Nov. 9, 12, 16, 23;
Milward, pp. 39, 548.
[3] *C.J.* viii. 659; *Milward*, p. 56.
[4] In 1662 and 1663, supra, pp. 5, 17 notes 4, 1.
[5] *Pepys*, vi. 88, Dec. 8.
[6] *C.J.* viii. 659, Dec. 9. This caused Arlington more dismay than any
previous action in this session, Carte MSS. 46, f. 412, Dec. 8.
[7] Seymour and Garraway were tellers for the proviso. Pepys names
Howard as its proposer, vi. 88; Milward gives the responsibility to Garraway
as does John Wynn, *Calendar of Wynn Papers* (1926), p. 389, Dec. 8, but

As in earlier and later sessions personal intervention by
Charles produced at least a temporary increase in the effectiveness of the court. Exhorting his party to action, the King let it
be understood that if the obnoxious clause were not removed he
would sacrifice the money and veto the bill.[1] Meanwhile
Christmas was approaching and a number of members, of
whom a majority may be presumed to have belonged to the
country, were preparing to leave London. As the numbers at
divisions dropped, the court counter-attacked: on December 11
they secured the removal of the 'tacking' proviso, and its
incorporation in a separate bill which was completed within
twenty-four hours and sent straight to the Lords.[2] Here it
received two readings but on December 19, acting on the
Chancellor's advice, the Lords abandoned it, and instead
agreed to petition the King for an accounts commission to be
appointed as an act of grace. Charles accepted this petition and
a list of commissioners was quickly published. The inclusion of
several leading members of the Commons failed, however, to
compensate for the omission of Buckingham; thinking, perhaps rightly, that the new commission would be ineffective, the
Commons continued to remind the Lords of the original but
now neglected bill.[3]

Relations between the King and the Lords on one side, and
the Commons on the other, were now worse than at any previous period in the reign. The Commons were determined to
push through both the unamended cattle bill and the bill for the
inspection of accounts, whilst they were also much concerned
with the Canary Patent and the attack on Mordaunt. Meanwhile the court wanted the supply bills finished and an end to
the session. Their best hope lay in the fact that as numbers fell
their chances of securing a majority were likely to increase: a
division on December 12 showed a total attendance of only 108

Howard may well have added his support. On these men's links with Buckingham, see Clarendon, *Life*, iii. 132–3.

[1] *Pepys*, vi. 90, 92, Dec. 10, 12.

[2] *Pepys*, loc. cit.; *C.J.* viii. 661, Dec. 11, 12. Clarendon's account, in *Life*,
iii. 131–2, is chronologically inexact.

[3] *L.J.* xii. 46–7, 52–4, 56–7, 88–9, Dec. 14, 19, 20–29; Jan. 14, 24; *C.J.*
viii. 670, 672–3, 683, 691, Jan. 3, 8, 24, Feb. 8; *Milward*, pp. 58, 81–2, Jan.
9, Feb. 7. The names of Charles' proposed commissioners are in *Cal. S.P.
Dom. 1667–8*, p. xlviii.

whilst the court strength was still in theory about 140.[1] Charles therefore sent a message announcing that in view of the urgent need to provide for a spring fleet there should be no Christmas recess but that the House should remain sitting, except for the chief festival days.[2]

Both sides saw this as a device to rush the remaining supply bills through whilst the country members were enjoying Christmas in their homes.[3] The opposition leaders at once ordered a check on absenteeism, and sent messengers to recall members who had already left.[4] Meanwhile the court hurried the main supply bill—for an eleven months assessment—into Grand Committee, and managed to reduce the estimated yield of the Poll Bill, thus encouraging the House to vote more money to make up the gap.[5] The opposition used every possible delaying tactic, keeping the House sitting till four, five or even nine o'clock. On December 18 they revived Mordaunt's affair and managed to spend a considerable time discussing his impeachment, but despite their efforts the assessment bill continued to make progress and the ministers took on new hope.[6]

In one week more the supply bills might have been finished, but steady application to business seemed beyond most members of the court. Already they had wasted a long debate, carrying the second reading of the bill to tax 'sealed paper' only to abandon it entirely on the following day.[7] Now they allowed their own numbers to drop so rapidly that on December 20 a proposal to adjourn produced a tied vote of 33 to 33, only the Speaker keeping the session alive. On December 22 a proposal to adjourn for ten days was lost by one vote, but an adjournment to December 29 was approved, and on that day the only business concerned Mordaunt. In effect it was January 2 before

[1] C.J. viii. 662; Carte MSS. 35, f. 171, Broderick, Dec. 15.
[2] C.J. viii. 663, Dec. 15.
[3] Carte MSS. 35, ff. 171, 238, Broderick, Dec. 15, Jan. 5.
[4] C.J. viii. 663, Dec. 15.
[5] C.J. viii. 663-4, Dec. 15, 17.
[6] C.J. viii. 663-6, Dec. 15-21. The filibustering tactics of the opposition are described with indignation by Sir John Nicholas, B. M. Egerton MSS. 2539, ff. 76-7, letter of Dec. 19.
[7] C.J. viii. 661-3, Dec. 12, 14-15; Pepys, vi. 97, Dec. 15. Temple seems to have had a hand in this, B.M. Egerton MSS. 2539, f. 77, Nicholas, Dec. 19. See also E. Hughes, 'English Stamp Duties, 1664-1764', Eng. Hist. Rev. lvi. (1941), 234-5.

they got back to work: what might have been a really successful move had failed completely.[1]

The new year opened sadly:

Our enemies, French and Dutch, great and grow more by our poverty. The Parliament backward in raising, because jealous of the spending, of the money . . . A sad, vicious, negligent Court, and all sober men there fearful of the ruin of the whole kingdom this next year; from which, good God deliver us![2]

To meet this situation three separate lines of conduct were considered by the court. Viscount Conway pinned his hopes on an Irish army: 10,000 men could easily be raised and soon taxes could be collected without consulting Parliament, as had been done in the happy days of Henry III.[3] The Duke of York, Clarendon, Anglesey, and Archbishop Sheldon, were for entrenching themselves behind the constitutional rights of the House of Lords and bringing the upstart, but fundamentally loyal Lower House to its sense by means of a few sharp words.[4] Arlington and Sir William Coventry were for yielding on Irish Cattle, and even, if necessary, on accounts; by this they hoped to regain the good will of the Commons.[5] Charles' later manœuvres suggest that Conway's rather drastic remedy might well have proved attractive; in fact, however, he alternated, not very happily, between the courses urged by Clarendon and Arlington.

At the beginning of January there was an invasion scare as the French moved ships and men towards the Channel ports. Having reminded Charles of his powerlessness to defend his coasts they moved away, leaving members muttering, quite unfairly, that this had been nothing but a court scare to hasten supply.[6] The Lords and Commons meanwhile settled down to

[1] *C.J.* viii. 665–9. Meres and Lee were tellers for the opposition. This abortive attempt to produce a 'Christmas' majority seems to have been remembered in later years, infra, p. 96 note 6.

[2] *Pepys*, vi. 113, Dec. 31.

[3] Carte MSS. 35, ff. 120, 240, Nov. 10, Jan. 5. Not surprisingly he asked Ormonde to burn these letters, which the latter neglected to do.

[4] Carte MSS. 35, f. 240, 30, Conway, Jan. 5, 14; 217, f. 366, Anglesey, Jan. 5; 47, f. 138, Anglesey, Jan. 15; Clarendon, *Life*, iii. 163–9.

[5] Carte MSS. 46, ff. 428, 434–5, 440, Arlington, Dec. 22, Jan. 5, 19; 47, f. 464, Sir William Coventry, Sept. 22, 1666.

[6] Carte MSS. 35, f. 240–1, Conway, Jan. 5; 217, f. 364, Anglesey, Jan. 1; Verney MSS. Claydon, letter of Sir Ralph Verney, Jan. 3. The fear had

hear their leading orators do battle in a series of conferences—
a contest thought by Pepys to provide far better entertainment
than a play. These conferences covered all the main matters in
dispute; agreement was reached on none. On January 13 the
cabinet council met again to try and find some way to break
the deadlock.[1]

On January 14 the Lords were due to debate the cattle bill
again, and in particular the Commons' demand that the word
'nuisance' should be retained. Clarendon had already enjoyed
himself at the expense of this proposal: if 'felony' or 'prae-
munire' would not serve as alternatives then perhaps 'adultery'
would meet the case.[2] In good hope of a rejection the Archbishop of Canterbury made ready to cross the ice from Lam-
beth Palace to vote in the debate,[3] but all was made vain by
the eventual decision of the council. Arlington's advice was
accepted: the Duke of York was ordered to inform his fellow
peers that the King did not wish the proviso opposed, and
after a few diehards had withdrawn from the debate the unamended bill was passed.[4]

The friends of Ormonde and Clarendon were appalled.
Bitterly they wrote that Arlington had assumed 'the odious
name of undertaker', promising Charles that all would now go
well.[5] Unabashed Arlington himself wrote to Ormonde, explaining the necessity of yielding, and predicting rapid progress
in supply.[6] To the angry delight of his opponents such progress
did not come. Having resolved to proceed at once with supply
the Commons wasted two days on minor bills and Charles
began to think that he had made the wrong decision.[7] On
January 18 he resolved, for the first time since the opening, to

---

been real enough, £100,000 would have provided twenty frigates but there
was not £1,000 to be had, Carte, MSS. 35, f. 246, Broderick, Jan. 12.

[1] *C.J.* viii. 671–5, Jan. 4–12, passim; *L.J.* xii, 60–73, passim; *Pepys*, vi.
114–15, 120–1, Jan. 2, 3, 9. Pepys mentions Swinfen and Meres as prominent amongst the Commons' delegation.

[2] Carte MSS. 35, ff. 197–8, Conway, Dec. 29.

[3] Carte MSS. 47, f. 138, Anglesey, Jan. 15.

[4] Carte MSS. 35, f. 30, Conway, Jan. 14; *L.J.* xii. 74.

[5] Carte MSS. 35, f. 259, Conway, Jan. 19.

[6] Carte MSS. 46, f. 440, Jan. 19.

[7] *C.J.* viii. 676–8, Jan. 15, 17. According to Conway's highly partisan
account he would have been prepared to 'eat his own flesh' if that would recall his consent to the Cattle Bill.

address the House in person, and at last Clarendon heard that 'touch of sharpness' for which he had waited so long.[1]

The occasion for this rebuke was, or should have been, a happy one. The Poll Bill, not a large supply but at least a beginning, was at last ready for passing, and was presented on this day. Charles thanked the Houses for it but expressed regret that this was all that had been offered. He had been forced to anticipate revenue to pay off last year's fleet; as for the coming spring: 'what time I have to make . . . preparations . . . you can well enough judge.' Denying, with more indignation than truth, that there was any prospect of a peace,[2] he was:

not willing to complain you have dealt unkindly with me in a Bill I have now passed, in which you have manifested a greater distrust of me than I have deserved. I do not pretend to be without infirmities; but I have never broken my word with you and if I do not flatter myself the nation has never had less cause to complain of grievances . . . than it hath had in these seven years it has pleased God to restore me to you. I would be used accordingly.

As before, when his policy was adopted Clarendon eagerly recorded its success, and as before his account was not entirely accurate.[3] When the Commons returned to their chamber, Sir William Coventry proposed that they should proceed at once to supply, but 'the faction' insisted that they should first complete their interrupted business, which was to take a roll call of the House. Pushed to a division they yielded, but by then it was too late to begin work on the supply.[4] Next day two new provisos were proposed for the assessment bill. The first, which was carried, appropriated the sum of £300,000 for payment of the seamen, £1,200,000 having at one point been considered; the second, of which no more was heard, would have cancelled half the new supply in the event of sudden peace.[5] After this

---

[1] *L.J.* xii. 80–1, Jan. 18.

[2] St Albans, by his own account, left on a mission to France five days after this speech, Carte MSS. 35, f. 275, Jan. 23. Arlington had admitted in December that a peace was quite likely to be agreed but that Parliament would not be informed of this, Carte MSS. 46, f. 426, Dec. 18. See also *Cal. S.P. Ven. 1666–8*, p. 130, Feb. 15, for the Venetian ambassador's suggestion that Charles might be asking Louis to help him escape from his subservience to Parliament.

[3] Clarendon, *Life*, iii. 179–80.

[4] *Milward*, p. 66, Jan. 18; *Pepys*, vi. 128–9, Jan. 18.

[5] *Milward*, p. 67, Jan. 19; Carte MSS. 46, f. 440, Arlington, Jan. 19.

the bill was engrossed and on January 25 passed the Lower House.[1]

The last fortnight of the session was taken up with a bill for rebuilding London, pushed through despite strong opposition from vested interests in the Common Council.[2] It might have been finished more quickly but for the fact that the arguments over Mordaunt's impeachment were now at their height, and conferences interrupted other business almost every day.[3] On February 8 Charles was at last able to pronounce the prorogation, with a word of thanks for the main supply bill, and a sharp aside about 'the new fashion in provisos'.[4] He asked members to return to their 'countries', assist in collecting taxes, and endeavour to remove jealousies for which there was, he declared, no cause.

When we have done the King's business we shall go home like fools as we came.

Many say we shall have peace; many fear we are juggled withall.

The Parliament shall not sit long; they are as cross to him as cannot be imagined.

They are parted with great heartburnings, one party against the other.[5]

Could this be the same House which King and Chancellor had welcomed so delightedly in the spring of 1661? Throughout letters and diaries references are made to faction and to opposition;[6] the concept of 'two sides of the House' was already far from a novelty when, in 1673, Meres referred to it and was

---

[1] *C.J.* viii. 683. Some members had tried to delay this bill until the Lords had yielded on Mordaunt and on the Canary Patent, *Milward*, p. 71, Jan. 25.

[2] *C.J.* viii. 684–92, Jan. 26–Feb. 5, passim; *Milward*, pp. 71–8, passim; Carte MSS. 35, ff. 271, 281, 292, Broderick, Jan. 22, 26, Feb. 2. The bill itself, passed as 18 & 19 Car. II, cap. 8, was long and complicated.

[3] *C.J.* viii. 685–92, Jan. 29–Feb. 8; *L.J.* xii. 92–107; *Milward*, pp. 71–82.

[4] *L.J.* xii. 109–11.

[5] Broome Whorwood, member for Oxford, *Milward*, pp. 40–1, Nov. 12, 1666; Dr Denton to Sir Ralph Verney, April 4, 1667, *H.M.C. 7th Rep.* p. 485; Richard Legh, Jan. 3, 1667, Legh MSS., John Rylands Library; *Pepys*, vi. 157, Feb. 8.

[6] For example *Milward*, pp. 16, 20, 21, 24, 25, 33, Oct. 6–29; *Pepys*, vi. 36, 97, 129, Oct. 25, Dec. 15, Jan. 18; B.M. Egerton MSS. 2539, ff. 76–7, letter of Sir John Nicholas, Dec. 19; Carte MSS. 35, ff. 171, 238, Broderick, Dec. 15, Jan. 5, ff. 240–1, Conway, Jan. 5; Marvell, i. 144–8.

censured for so doing.[1] Party warfare had been open during the
procedural struggle of December. In January a bill concerning
parliamentary candidature, making residence an essential qualification, had been seen by the court as an opposition counter to
their 'carpet-baggers', and opposed accordingly.[2] Had Harring-
ton's prophecy come true and had the cavaliers become, in
seven years, commonwealthsmen indeed?

To answer this we have to distinguish between two groups
within the 'opposition'. On the one hand there were those
praised by Marvell, the

> Gross of English Gentry, nobly born,
> Of clear Estates and to no Faction sworn;
> Dear lovers of their King, and Death to meet,
> For Country's cause, that Glorious think and meet;
> To speak not forward, but in action brave;
> In giving generous, but in Counsel Grave;
> Candidly credulous, for once, nay twice;
> But sure the Devil cannot cheat them thrice.[3]

On the other were the officers of this troop:

> . . . Temple, conqueror
> Of Irish Cattle and Solicitor;
> Then daring Seymour, that with Spear and Shield
> Had stretched the monster Patent in the field;
> Keen Whorwood next in aid of Damsel frail
> That pierced the Giant Mordaunt through his Mail;
> . . . Great Garraway and great Littleton. . . .[4]

As far as the first, silent group is concerned, we can offer only
conjecture. The meagre evidence of these men's views that has
survived does not, however, point to their having become conscious enemies of the Crown. Colonel John Milward supported
the Cattle Bill and the Committee of Accounts but drew the line

---

[1] Too much has been made of Henry Coventry's rebuke to Meres when
the latter referred to divisions within the House. Able parliamentarian that
he was, Coventry was in this appealing to a vanished age, *Dering*, p. 128,
Feb. 22, 1673.

[2] Carte MSS. 35, ff. 271-2, Broderick, Jan. 22. Bab May and Joseph
Williamson were two court candidates who found letters of recommendation
little help, *Pepys*, vi. 32, Oct. 21; *Cal. S.P. Dom. 1666-7*, pp. 378-80, 440,
443, 446, 449-54, 470, 473, Dec. 30-1, 1666, Jan. 5-26, 1667.

[3] Marvell, i, 148.

[4] Ibid., i, 147.

at the 'tack'. He was near to tears on the anniversary of
Charles I's martyrdom, referred with loathing to the 'old parliamentary gang' yet showed extreme reluctance to give the King
a halfpenny more than was absolutely necessary.[1] Sir John
Holland had favoured the repeal of the Long Parliament's
Triennial Bill; he was soon to appear among Clarendon's
defenders, but when it came to excise or assessment his voice
went against the court.[2] Sir Ralph Verney and his son were
staunch loyalists who yet saw the Cattle Bill as the only remedy
for the decline in English rents.[3] Men with such views could
cause extreme embarrassment and annoyance to the Crown,
yet to call them 'commonwealthsmen' would be very wide of
the mark.

As for their leaders, the answer may be sought in the later
comments of their panegyrist Andrew Marvell. Seymour, Garraway, and Temple, are found to have apostasized, 'fallen to
head the King's business',[4] and they have been preceded in their
defection by Littleton who took office, with Osborne, in 1668.[5]
These were again no 'commonwealthsmen', but skilled professional politicians, hungry for office.[6] Such men could be
bought off; if this were done, and the prejudices of the central
block respected, there might still be found a wealth of loyalty in
the House. This was the true lesson to be learnt from these
debates.

[1] *Milward*, pp. 9, 14–16, 20–1, 24, 27, 47, 53–6, 75, 128, Sept. 28, 1666–
Jan. 30, 1667, Nov. 14, 1667.
[2] Tanner MSS. 239, ff. 49–51; *Milward*, app., pp. 307–20.
[3] Verney MSS., Claydon, letters of Jan. 10, 17, 1667. Compare the
comment of Richard Wynn, *Calendar of Wynn Papers* (1926), p. 387, Oct. 27.
[4] In a letter to Popple, Nov. 28, 1670, Marvell denounces Seymour,
Temple, and Holles, *Poems and Letters*, ii. 305, and compare Aug. 9. 1671,
ibid., ii. 310. Garraway's turn came in the poem 'Britannia and Raleigh',
written some years later, ibid., i. 185.
[5] A. Browning, *Danby*, i. 64–5. They became joint treasurers of the navy.
[6] More is said of this infra, Chapter IX and Conclusion.

CHAPTER VI

CLARENDON AS SCAPEGOAT

In the session of 1666-7 the initiative had passed from the hands of the court. Supply had been thrown to them, almost contemptuously, by the opposition. They had yielded on Irish Cattle and had barely staved off an enquiry into accounts. The alleged misdeeds of Lord Mordaunt, the supposed irregularity of the Canary Company's charter, had produced criticism to which no effective answer had been made. On all these topics the country centre had listened to the trouble-makers rather than to the court. No session was due until the autumn, but in June came the humiliating Dutch raid on Chatham, bringing with it the threat of invasion. An army was scraped together but there was no money with which to pay it. Only Parliament could provide supply and so, once again, the King's advisers argued over policy.

Clarendon had made his name as a member of the Commons. In 1660, as in 1641, he had worked for a constitutional settlement. Unnerved however by the campaign against him at court, distressed by the death of his friend the Treasurer, he allowed himself to make some very dangerous proposals. Aware as a lawyer that a parliament prorogued to October could not properly be recalled before that time, he advocated raising money by prerogative, or, if that were rejected, holding new elections. In the heat of the moment he spoke scathingly of 'four hundred men, fit only to grant money', and his remarks were noted down by those who hoped for his destruction. Charles overruled him, Parliament was summoned, and on July 25 it met.[1]

Between two and three hundred members made the journey to Westminster, sweating in the heat but spurred on by their angry constituents.[2] By this time the peace treaty was virtually

[1] Clarendon, *Life*, iii. 252-8 and infra. *Pepys*, vi. 342-3, 368-9, June 13, 25.

[2] Tanner MSS. 45, ff. 202-4, letters of Roger Pepys, July 2, 25; Carte MSS. 35, f. 568, and 215, f. 359, Broderick, July 23, 30; *Pepys*, vii. 11, 34-5, July 7, 25.

concluded, and it had been hoped to prevent discussion until the terms had been announced.[1] This hope proved vain. Thomas Tomkins, 'the fittest man to start what others would continue', rose to move the immediate disbandment of the army.[2] Garraway followed, explaining that this request was only made on the understanding that a peace was imminent. Alone of the court Sir William Coventry dared to point out that this would hardly strengthen our negotiators at Breda; Littleton retorted that 'some about the King' might try to keep the army in time of peace, whilst if the Commons postponed their address they might then find themselves prorogued. The motion for the address passed *nem. con.* and only then did the House adjourn.[3]

On July 29, as on several subsequent occasions, the Speaker came very late to the House. No sooner had he appeared than he was followed by Black Rod, calling members to attend the King.[4] Charles told them briefly that he was sorry to have given them the trouble of a journey but that he no longer required their attendance. Denying strongly any intention to keep up his army, he announced both the conclusion of the peace and the immediate disbandment of the troops. He hoped to see members again in October, by which time he would have done several things that he believed would please them. Until then their session was prorogued.[5]

The mood of the Commons must certainly have alarmed the court. In all fairness the Chancellor could hardly have been held to blame, yet, having done everything he could to prevent the session, he was now made the scapegoat for its failure. Arlington, Sir William Coventry, and, emerging at last into a full political role, the Duke of Buckingham, were resolved upon

---

[1] *Pepys*, vii, 34–5, July 25.

[2] Ibid.; *Milward*, p. 83. William Coventry had picked out Tomkins as a likely trouble maker in the previous year, *Cal. S.P. Dom. 1666–7*, p. 144, Sept. 22, Marvell, not surprisingly, admired him. *Poems and Letters*, i. 161.

[3] *Milward*, pp. 83–4; *C.J.* viii. 692; *Pepys*, vii. 34–5, July 25. The troops had been put under Parliamentary officers such as Manchester and Fairfax in an effort to placate opinion, Ogg, op. cit., i. 313. Sir John Nicholas thought the Commons' vote superfluous since there was no means of paying the army if it kept together, B.M. Egerton MSS. 2549, ff. 105–6, July 25.

[4] *Milward*, p. 84; *C.J.* viii. 692.

[5] 'The Speaker . . . came rubbing his eyes with his handkerchief all the way to his coach and looked between anger and pity.' *HMC Hastings MSS.* ii. 154, Ferdinando Davy, July 30. See also *Pepys*, vii. 41–3, July 29.

his fall.[1] 'Proud of a good conscience' Clarendon refused to resign. As with Ormonde two years later, Charles shrank from dismissing so obviously loyal, if exasperating, a servant, and for several weeks Clarendon's friends believed that he might still escape. At last the rather shabby decision was made, and on August 31 Clarendon surrendered the seals.[2]

The first phase of this reign's parliamentary history was over. A new and even more confused one was about to begin. In place of Clarendon there were now three leading ministers, Arlington, Buckingham and, less powerful but active both at the Treasury and in the Commons, William Coventry. The first two hated each other but were to work together for seven years. The third distrusted his colleagues, was disliked by them, and was to be driven from power before two years had passed. As they discussed tactics for the autumn session the rift between them was already apparent. Buckingham wanted Clarendon's prosecution on a charge of treason; Coventry opposed this; Arlington hovered undecided.[3] Buckingham favoured enquiries into the 'miscarriages' of the war; he had held no office of importance and had nothing to hide, but either of his colleagues might have to face some embarrassing questions.[4] Coventry seems to have hoped that financial stability could be improved by economy at the Treasury;[5] Buckingham hoped to present Charles with large new grants of supply.[6] On religion all three were for

---

[1] The rise of this triumvirate, the circumstances of Clarendon's dismissal, and the attempt to have him impeached, are admirably described in an article by Dr Clayton Roberts in *Cambridge Hist. Journal* xiii (1957), 1–18. Dr Roberts refers to Buckingham's rise on pages 6–7; for contemporary comment see *Pepys*, vii. 26, 31, July 17, 22; PRO 31/3/116 f. 76, Ruvigny, Sept. 9. Arlington, Coventry and Charles himself all excused the removal of Clarendon on the grounds that this was the only means of revitalizing the administration, and at the same time of pacifying Parliament: Carte MSS. 46, ff. 540–3 and 75, f. 553, Arlington, Aug. 27, 31, Sept. 5; *Pepys*, vii. 86–9, Sept. 2; *The Letters of King Charles II*, ed. A. Bryant (1935), pp. 204–5, Sept. 15.

[2] Clarendon, *Life*, iii. 267, 282–94; Carte MSS. 35, ff. 657, 682, Carlingford, Aug. 24, Broderick, Aug. 27; 46, ff. 540–1, Arlington, Aug. 27; 217, ff. 404, Anglesey, Aug. 27.

[3] Roberts, op. cit., pp. 5–7.

[4] PRO 31/3/116, f. 96, Ruvigny, Sept. 30.

[5] On his works and aims as a Commissioner of the Treasury see Roseveare, pp. 146, 154–6.

[6] Roberts, op. cit., p. 2.

toleration, though no move was to be made towards this until Clarendon had been removed.[1] On foreign policy the various ambassadors tried vainly to establish any minister's views.[2]

Mention of these ambassadors recalls that this was probably the first session of this Parliament in which foreign money was used in an attempt to influence the course of debates. Ruvigny was sent from Paris, with a rather limited supply of money and instructions to build up a party in both the Council and the House of Commons.[3] Lisola, Spanish envoy and pamphleteer, was ready to meet him on his own ground and worked hard to complete the ruin of the supposedly pro-French Clarendon.[4] Even such an apparently domestic matter as the disbanding of Charles' militia after the July invasion scare concerned outsiders: Lisola was reported as rejoicing at a chance to recruit unemployed trained soldiers for the defence of Flanders.[5] Prussian and Dutch envoys were also hovering around Westminster: how far these various diplomats had any real influence over Parliament's proceedings will be considered later.[6]

Parliament met on October 10 to learn, officially, that Clarendon had been dismissed.[7] They were also informed that the Canary patent had been recalled, proclamations put out against smuggled Irish Cattle and against the growth of popery, and that the King was prepared to authorize a Parliamentary commission to inspect the Treasury's accounts. It was natural that so gracious a speech should draw a rapid vote of thanks but the terms of this vote were not agreed without a debate.[8] Clarendon's enemies proposed specific thanks for his removal,

---

[1] Infra, Chapter VII.

[2] Throughout the despatches of the French ambassador, PRO 31/3/116–118, estimates of Buckingham's and Arlington's position fluctuate wildly. Coventry seems to have taken little interest in foreign affairs until a much later stage in his career.

[3] PRO 31/3/116, ff. 76, 82, 90, Ruvigny, Sept. 9, 16, 19.

[4] *Cal. S.P. Ven. 1666–8*, pp. 183–4, Sept. 13, 20 (the first of these reports came from France); PRO 31/3/116, f. 82, Ruvigny, Sept. 16. *Cal. S.P. Ven. 1671–2*, p. 65, memorandum on parliamentary proceedings; A. F. Pribram, *Lisola* (1894), pp. 366–9. See also infra p. 71.

[5] *Cal. S.P. Ven. 1666–8*, p. 180, Aug. 23. (This report came from Paris.)

[6] Infra, Conclusion. See also Feiling, *British Foreign Policy 1660–1672*, p. 231.

[7] *L.J.* xii. 115–16.

[8] *Milward*, app. ii, pp. 328–9; *Calendar of Wynn Papers* (1926), p. 392, Oct. 15.

to pave the way for a full-scale parliamentary attack. In favour of this were Littleton and Trevor, both place hunters, Vaughan, soon to become Chief Justice of Common Pleas, and Sir William Coventry, reaffirming his principle that the King should not retain a minister 'not liking to himself and to his people'. With the exception of Coventry, who changed sides when it came to the question of an impeachment, by far the bitterest, indeed almost the only attacks on the Chancellor came from those who hoped to win a place in the administration. On this first day not only cavaliers like the two Goodricks, but Maynard, Holland, even Marvell and Birch, took Clarendon's part—indeed the presbyterians, though often thought to take their cue from Buckingham, now supported the unfortunate ex-Chancellor throughout every debate.[1] Nevertheless the defence did not, it seems, feel strong enough to press for a division, and the more hostile version of the address was finally approved. Charles replied that he would never employ the Chancellor again,[2] and the hunt was called off for ten days whilst the Commons considered various blunders, or alleged blunders, of the recent war.

'We have not been beaten by power and force, but by cheating and cozening.'[3] This was the theme of the long laboured inquest which was to continue for another two years. 'A fact done, somebody must be presented, and who but the most probable person.'[4] This could be used against Clarendon, against Pett, Brunkard, Carteret, even against Arlington and Sir William Coventry who were, with Buckingham, supposed to be controlling these debates. Despite all the angry speeches not one of the accused was ever brought to trial,[5] and the accuracy of most of the charges remains still in doubt. All that can be said, in passing, is that comparison of the records kept by Sir William Coventry and Pepys with those accounts, by Rupert and Albemarle, which were enshrined in the respectability of the Commons Journals suggests that much of the history of the

[1] Roberts, op. cit., 5–6, makes this point, quoting *Reliquiae Baxterianae* (1696), part iii, 20.

[2] *Milward*, p. 88, Oct. 15.

[3] Sergeant Maynard, *Grey*, i. 98, Feb. 28, 1668.

[4] Sir Richard Temple, *Grey*, i. 28, Nov. 7.

[5] Pett spent some months in the Tower, Brunkard was expelled from the House and Carteret forced to resign his post but none of these stood trial.

war merits re-examination.[1] The point so far as we are concerned is that these enquiries raised the temper of the House,
made members more ready to accept wild accusations, and
made it difficult for moderates to speak without having some
charge levied against themselves.

During this first period of the session recriminations swamped
all other business. If Buckingham had hoped to secure a quick
grant of money he was forced to change his plans. Supply was
in fact completely ignored; so too was foreign policy. A debate
on a bill for general naturalization revived, for a moment, the
old arguments for and against religious toleration,[2] but the
topic was not pursued. Everything hung fire whilst members
argued over the war and at the same time waited to see how
Clarendon's enemies would fare in their attempt to compass his
destruction.

On October 20 Charles had at last yielded to Buckingham
and agreed that the former Chancellor should not merely be
kept out of power but prosecuted as a criminal.[3] On October
25, perhaps to test opinion in the House, the charge against
Clarendon's friend, Lord Mordaunt, was revived from the
previous session.[4] On the following day Seymour opened the
indictment of Clarendon, followed by Littleton, Temple, Vaughan, Osborne and Wheeler.[5] All kinds of charges were put
forward and there was much talk of money: £4,000 for the
Canary Patent, £120,000 from the Treasury, £50,000 from
Ireland. Perhaps the most serious charge referred to Clarendon's

---

[1] Compare for example Albemarle's account of his defence of Chatham,
C.J. ix. 12–13, Oct. 31, with his assurances at the time of the security of the
defences, Coventry MSS. 95, f. 323, June 11, 1667, and Pepys, vi. 339, June
12. In Coventry MSS. 95, ff. 214–15, 384–96, Coventry gives an account
of the division of the fleet in 1666 which differs markedly from that accepted
by the Commons and quoted, from the Journals, by Ogg, op. cit., i. 298–9.
Another version of Coventry's defence can be found in B.M. Add. MSS.
32,094, ff. 196–209.

[2] Grey, i. 56, Dec. 3. An earlier bill against catholics had been attacked as
too severe, and tacitly abandoned, C.J. ix. 4, 10, Milward, pp. 88, 104–5,
Grey, i. 1–2, Oct. 16, 30. Waller, Vaughan, and Morrice had opposed this
bill which had been drafted by Sir Thomas Clarges, B.M. Add. MSS. 36,916,
f. 11, Starkey newsletter, Oct. 31.

[3] PRO 31/3/116, ff. 96–7, 117, Ruvigny, Sept. 30, Oct. 23.

[4] Milward, p. 98. No further action was taken on this, a fact which sup-
ports the possibility of its having been merely an emotive gesture.

[5] Ibid., pp. 99–102 and app., p. 331.

alleged support for a standing army, coupled with his scorn of the 'four hundred men . . . only of use to raise . . . money, but . . . not fit to meddle with state affairs'.[1] Other of the accusers' inspirations were less happy: the charge that he had alienated the King from the Duke of York went oddly with the latter's vigorous moves in his support, and though the Duke was at this time kept from Westminster by sickness[2] Broderick and Sir Philip Warwick were present to refute categorically another assertion, that there had been friction between the Chancellor and the late Treasurer, Southampton. Henry Coventry insisted that witnesses should be produced before an impeachment was approved, and the House seemed

to think it something irregular to confine and impeach a person (out of favour with his prince and so not in danger of obstructing these proceedings) before proof were made.[3]

The debate was adjourned for three days and a committee was set up to search for precedents.

The first attack had failed: despite an avalanche of accusations no final vote had been secured, and the managers were aware that it would be ruinous if an impeachment was to depend on a prehearing of witnesses, since these did not exist. On October 29 the Commons had a chance to display their antiquarian scholarship with references to Earl Godwin, Thomas Arundell, and Michael de la Pole.[4] When it came to capital impeachments, however, the only precedents to be found were the less comfortable ones of Laud and Strafford and, significantly, it was stressed that the latter at least had been attacked with the King's nominal permission.[5] The main point to be settled was whether impeachment was to be justified by 'common fame', by a select committee which would report directly to the House of Lords, or by the committee of grievances

[1] *Milward*, p. 99, and supra.

[2] *Milward*, p. 101. The Duke's illness was smallpox, *Pepys*, vii. 177–8, Nov. 8, 10. For his support of Clarendon see ibid., vii. 164, 171. Oct. 28, Nov. 4; J. S. Clarke, *James the Second* (1816), i. 430.

[3] *Milward*, p. 101 and app., p. 331.

[4] *Milward*, pp. 102–3; *Grey*, i. 6–14.

[5] *Grey*, i. 6. This point was made by Vaughan. Prynne, who was also prominent in this debate, had carried up Strafford's impeachment; now however like other presbyterians he was for the defence.

which would report back to the House.[1] The managers were anxious to secure the adoption of the third course—it might be easier to advance vague charges in the House than in the less emotional atmosphere of a committee—and, with the help of some Old Testament rumblings from Temple,[2] this object was achieved. There was now another pause whilst the committee prepared its preliminary report.

At this stage Clarendon was still feeling reasonably confident, whilst the new 'ministry' was already cracking badly.[3] The Duke of York had shamed Charles into denying publicly that there was any substance in the 'standing army' charge,[4] and there was little in the remaining articles to warrant a conviction. Against this, however, must be set the general atmosphere of 'sauve qui peut'. Coventry and Arlington, who had opposed the impeachment in council, had already come under attack for their conduct during the war.[5] Petitions from a certain Alderman Barker, and from the City of Dublin, helped to immobilize the Ormonde faction, whilst Ormonde himself was prepared to make terms with at least the less violent of his friend's supplanters.[6] On a humbler scale Sir John Nicholas, son of Sir Edward, and a strong supporter of Clarendon, was distracted from the latter's defence by a private petition striking at his father's lands.[7] Possible reluctance by the Lords to accept unsubstantiated charges had been anticipated by reviving

---

[1] *Milward*, p. 332.

[2] *Grey*, i. 13. 'Let not this son of Zeruiah be too strong for King and Parliament.'

[3] Carte MSS. 36, f. 25. Conway, Nov. 5.

[4] PRO 31/3/117, f. 14. Ruvigny, Nov. 1.

[5] Arlington and Coventry had both been concerned in the division of the fleet before the Four Days' Battle of 1666, supra, p. 66 note 1. This had been discussed on Oct. 19, 22, 24, Milward, pp. 90, 93–4, 97. See also B.M. Add. MSS. 36,916, f. 5. Starkey, Oct. 24.

[6] The campaign against Ormonde is referred to in numerous letters. Typical are Carte MSS. 46, f. 544, Arlington, Sept. 3, 36, f. 25, Conway, Nov. 5; 69, f. 137, Orrery, Oct. 12; and 220, f. 286, Ossory, Sept. 24. See also B.M. Add. MSS. 36,916, f. 11. Starkey, Oct. 31 and T. Carte, *Ormonde*, iv. 311–18. Ormonde was on friendly terms with Arlington; his son Ossory was Arlington's brother-in-law, Barbour, *Arlington*, pp. 21, 22, 51, 99. On Sept. 9, after he had received news of Clarendon's fall Ormonde instructed his son to open negotiations with Clifford and William Coventry, Carte. MSS. 48, f. 219.

[7] B.M. Egerton MSS. 2539, ff. 135–40, letters of Nicholas, Nov. 12, 13, 14.

memories of their stubbornness over the 1666 accounts bill;[1] the presbyterians, who had proved generally sympathetic to Clarendon were given a more immediate object for their pity in the unfortunate Peter Pett,[2] and, if Conway is to be trusted, the Duke of York himself was threatened by talk of Monmouth's recognition as Charles' legitimate heir.[3] How far there was a co-ordinated campaign cannot be known but all these pressures coupled with the King's now open hostility, went into the as yet still balanced scale.

On November 6, after the House had been warmed up by a petition against the hearth tax collectors, Littleton brought in a formal list of charges drawn by the committee.[4] The savagery of many speeches may reflect the authors' fears for their own safety: as Howard put it, 'if the charge be not true, each member that delivered the charge' might be 'exposed to ruin'. 'The earth groans under his building', cried Seymour; 'he whined after peace' and made no preparations for a war, declared Littleton. Parliament—the Grand Inquest of the Nation—could surely override inconvenient points of law.[5] The defence remained uncowed: Atkins, Cornbury, North, Walpole, Henry Coventry and Holland all pressed for witnesses to be produced, but the answer came pat:

the witnesses are not to be known, and the thing in the Commons' House to be carried on with all privacy imaginable, because great men may hinder the prosecution by their great power, or otherwise may break the Parliament, and no injustice is done to them as long as they are brought to their trial by their peers.

By 194 to 128 the proposal to refer the charges back to the

---

[1] *Grey*, i. 3–5, Oct. 26; *Pepys*, vi. 341, 354, June 13, 18, vii. 71, 181, Aug. 22, Nov. 13; Marvell, i. 159–60.

[2] *Milward*, pp. 93, 127–8, Oct. 22, Nov. 13, 14.

[3] Carte MSS. 36, f. 25, 35, f. 873, Conway, Nov. 5, 30.

[4] *C.J.* ix. 15–16. For the ensuing debate see *Milward*, pp. 110–14, and *Grey*, i. 14–23.

[5] 'The House of Commons is in the nature of an Inquest, or Grand Jury, which is that if any of the Jury affirm the fact it is enough to find the bill . . . then upon his impeachment he has his fair trial before his peers . . .', *Milward*, app. 333, Nov. 6. Compare Broderick's comment on the attack on Mordaunt where, after describing how little evidence had been found of the latter's guilt, he comments that 'little proof is necessary where the matter hath been found by the Grand Inquest of the Nation', Carte MSS. 35, f. 281, Jan. 26, 1667.

committee was rejected and their reading over was begun, each in turn being affirmed by one or more members of the House.[1]

November 7 and 8 were spent hearing these charges and discussing whether they might offer reasonable grounds on which to present an impeachment to the Lords.[2] Osborne complained bitterly of the Chancellor's pride—'threatens every man that gave advice—no hand but his on the helm or rudder'—and got in, surely not by chance, a side shot at Sir William Coventry, who had not only scorned to join in the hunt but was prepared to speak in his old enemies' defence.[3] Marvell demanded solemnly that Clarendon's alleged stricture upon the King as 'an unactive person' should be read in full, at which Howard called on Seymour as a witness, Seymour pointed at Denham, and Denham 'affirmed he had it from another'.[4] Henry Coventry recalled how Charles I had spoken at his death of Strafford, but on the other side was Waller, claiming that Burleigh plodded fifty years for what Clarendon had got in five. After two days' fierce debate the House agreed that an impeachment was warranted; at last the managers seemed to be nearing their goal.

Appearances were deceptive. If these managers had thought more carefully about Strafford's impeachment they might have realized that it was one thing to abuse a minister in debate but quite another to prove specific charges in a court of law. When, on November 9, they produced their first article—that the Chancellor had advised the King to govern by a standing army—they were faced by a statement from their most respected lawyer, Sergeant Maynard, that this did not fall within the statute of 25 Edward III.[5] Despite some talk of 'government by bashaws', a majority of members stuck to this question of law, and even Vaughan, a bitter enemy of Clarendon but a lawyer before a politician, changed sides and denied that the offence

---

[1] The editor of Milward's *Diary* has a note comparing different lists of charges, *Milward*, pp. 113–14.

[2] *Milward*, pp. 114–19, and for Nov. 7 only, *Grey*, i. 23, 27–8.

[3] *Grey*, i. 23. Coventry refused to shelter behind the Chancellor even if this would clear him on the division of the fleet, infra p. 71.

[4] *Milward*, p. 116.

[5] *Grey*, i. 29–32; *Milward*, pp. 119–22. Maynard had played a leading part in the impeachment of Strafford, C. V. Wedgwood, *Thomas Wentworth, First Earl of Strafford* (1961), pp. 338–50. He was now exactly reversing his earlier views.

was treason.[1] Some members, groping after the concept of Parliamentary sovereignty, claimed that Parliament could declare treason retrospectively, but this was not accepted and the article was rejected by 172 to 103.

The situation was now somewhat similar to that of April 1641,[2] and though Clarendon was no Strafford his enemies clearly felt that they had gone too far to draw back. The King was putting heavy pressure on members to support the attack,[3] conduct which makes his father's weakness seem almost heroic by comparison, and after a break for Sunday the managers made a new effort on November 11.[4] Charges 2 to 16 were read, one after the other, and a rash reference by Dowdeswell to 'a violent stream against the Chancellor' brought a storm upon his head. Still the presbyterians, Prynne, Swinfen, and Birch spoke up for Clarendon; Sir William Coventry, though in great anxiety for himself, refused to shelter behind the fallen minister;[5] Henry Coventry suggested that the sale of Dunkirk was no different to disbanding the guards, since both sprang from inadequate grants of supply.[6]

Then came the turning point of the struggle. Lisola, the Spanish ambassador, had been waiting with impatience for the Commons to turn from Clarendon to consider the French threat to the Netherlands. He appears now to have approached the managers and to have offered them 'proofs', in the shape of intercepted letters, that the Chancellor had betrayed council secrets to the French.[7] Lord Vaughan seized on this and produced, as an additional article, the charge of 'corresponding with the King's enemies'.[8] For once there was no doubt that the

---

[1] PRO 31/3/117, f. 23. Ruvigny, Nov. 11; B.M. Egerton MSS. 2539, ff. 135–6, Nicholas, Nov. 12. Vaughan's speech as reported by Milward, p. 121 and Grey, i. 30, seems however rather ambiguous.

[2] Wedgwood, *Strafford*, 326–9, 337, 355.

[3] *Pepys*, vii. 186–7, Nov. 16; Carte MSS. 35, ff. 764, 778, Conway, Oct. 15, 22; Thynne MSS., Longleat, 16, ff. 477, 479, letters of Henry Coventry, Oct. 15, Dec. 2.

[4] *Grey*, i. 32–7; *Milward*, pp. 122–5, and app., 336–8.

[5] *Grey*, i. 36. This was on the question of the division of the fleet in 1666, supra p. 70.

[6] *Milward*, p. 125, and compare Secretary Morrice after Christmas, *Grey*, i. 75, Feb. 15, 1668.

[7] Roberts, op. cit., 13–14 and supra, p. 64 note 4.

[8] Lord Vaughan does not appear to have been any relative of the 'Mr

offence, *if proved*, amounted to treason. Clarendon's friends made a last effort, recalling Gondomar's part in procuring Raleigh's death and demanding to know if the witnesses to prove this article would be English or foreign.[1] Their arguments, though maintained for some three hours, were unsuccessful, and at the division the article was accepted as a basis for impeachment by 161 votes to 89.[2]

In some ways this concluded the House of Commons' dealings with Clarendon. The impeachment was carried up to the Lords by Edward Seymour—it was decided not to send the Speaker for fear of a snub[3]—and as he handed it over he added the request that Clarendon should be committed to custody until, 'within a reasonable time', the Commons should make good their charge.[4] The Lords' response was somewhat disappointing: they would take the message and the articles of impeachment into consideration and return answer by messengers of their own. When, on November 15, these messengers informed the Commons that since no exact charge had been made they were not prepared to commit Clarendon to custody, the issue ceased to be one of justice or even of politics and became just a round in the long struggle for precedence between the Upper and Lower Houses. In one way this was in Clarendon's favour, since it very much reduced the likelihood of the impeachment's going forward. On the other hand an impeachment on charges that could not be proved was not a very serious threat, and it soon appeared that the managers were doing their best not to heal but to widen the breach between the Houses for a purpose of their own.[5]

Vaughan' who has been mentioned several times above. He had not been prominent in the earlier sessions and he died in 1668.

[1] *Grey*, i. 35; *Milward*, pp. 317, 337, speeches by Holland and Prynne.

[2] Milward's own attitude seems to have changed considerably since the previous debate, *Milward*, pp. 122, 125, Nov. 9, 11. According to Broderick the turning point of the debate came about three o'clock, Carte MSS. 35, f. 851, Nov. 16. Feiling, *History of the Tory Party*, p. 122 draws unjustified conclusions from a comparison of this division with two others where the issue was quite different.

[3] *Milward*, pp. 126–7, Nov. 12.　　　　[4] Ibid.; *C.J.* ix. 19; *L.J.* xii. 135.

[5] For evidence of this see the speeches of Seymour, Howard, Temple, and Littleton in the debates cited infra p. 73 note 3. Sir Ralph Verney, in a letter of Nov. 28, Verney MSS., Claydon, makes clear his own view that this was basically an inter-House dispute, and compare B.M. Egerton MSS. 2539, ff. 139–46, letters of Nicholas, Nov. 14, 19, 21, 27.

The Commons discussed the Lords' procrastination on nine occasions between November 16 and December 2.[1] At one point the two Houses indulged in a long procedural wrangle, the Lords wanting to hold formal conferences limited to the discussion of a single point, whilst the Commons wanted a free conference at which they could plead other relevant issues.[2] Much dignified abuse was bandied to and fro; each side told the other that its behaviour was 'not Parliamentary' and there was endless argument over precedents, without any conclusion being reached. The Presbyterians, Swinfen and Prynne were for moderation, as were Sir Edward Walpole, Sir William Coventry, and the cavalier Heneage Finch. Temple, Littleton, Howard and Waller, however, were bitter against the Lords, the latter making a strong constitutional claim: 'the people are at home nowhere but in the House of Commons, knock when you will'.[3]

All this time the King was making every effort to secure his former minister's destruction.[4] Clarendon's friends, aware of his royal displeasure, received another warning from an attack on one of their number, Sir John Ashburnham, for accepting bribes from wine merchants in return for licences to import French wines. That Ashburnham had taken the money was rapidly established: as often happened an official fell foul of the double standard of conduct which made the acceptance of bribes almost universal yet still a technical offence, and after a debate in which he was not without defenders he was expelled from the House.[5]

During this fortnight's deadlock the House at last found some time for other business. Sir John Knight of Bristol made a practical suggestion that prize ships should be 'naturalized', to

---

[1] *Milward*, pp. 129–34, 136–8, 140, 142–51; *Grey*, i. 41–5, 48–54; Nov. 16, 18, 21, 23, 26, 27, 28, 29, Dec. 2.

[2] Ruvigny, the best informed of all Louis' ambassadors when it came to parliamentary affairs, grasped the point of this rather complicated dispute, PRO 31/3/117, f. 46, Nov. 26.

[3] *Grey*, i. 43, Nov. 16.

[4] *Pepys*, vii. 183–4, 186–8, 202, Nov. 15, 16, 27.

[5] *Grey*, i. 46; *Milward*, pp. 131–2, 134–5 and note, Nov. 18, 19, 22. Nicholas suggests that Ashburnham was distrusted because of his equivocal conduct during the Civil War, but also makes it clear that he was a personal friend of old Sir Edward Nicholas, a staunch Clarendonian, B.M. Egerton MSS. 2539, ff. 141–2, 145–6, Nov. 19, 27. *Milward*, p. 139, Nov. 27.

bring them within the limits of the navigation acts.[1] Ways of apprehending highwaymen were discussed, the advisability of allowing tanned leather to be exported, the condition of our prisoners at Flushing, and the possibility of free trade between England and Scotland.[2] One curious constitutional gesture was the rescinding, by a resolution of the House, of the judgement given against the 'Five Knights' in 1627.[3] Another matter was an enquiry into the alleged intimidation of juries, Chief Justice Keeling being particularly named.[4] Unfortunately, but very naturally, the various correspondents and even the diarists,— Milward rather less than Grey—pass over these debates in their anxiety to give the latest news about Clarendon. For reasons of clarity and space we shall do the same but it must not be forgotten that this 'minor business' was probably of as great concern as the impeachment to a large proportion of the House.

Meanwhile the settlement of Clarendon's case could not be postponed indefinitely. Had he stayed on and demanded a trial it was probable that no majority in the Lords could have been found to convict him. Two things seem to have decided him against this course: he did not wish to be a source of discord between the Houses,[5] and perhaps more important, he feared that Buckingham would persuade the King to dissolve Parliament and appoint a court of twenty-five selected peers, who would try, convict and sentence him without his having any

---

[1] *Milward*, p. 139 Nov. 27. This eventually became law as 19 & 20 Car. II, cap. 3.

[2] *C.J.* ix. 26–7, Nov. 27, 28; *Milward*, pp. 139–40, Nov. 27. Free trade with Scotland had been suggested by the King in his opening speech. A committee was set up to study detailed proposals but little progress seems to have been made.

[3] This took place on Nov. 23, *C.J.* ix. 25. No debate is recorded and no correspondent seems to have thought the vote worth a comment. It seems in fact only to have confirmed a clause in one of the Long Parliament's acts, Howell, *State Trials*, iii. 1–59; W. S. Holdsworth, *History of English Law*, vi. 32–7, 112.

[4] *Milward*, pp. 88–9, 159–60, 162–3, 166–70; *Grey*, i. 62–4; Oct. 16, Dec. 9, 11, 13, Keeling was heard at the bar and a resolution against the intimidation of juries was passed, anticipating the famous judgement of Chief Justice Vaughan in Bushell's case three years later, *C.J.* ix. 37, Dec. 13.

[5] Clarendon, *Life*, iii. 332–4 and see also the paper of justification he left behind, printed in *L.J.* xii. 154–6, Dec. 3.

right of appeal.[1] For several weeks he hesitated; then, on November 29, he took ship for France. Four days later the Commons were interrupted in their debate by two judges, sent from the Upper House with the news that Clarendon had 'withdrawn himself', and had left behind a long paper containing a full apology for his past and present conduct.[2] 'Lord Clarendon makes the fire betwixt the two Houses and goes away in the smoke';[3] the Commons now felt convinced that a criminal had escaped justice through the negligence of the Lords, and after the gesture of stopping the ports, they ordered a committee to draw up a full account of all their proceedings 'and so to give satisfaction of their fidelity both to King and people'.[4]

On December 4 the Lords called a conference and Buckingham handed over Clarendon's vindication, which at once became the target for much bitter irony.[5] After some debate this paper was voted scandalous and a reproach to 'the public justice of the nation'—a vindication of something that had been nearer to lynch law than anything out of the statute book—but having ordered it to be burnt by the public hangman the Commons' anger began to cool. Even when, on December 5, they passed a resolution denouncing the failure to commit Clarendon it was framed in general terms and contained no specific reproach against the Lords.[6] Significantly several of the late managers, who had been breathing fury against the Lords only a week before, had changed their tune.[7] With Clarendon out of the way a quarrel between the two Houses would only have impeded public business, and they had still to perform the rest of their bargain and secure a supply.

[1] This was the explanation given by Clarendon's son to Ormonde, Carte MSS. 36, f. 84, Cornbury, Dec. 8.

[2] *C.J.* ix. 29; *Milward*, pp. 152–3, Dec. 3. Clarendon's ship was forced to wait three days for the wind, yet the news of his flight seems only to have become known after he had landed in France, *Life*, iii. 323.

[3] Temple's comment, *Grey*, i. 65, Dec. 13.

[4] *Milward*, p. 153, Dec. 3.

[5] *C.J.* ix. 30–2; *Milward*, p. 154; *Grey*, i. 58–9; B.M. Add. MSS. 36,916, f. 34. Starkey, Dec. 5. (Starkey's letter is interesting in that it shows exact knowledge of the words spoken at the conference, and also that the writer was getting much information from the diarist, Anchitell Grey.) Ormonde's son, Ossory, disapproved of Clarendon's vindication, Carte MSS. 220, f. 312, Ossory, Dec. 13.

[6] *Milward*, pp. 155–6.

[7] Temple and Littleton for example, *Milward*, loc. cit.

No move in this direction was, however, possible before the Christmas recess. Instead the main business was to complete the bill setting up an accounts commission, for which Charles had given permission at the beginning of the reign, and which had been discussed briefly as early as October 26. The King had 'no prerogative that he may be cheated';[1] this was the prevailing argument, and there had already been some criticism of the Lords' action in defeating the bill of 1666.[2] By December 2 the Commons had got so far as to establish that no member of their House should sit on the new commission and rumours began to circulate that it would contain men as notorious as John Wildman, republican plotter and now Buckingham's henchman. Wildman was in fact nominated, but this led to an outcry and the list was hurriedly revised.[3] Despite fears that the bill would be abandoned the new committee was at last agreed upon, and the act establishing its authority received the King's consent on December 19.[4]

Also presented to the King was a bill for the banishment of the Earl of Clarendon. The first bill, drafted by the Lords, had been angrily rejected by the Commons, who declared that after years of fraud it left him free to enjoy his ill-gotten gains in a foreign country.[5] However, by this time the House was getting thin[6] and, perhaps because of this, his friends were able to stage a counter-attack amending the new bill to allow him up to February 1 to surrender and stand his trial.[7] For a time it was thought that he would avail himself of this concession[8] but, unwisely perhaps, he did not do so and apart from a few petty attacks which his son had little difficulty in fending off[9] the House had done with him.

---

[1] Temple, *Grey*, i. 3, Oct. 26.   [2] *Grey*, i. 4–5, Oct. 26.

[3] *Milward*, p. 164, Dec. 12; *C.J.* ix. 28, 36, Dec. 2, 12; *Pepys*, vii. 216, 218, 222, Dec. 7, 8, 12; Verney MSS., Claydon, letter of Sir Ralph Verney, Dec. 19; Carte MSS. 47, f. 174, Anglesey, Dec. 20; B.M. Add. MSS., 36,916, f. 44, Starkey, Dec. 12. For Wildman's activities at this time, and for his connection with Buckingham, see M. P. Ashley, *John Wildman*, pp. 184, 206–7.

[4] 19 & 20 Car. II, cap. 1.   [5] *Milward*, pp. 165–6, Dec. 13.

[6] So at least Starkey reported, B.M. Add. MSS. 36,916, f. 47, Dec. 17, though on Dec. 16 a division of 101 to 65 was recorded, *C.J.* ix. 40.

[7] *Milward*, p. 176, Dec. 18.

[8] B.M. Add. MSS. 36,916, f. 59, Starkey, Jan. 23.

[9] For examples of this see *Milward*, pp. 152, 203, 242, Dec. 3, March 2, April 2.

Ten weeks had passed since the session had begun. The first phase of the new parliamentary programme—the completion of Clarendon's disgrace—had been successful, but this had been brought about at least as much by his own conduct as by any skill in management.[1] During the early debates it had been the one time trouble makers, future holders of office, who had led the prosecution, followed without much apparent enthusiasm by the centre, and opposed not only by leading cavaliers but by a number of Buckingham's supposed friends, the presbyterians. The only votes recorded against the Chancellor had been that *if guilty* of betraying secrets to our enemies he had committed treason, and later, that he had done wrong to flee the country instead of remaining to stand trial by his peers. This was not by any means the emphatic repudiation of the minister for which the new managers had hoped or which has been described by some later writers. As for the other feature of these weeks, the enquiries into our failures in the war, they may have increased Buckingham's popularity but they were also producing even greater reluctance to consider supply than had existed in the previous year. With Coventry turning back to straight administration and the rift between Arlington and Buckingham reopening the prospect for the future was not good.[2] By the adjournment of December 19 the managers were left with just seven weeks to find a policy which would commend itself to the Commons, and perhaps produce both toleration and a much needed grant of supply.

[1] This was certainly the opinion of *Pepys* and his gossipy friend Captain Cocke, vii. 215, Dec. 6.

[2] PRO 31/3/117, f. 40v., Dec. 3; *Pepys*, vii. 238, Dec. 30.

CHAPTER VII

THE FAILURE OF THE 'UNDERTAKERS'

AT the beginning of the reign Clarendon had approached the problem of 'management' on good Elizabethan lines. He explained, through his subcommittee, what the King required, and the members, in theory, hastened to comply. This system had failed: now it was for Clarendon's supplanters to try their skill. A good guide to the way their minds were working is provided by some notes made by Sir Richard Temple, probably in May 1668.[1] Though not yet in office Temple was already linked with Buckingham,[2] and his comments accord very well with the policy announced in the King's speech of February 1668. The Commons, so Temple declared, could be divided into four main groups: 'the Clarendonians', diehard anglicans; 'the anti-Clarendonians', among whom he would presumably have numbered Seymour, Howard, Osborne, Littleton, and himself; 'the Presbyterians', men like Holland and Birch; and the central mass of country gentlemen, whose votes he believed, rightly, to be the key to parliamentary success. It was his hope that, having crushed the first group, the last three could be welded into an alliance, and to judge from the King's speech, and from the debates which followed, something of this kind was indeed the new managers' intention.

Translating this strategic outline into specific proposals, and anticipating our later narrative, we find that the court offered two main concessions, and asked for two in return. A new foreign policy had been devised, based on an alliance with Sweden and with our recent enemies the Dutch, and having as its object the preservation of the Netherlands, and the administration of a check to catholic France.[3] For those

---

[1] These have been printed from B.M. Stowe MSS. 304, by Dr Clayton Roberts in *Hunt. Lib. Quart.* xx (1956–7), pp. 137–44. The assessment they give tallies closely with those made by Ruvigny on Sept. 30, 1667, and Feb. 23, 1668, PRO 31/3/116, f. 95, and 31/3/118, f. 70.

[2] Dr G. R. Abernathy, who has been making a full study of Temple, feels that his connection with Buckingham may have been exaggerated but their names were quite frequently linked at the time.

[3] Feiling, *British Foreign Policy,* pp. 255–6.

whose interests lay nearer home, the Commission of Accounts was to be allowed its head, further investigations were to be permitted, and new safeguards provided against incompetence on the part of government officials.[1] In return Parliament would be asked to provide some form of toleration—itself a concession rather than a request so far as the presbyterians were concerned—and at the same time it was hoped, for the first time since the previous spring, to coax forth a supply.[2] As an example of how to plan a session this made Clarendon's committee look somewhat primitive. Unfortunately it lacked the one thing that Clarendon might have contributed: a true understanding of the vital centre group within the House.

Several weeks before Parliament met there was already discussion of a new design for toleration, and if Charles could look for little support from his Archbishop other senior clergy were said to favour the proposals.[3] Unfortunately this attitude was not shared by a majority in the Lower House. On the first day of the session Charles failed to appear, and a hasty resolution was pushed through the Commons that no new business should be taken until the House had been called. To more than one observer it appeared that this was done with the deliberate intention of preventing any attempt by the managers to introduce a toleration bill before all the country members had arrived.[4] When Charles did arrive, five days later, he announced the new alliance[5] but this 'Triple League', often recalled with admiration when our foreign policy had drifted the other way, aroused at the time very little response. It is true that public opinion seems to have been hostile to France, even perhaps in favour of an alliance

---

[1] For this see Temple's memoir, *Hunt. Lib. Quart.* xx (1956–7), pp. 139, 143 and compare speeches by Seymour, Temple, and Howard, *Milward*, pp. 188, 299, Feb. 17, May 7, and *Grey*, i. 75, 80, 138, Feb. 15, 17, April 16.

[2] Toleration and Supply were both mentioned in the King's opening speech, *L.J.* xii. 181, Feb. 10.

[3] B.M. Add. MSS. 36,916, ff. 59, 60, 62, Starkey news letters, Jan. 23, 28, Feb. 4; Verney MSS. Claydon, letter of Sir Ralph Verney, Feb. 2; *Pepys*, vii. 228–9, 272, Dec. 21, Jan. 23.

[4] *Milward*, p. 179, Feb. 6; B.M. Egerton MSS. 2539, ff. 155–6, Sir John Nicholas, Feb. 19; *Pepys*, vii. 292, Feb. 10; *H.M.C. Kenyon MSS.*, p. 81, letter of G. Ayloff, Feb. 11. Starkey noted that Littleton had opposed this resolution, B.M. Add. MSS. 36,916, f. 66, Feb. 11.

[5] *L.J.* xii. 181, Feb. 10.

to preserve the Netherlands, though some would have preferred that we should have remained neutral and taken over the trade of all contending parties.[1] The whole question of foreign policy was, however, quite overshadowed by that part of Charles' speech which contained his plea for toleration. Reverting to their ungracious attitude of 1666 the Commons failed to vote him thanks and postponed consideration of his speech.[2] They then turned back to their dissection of our failures in the recent war.

To allow this inquest to continue was part of Buckingham's policy, and it may not have grieved him very much that the first matter to be considered involved Arlington and Sir William Coventry. This matter was the delay in orders sent to the fleet before the Four Days Battle of 1666.[3] Arlington kept silence, hoping that the enquiry would come to nothing, whilst his able if somewhat self-righteous colleague, Coventry, produced a mass of papers and cleared himself completely.[4] The failure to fortify Sheerness and the payment of seamen by ticket were also debated, but the House was not really a suitable place in which to conduct a detailed enquiry and amid a babble of accusations and denials no positive conclusions were reached.[5] One result, however, was to promote a mood of widespread hostility towards the wartime administration, and this seems to have developed into a general reluctance to trust any administration further than was absolutely necessary. In the heat of debate Sir Rupert Brooke declared that the proper body to advise the King was not the Council but Parliament;[6] nothing came of this, but there was enough grumbling and protesting to cause one moderate, Sir Robert Atkins, to declare that things would soon be as bad as in the days of '41.[7]

[1] B.M. Add. MSS. 36,916, ff. 45, 58, 59, 62, Starkey, Dec. 11, Jan. 18, 23, Feb. 4; *Pepys*, vii. 248 and note, 269, Jan. 2, 20.

[2] *C.J.* ix. 44. This was commented on by Starkey, B.M. Add. MSS. 36,916, f. 66, Feb. 11; and Ruvigny, PRO 31/3/118, f. 62, Feb. 10. Arlington's disappointment appears in his letter of Feb. 15, Carte MSS. 46, f. 598.

[3] *Supra*, Chapter VI.

[4] *Milward*, pp. 185–8; *Grey*, i. 74–81, Feb. 15, 17. Part of the debate given by Grey under this date took place in fact on March 5.

[5] For these debates see *Milward*, pp. 184–9, and *Grey*, i. 70–82, Feb. 14, 15, 17. See also *Pepys*, vii. 300–4, Feb. 14, 17.

[6] *Grey*, i. 75, Feb. 15.   [7] *Ibid.*

Faced with this mood among the country backbenchers Temple decided that it was again time to play the tribune of the people. In 1664 he had been a passionate opponent of the Triennial Act's emasculation; he now brought forward a bill which would have restored the sanctions originally imposed in 1641.[1] Supporting him in this were Howard, Littleton, and Sir Robert Carr, the first a rather doubtful Buckinghamite, the last two of the Arlington faction, and all, like Temple, future office-holders. To their annoyance they found their 'country' measure firmly rejected by the genuine country members.[2] Littleton, who spoke of 'compelling the King', was forced to explain that 'thing' was the word he had intended; feeling in the House was clearly against the bill, and it was only by getting hasty permission to withdraw it that its supporters were able to avoid a humiliating defeat.[3]

That this abortive proposal was intended to soften the mood of the centre is supported by the fact that supply, or at least that part of the King's speech which concerned supply, was due to be debated on the following day. On that day Temple was joined by Seymour in requesting a grant and in asking for a resolution approving the new foreign policy.[4] Solicitor-General Finch now showed that, as a past friend of Clarendon, he preferred scoring off Temple to advancing the King's business, and declared that for the House to approve the alliances would be for it to invade the royal prerogative. The Commons appeared to accept this assertion: the topic was dropped, and nothing more was said of foreign policy during this session. The next time the Triple League was mentioned was in October 1669.[5]

Whilst Finch had attacked the unfortunate Temple on

[1] *Milward*, p. 189, Feb. 18; *Pepys*, vii. 306, Feb. 18, over-estimated Temple's chances of success.

[2] *Milward*, pp. 189–90; *Grey*, i. 82–4. This is one of several occasions on which Grey's bias may have led him to record an unrepresentative selection of speeches.

[3] *Milward*, loc. cit.; B.M. Add. MSS. 36,916, ff. 72–4, Starkey, Feb. 18, 20; Egerton MSS. 2539, ff. 155–6, Nicholas, Feb. 19. Arlington blamed the 'Clarendonians' for the defeat of the bill, Carte MSS. 46, f. 600, Feb. 18.

[4] *Milward*, pp. 191–2; *Grey*, i. 84–5, Feb. 19.

[5] *Milward*, loc. cit.; *Grey*, loc. cit.; PRO 31/3/118, ff. 72, 76, Ruvigny, Feb. 22, 26.

constitutional grounds, the latter's recent ally, Littleton, had undermined his attempt to secure a supply by reviving the old argument that there might still be enough money left from previous grants.[1] When, on February 21, the House went into committee of supply for the first time for over a year, this question of money remaining in the Treasury was referred to a sub-committee and progress was delayed for another five days.[2] At last, on February 26, a long, fierce debate took place, in which anonymous opponents of supply tried to push through a resolution that no money at all should be given in this session.[3] They chose a time when the House had grown thin, and came near to carrying their proposal. Temple and his friends seem to have been silent; the only courtiers known to have spoken are Sir William Coventry and Sir Charles Harbord, but on this occasion the silent centre, including at least some staunch Clarendonians, rallied to the crown. Late in the evening—so late that Sir John Nicholas went without his dinner—the welcome, if somewhat grudging, resolution was carried that there should be a supply, 'not exceeding £300,000', of which no part should be raised by an excise. With this the new managers were forced to remain content.

Against this rather meagre success had now to be set an unequivocal defeat. On February 28, March 4, 11, and 13 the Commons discussed religion, with Littleton, Seymour, and Clifford joining the presbyterians Birch, and Swinfen in a powerful plea for some form of toleration.[4] Against them, and against the King's known wishes, were such loyal cavaliers as Henry Coventry, Giles Strangeways, and Sir John Birkenhead, together with Sir Thomas Meres and a significantly large number of 'backwoodsmen', whose names do not appear in the records of any other debates.[5] The arguments were as

[1] *Milward*, p. 191, Feb. 19. It may be significant that Littleton's patron, Arlington, was said to be welcoming Finch as an ally at about this time, *Cal. S.P. Dom. 1667–8*, pp. 258–9, Conway, Feb. 1668.

[2] *C.J.* ix. 54; *Milward*, pp. 194–5; *Grey*, i. 89–90, Feb. 21.

[3] *Milward*, p. 198; *Grey*, i. 93–4; B.M. Egerton MSS. 2539, ff. 160–1, Nicholas, Feb. 27; *H.M.C. 7th Rep.* Verney MSS., p. 486, Denton, Feb. 26.

[4] *Milward*, pp. 180, 201, 206, 214–22; *Grey*, i. 97, 103–6, 110–16. The debate on March 11 was particularly long, *H.M.C. 7th Rep.* Verney MSS. Denton, March 12; *Pepys*, vii. 321, 334–5, Feb. 28, March 11.

[5] Among these were Sir Hugh Windham, Sir John Arnly, Mr Chune, Lord Gorges, Mr Ratcliffe, Sir John Cotton and Lord Fanshaw. Once again

before: the Breda promises, the advancement of trade, protestant unity, set against the subversion of good order and the
fear of anarchy or military dictatorship.[1] Both sides quoted
precedents, neither would appear to have made many converts, but when it came to a vote the King's proposals were
put aside for a month, whilst a new bill against conventicles
received its first reading on March 13.[2]

Scarcely less frustrating for the court was the time still spent
on minor business. The export of horses to France, the reform of the Silk Throwsters Gild, the new regulations for
the Forest of Deane, the case of Carr versus Gerard, not only
produced long debates in the House but gave rise to petitions
and counter petitions which demanded the attention of both
Commons and Lords.[3] Nevertheless supply, unlike toleration,
continued to make progress, although agreement on a sum
did not preclude long arguments on methods. A majority among
the court believed that if a tax was collected inland instead of
at the customs-house the possibility of smuggling would be
much reduced, and the yield increased.[4] This, however, led
them towards an excise, and home excise had been specifically
barred by the original resolution of February 26.[5] On March 1
this ban was extended—by a snap vote in a thin House—
to an excise on foreign commodities. In Milward's opinion
the opposition were again moving towards a land tax which
would produce such discontent that Charles would be forced
to order a dissolution.[6]

Grey's notes present a rather different picture of the debates from that given
by Milward.

[1] For a good example of the speeches against the bill see the one by Birkenhead, *Milward*, pp. 218–20, March 11. Though this sometime editor of
Mercurius Aulicus had lost most of his sparkle he was to be one of the few
reliable court speakers during the difficult years after 1671. Strong speeches
on the other side were made by Littleton, Seymour, and Swinfen, *Milward*,
pp. 215, 216, 218, 221, March 11 and *Grey*, i. 104, 112, 114, March 4, 11.

[2] *C.J.* ix. 66; *Milward*, p. 180.

[3] *Milward*, pp. 181–2, 194–6, 198–9, 211; *Grey*, i. 88–9, Feb. 11, 12, 21,
22, 27, March 9. For petitions concerning these and other measures, see
H.M.C. 8th Rep., House of Lords, pp. 115, 116, 118, 124.

[4] Chandaman, i, 79, 143. This was the view of Finch, Howard, William
Coventry, and Clifford, who saw taxation as a purely fiscal matter. Mercan-
tilists such as Downing supported the customs, as did Littleton and Temple,
Milward, 202, 224, 228, Feb. 29, March 12, 17.

[5] *Supra.*   [6] *Milward*, pp. 201–2.

On March 10 the resolution against any form of excise was rescinded, after yet another long and bitterly contested debate.[1] This still left the way open for the usual freak proposals:[2] loans from rich men; a tax on all found to have cheated the King; a loan from the City of London. Local patriotism was still strong, as was shown when Sir William Thomson proposed that an excise should be levied everywhere except in London, and Meres retorted that it should be levied in London alone. On March 14 a sub-committee suggested that the whole sum should be raised by an excise on wine and tobacco,[3] the solution favoured by the court—but two days later, when many members had drifted away, it was agreed that a part should be transferred to an additional customs duty, and later still a poll bill was proposed.[4] Further complications arose when Prynne proposed a tax on duelling, an obvious hit at Buckingham who had just been involved in the most notorious duel of the reign.[5] Littleton defended Buckingham, and put forward a counter proposal of a new tax on the clergy; Finch and William Coventry rose in the latter's defence, and by a final hurried resolution it was agreed to raise the money partly by a tax on the vintners, another part by a poll bill, and the remainder at the custom house.[6] In this unsatisfactory state the matter was left when the House rose for the Easter recess.

In almost every debate, on almost every topic, Temple, Seymour, Littleton, and Howard had appeared on the losing side.[7] For the limited success that had been achieved Charles had to thank the friends not of Buckingham, but of

[1] *Milward*, p. 213; B.M. Egerton MSS. 2539, ff. 166–7, Nicholas, March 10.

[2] *Milward*, pp. 223–4, March 12.

[3] Ibid., pp. 226–7.

[4] Ibid., pp. 228–31, March 17, 18.

[5] *Milward*, pp. 230–1; *Grey*, i. 118–19, March 18. On the duel see Winifred Gardner, *George Villiers, Second Duke of Buckingham*, pp. 190–7.

[6] *Milward*, pp. 230–1; *Grey*, i. 118–20, March 18; Verney MSS. Claydon, letter of Dr Denton, March 19. Although the clergy were left to tax themselves Nicholas feared that they might be heavily assessed in the proposed Poll Bill, B.M. Egerton MSS. 2539, ff. 174–5, March 19.

[7] For comments on their discomfiture see B.M. Egerton MSS. 2539, ff. 155–6, 170–1, Nicholas, Feb. 19, March 14; *Pepys*, vii. 301, Feb. 14; Carte MSS. 36, ff. 153, 167, Forster, and Broderick Feb. 11, 18. Nicholas and Pepys both use the 'odious name of undertaker' echoing Clarendon's comment of some years earlier, *Life*, ii. 209.

Clarendon, a fact which he admitted ruefully to the French ambassador.[1] Logically Charles should have dismissed his new ministers and recalled the ex-Chancellor, since the main reason he had given for the latter's dismissal had been the need to smooth relations between Crown and Parliament.[2] If this was too much to expect Charles could at least have adopted an avowedly anglican policy: that he delayed doing this for another two years may be attributed to his devotion to the ideal of toleration, to his enslavement by Buckingham, or to the notorious discrepancy between his actions and his words.

Whatever the reason, Buckingham remained his confidant, though it was the cavaliers who did most of the talking during the remaining debates on supply. On March 28 Finch produced a draft bill for the tax on wine retailers, in all but name an excise.[3] This had been intended, it will be recalled, to produce only a third of the total sum: to extend it to cover the whole £300,000 it was necessary to get the Poll and Customs Bills laid aside and this might well have taken a considerable time. Fortunately, however, the court for once seem to have maintained party discipline and to have attended in strength, whilst the opposition were slow to return from their Easter vacation.[4] On April 1, in a thin House, it was agreed that the whole sum should be raised by Finch's tax.[5]

With this decision the battle over supply was virtually concluded. The vintners, it is true, had struck up an alliance with the presbyterians,[6] and their combined opposition produced irritating delays. Three hours were spent deciding on the correct description of various 'strong liquors', and four hours on one other paragraph of a bill which contained thirty paragraphs in all.[7] Nevertheless progress continued, and by

[1] PRO 31/3/118, f. 87v, Ruvigny, March 19.
[2] Supra, p. 63 note 1.
[3] Milward, pp. 236–7.
[4] This can be deduced from Nicholas' comment on the thinness of the House, B.M. Egerton MSS. 2539, ff. 182–3, March 26, and from the evidence of the court's success, Milward, pp. 239, 241, March 30, April 1, and C.J. ix. 72, March 30.
[5] Milward, p. 241, April 1; C.J. ix. 73, April 1.
[6] Milward, p. 240, March 31.
[7] Milward, pp. 244–5, 258, April 4, 15; B.M. Egerton MSS. 2539, ff. 200–1, Nicholas, April 16.

May 1 the last amendments had been agreed. One last gesture from the opposition was the proposal of a strict appropriation clause, by which the money was to be paid into a separate treasury and issued only for the fitting out of an 'extraordinary' fleet—the term being chosen to emphasize the old country claim that the 'ordinary' charge of the navy should be met from the customs.[1] As a codicil the proposal of 1663 to appropriate the customs to the use of the Navy, was revived. Seymour, Littleton, and Howard, once again mistaking the mood of the House, supported this proposal, but it shocked the uncommitted centre and was rejected, after some debate, by 134 to 93.[2] The supply Bill passed the Commons, survived the disruption caused by inter-house disputes, and became law, a tribute more to the loyalty of the 'Clarendonians' and of the centre group, than to the ineffective, and at times harmful, intervention of the 'undertakers'.

If the cavaliers were prepared to grant money this did not mean that their views had in any way changed on Charles' other request, that there should be some advance towards toleration. The 'second part of the King's speech' was not debated again until April 8—by which time the new Conventicle Bill was already under way.[3] On that day three or four hours were spent going over familiar ground; eventually it was suggested that the matter should be left to the discretion of the King but this was rejected, by 170 to 70, and further discussion was postponed, first for a week and then indefinitely.[4] Two days later, on April 10, the Bill against Conventicles received its second reading.[5] It was agreed that since the conventiclers had not been cowed by imprisonment their goods should be distrained upon and the money given to the poor

[1] *Milward*, pp. 285–6; *Grey*, i. 148–50, May 1.

[2] *Milward*, loc. cit. For the earlier proposal see *H.M.C. Ormonde MSS.* new series, iii. p. 53, H. Coventry, May 12 1663.

[3] The Bill, ordered on March 13, had received its first reading on March 30, *C.J.* ix. 66, 71.

[4] *Milward*, pp. 248–50; *Grey*, i. 126–32, April 8. The topic was adjourned until April 15, but the time allotted to it was used for a new Conventicle Bill, *Milward*, p. 258, April 15. See B.M. Egerton MSS. 2539, ff. 189–92, April 7, 8, for Nicholas' eagerness for the rejection of toleration, and see also B.M. Add. MSS. 36,916, f. 91, Starkey, April 9.

[5] *Milward*, pp. 252–3. The draft of this bill which did not become law is summarized in *H.M.C. 8th Rep.*, House of Lords, p. 126, April 29.

of the parish: this would have the additional advantage of
providing informers with a strong incentive to reveal any
meetings that might take place. On April 24 and April 28
more progress was made.[1] A clause empowering officers to
break into buildings where an illicit meeting was suspected
passed by 124 to 58; a clause to include papists in the bill
was rejected—on the grounds that this would weaken rather
than strengthen existing laws against them[2]—and the completed bill was approved by 144 to 78. After so much discussion
the bill failed to pass the Lords[3]—ironically Birch was chosen
to remind their Lordships of its existence[4]—and, since the act
of 1664 expired with this session, dissenters had now two years'
grace to meet without fear of molestation.[5]

Religion was one matter on which the cavaliers showed
their strength. Another was the investigation of alleged mal-
practices, on the one hand by Ormonde and the Commissioners
for the Irish Settlement, and on the other by various naval
officers during the recent war. The first of these topics was
debated on April 20,[6] by which time two of the Irish Commissioners had been forced to return to Ireland, leaving
their colleague Henry Coventry to defend their good name.[7]
For counsel, however, they had Sergeant Scroggs, who showed
himself on this occasion a bold and intelligent advocate.
Howard of Escrick led the attack on the Commissioners, and
on the first day scored various tactical successes.[8] One of the

---

[1] *Milward*, pp. 277–8, 282–3; *Grey*, i. 146–7; B.M. Egerton MSS. 2539, ff.
208–9, 210–11, Nicholas, April 24, 29.

[2] *Milward*, p. 283, April 28. This does not seem to have been understood
by *Pepys*, vii. 384, April 28.

[3] Starkey attributed this to a speech by the Earl of Anglesey, B.M. Add.
MSS. 36,916, f. 95, May 2.

[4] *Milward*, p. 293, May 4.

[5] For evidence of their activity see B.M. Add. MSS. 36,916, ff. 107, 119,
140, July 4, Nov. 18, 1668, Aug. 7, 1669; Egerton MSS. 2539, f. 236, July
22; *Pepys*, viii. 74, Aug. 11. For the lapse of the original statute see 16 Car.
II, cap. 4, clause 20.

[6] *Milward*, p. 264. The matter had first been raised on March 16, *Milward*, p. 227.

[7] Churchill and Broderick were the two absentees, Carte MSS. 46, f.
616, Arlington, March 24.

[8] *Milward*, pp. 264–7; B.M. Egerton MSS. 2539, ff. 204–5, Nicholas,
April 21; B.M. Add. MSS. 36,916, f. 93, Starkey, April 21. Nicholas
sympathized with the commissioners; Starkey thought them monsters of
iniquity.

defence witnesses then failed to give the evidence expected of him,[1] but, rising above these setbacks, Scroggs demolished Howard's arguments in a vigorous speech, and only shortness of time forced a postponement of the enquiry in place of a triumphant acquittal.[2] A further attack had been planned, this time against Ormonde himself, but when it became known that the latter was preparing to come over and defend himself in person his enemies lost heart and the whole affair was left until the following session.[3]

No such escape was granted to those who had been accused of misconduct during the war. The failure to pursue the Dutch after the victory of 1665 and the 'breaking of bulk' in the autumn of that year were both discussed, and the return of a key witness, Admiral Harman, was eagerly awaited.[4] His evidence, given over two days, incriminated Henry Brounker, a member of the House, and on April 20 the latter fled the country, his expulsion, and token impeachment, being voted in absentia.[5] Next on the list was Sir William Penn, also a member, and unhappily for himself chosen in place of Prince Rupert as admiral of the proposed summer fleet. The charge against him was that he had shared in Sandwich's misappropriation of prize goods. His attempt to defend himself turned the friends of Sandwich against him, the cavaliers hated him as a survivor of the Interregnum, and despite a well argued and convincing defence he was formally impeached and the articles against him sent to the Upper House.[6] No action followed but he was left, like Sir George Carteret whose

---

[1] *Milward*, p. 267, April 20.

[2] Ibid., pp. 272–7; *Grey*, i. 144–5, April 23; B.M. Egerton 2539, ff. 206–7, April 23, for Nicholas' cheerful letter, written at 9 in evening, immediately after the House had adjourned; Carte MSS. 36, f. 304, Forster, April 25.

[3] B.M. Egerton MSS. 2539, ff. 204–5, Nicholas, April 21. An account of these attacks is given by T. Carte, *Ormonde*, iv. 311–20, 325–33.

[4] *Milward*, pp. 251, 254, April 9, 11; *Pepys*, vii. 372–4, April 9, 13, 14, 15.

[5] *Milward*. pp. 261–3, 269–70; *Grey*, i. 139–41, 143–4, April 17, 21; *C.J.* ix. 96, May 7; *Pepys*, vii. 375–8, April 18, 19, 20, 21; B.M. Egerton MSS. 202–3, 204–5, April 20, 21; B.M. Add. MSS. 36,916, f. 93, April 21.

[6] *Milward*, pp. 257, 259–60, 268–9, 278–9, 293–5; *Grey*, i. 133–9, 142–3, 145–6, April 14, 16, 21, 23, 24; *Pepys*, vii. 374–87, April 16–30. passim, May 1, 3; *C.J.* ix. 85–6, April 21; *L.J.* xii. 237–8, April 29; B.M. Add. MSS. 36,916, f. 87, March 21; Egerton 200–1, 204–5, April 16, 21; F. R. Harris, *Sandwich* ii. 191–4.

accounts had been queried, and Peter Pett already committed to the Tower, to await with anxiety the opening of the next session.[1]

Whether these impeachments had ever been intended as more than gestures of disapproval is not clear. Any effective prosecution of them was, at all events, prevented by the outbreak of one of the most celebrated of the many inter-House disputes which occurred during this reign. On April 17 the East India Company presented, by mediation of certain of their directors who were also members of the House, a petition concerning an injury done them by a Mr Thomas Skinner.[2] Skinner was an 'interloper', who had profited by the relaxation of the Company's monopoly during the Protectorate and attempted to invade their eastern markets. The company's servants had attacked his representatives and destroyed a large part of his stock, the damage being subsequently inflated in a manner worthy of Don Pacifico himself. By 1666 the case had reached the Privy Council who, at the King's wish, referred it to the Lords. In October 1667 the Lords enquired of the Judges if the matter was hearable in Westminster Hall and were told that it was not, since the alleged injuries had been suffered outside the Crown's dominion. On the grounds that there was no other court which could give Skinner justice the Lords then agreed to act as a court of first instance and, despite many delays, proceeded slowly towards judgement.[3]

Such was the situation when, in April 1668, the Company hit on a new line of defence. By his allegations against a company some of whose directors were also members of the Commons Skinner had, it was declared, violated the privileges of the Lower House. A committee, under Sir Robert Atkins, accepted this contention, and at the same time attacked the Lords for their attempt to act as a court of first instance.[4] The Lords at once retaliated by charging the Deputy Governor of the Company, Sir Samuel Barnadiston, with a breach of the privileges of their own House.[5]

[1] For Carteret see *Milward*, p. 272, April 23; *C.J.* ix. 88, April 24; *Pepys*, viii. 28–9, May 27. For Pett supra, Chapter VI, *C.J.* ix. 93, May 4.

[2] *Milward*, p. 260.

[3] The events of this dispute can best be followed in three main sources: *H.M.C. 8th Rep.*, app. 1, pp. 165–74; (J. Hatsell) *Precedents of proceedings in the House of Commons* (1818), iii. 38–377; T. B. Howell, *A Complete Collection of State Trials* (1816), vi. 710–64.

[4] *Milward*, p. 280, April 24.   [5] *H.M.C. 8th Rep.*, app. 1, 167, May 1.

During the last week of this session the dispute absorbed almost the whole time of both Houses, though it failed, surprisingly, to crowd out the bill of supply.[1] Buckingham backed the Lords, his former follower Howard urged on the Commons; Finch too was for the Commons, and only William Prynne, controversial to the last session of his career, declared that the Lords were very possibly in the right. The Commons tried to arrest Skinner but he eluded their Sergeant; the Lords were more successful and committed Barnadiston to custody. Conferences were held, precedents exchanged, but far from reaching any agreement both sides grew more and more irate. On May 9, after Charles had ordered both Houses to adjourn forthwith, the Lords returned to their Chamber and sentenced Barnadiston to remain in custody until he should have paid a fine of £300.[2] The Commons passed one last furious resolution—they had been debating the case until five o'clock that morning, after which both Houses did at last adjourn.[3]

Leaving this controversy to the lawyers we may briefly consider what progress had been made since the previous October. Up to Christmas such progress had been entirely negative—the removal of Clarendon—and had been offset by the establishment of the vexatious Commission which was to examine the administration's accounts. After February there had been one gain, a tax expected to produce £300,000, spread over a period of two years, and out of which Charles was expected to equip an 'extraordinary' fleet. Such was the sum total of the new managements' achievement. Small wonder, argue Charles' apologists, that he turned with disgust from dependence upon Parliament.[4] If the Commons would not agree to toleration, then it should be imposed by royal fiat. If they would not provide an adequate revenue then recourse must be had to the well stocked coffers of Versailles.

[1] Which passed the Commons on the afternoon of May 2, *C.J.* ix. 92 and the Lords on May 5, *L.J.* xii. 242.

[2] *H.M.C. 8th Rep.*, app. 1, pp. 167–74, May 1–9; Hatsell, op. cit., iii. 371–7; *Milward*, pp. 286–92, 295–6, 302–3, May, 1, 2, 4, 8; *Grey*, i. 150–6, May 1, 2; *Pepys*, viii. 1–10, May 1–10, passim; B.M. Add. MSS. 36,916, ff. 95–7, May 2, 7, 9; B.M. Egerton MSS. 2539, ff. 193–4 (misdated) 'April 12', f. 214, May 5.

[3] Howell, op. cit., vi. 763.

[4] W. A. Shaw, *Cal. Treasury Books 1667–8*, p. lxviii; A. Bryant, *King Charles II*, pp. 161–3 and see Feiling, *British Foreign Policy*, pp. 272–5.

The niggardliness and the religious bias of the Commons lead directly, so it is suggested, to Charles' reversal of his 'protestant' foreign policy—a policy which the Commons had in any case ignored—and to the opening of secret negotiations with France.

That Charles acted out of disgust with Parliament is very probable. What is not so clear is whether his reaction was entirely justified. When 'the undertakers', though linked with leading ministers and thus enjoying quasi-official status, had proposed to revise the Triennial Act, or to appropriate the Customs, it had been the central mass of members, led by the Clarendonians and cavaliers, who had rejected their proposals. The supply was admittedly a small one, but it was nevertheless a further addition to what had been an unprecedented series of 'extraordinary' grants. The enquiries into maladministration had never developed, as they were to do in later years, into criticism of royal policy. If the Lower House had refused to accept the leadership of Buckingham it had shown strong loyalty to the Crown, and, on every matter except toleration, a respect for the wishes of the King. Had Charles been prepared to abandon, perhaps only to postpone, his efforts to amend the religious settlement, and had he been willing to accept Ormonde, Finch and perhaps Sir William Coventry, as his councillors there is good cause to think that a new session might have produced a far happier relationship between the Commons and the Crown. Unfortunately these advisers were dull, pedantic, 'visionaire',[1] whilst Buckingham was a delightfully amusing companion. Buckingham, therefore, remained Charles' trusted councillor and first Coventry, then Ormonde was forced into retirement.[2] The next session opened, after seventeen months of prorogation, with the central group of cavaliers still lacking any ministerial link with a King whom they desired, in however muddled a way, to serve.

[1] For Charles' impatience with those who talked to him of the need for reform see *Pepys*, vii. 249, viii. 164, Jan. 2, Dec. 7, 1668; Lord Conway's letter of Feb. 1668 in *Cal. S.P. Dom. 1667–8*, p. 259; and Charles' own letter to his sister, Julia Cartwright, *Madame*, p. 285, March 7, 1669.

[2] For the circumstances of their dismissals see *Pepys*, viii. 229–39, March 4, 9, 1669, and T. Carte, *Ormonde*, iv. pp. 342–52.

CHAPTER VIII

THE CAVALIERS TO THE RESCUE

THE long recess, from May 1668 to October 1669, was punctuated by two well attended but abortive meetings: over a hundred members appeared in August 1668, and again in March 1669, only to be sent straight home again.[1] Before and after these meetings rumours of a dissolution circulated freely; it was understood that Buckingham and the 'presbyterians' wanted Charles to dismiss the existing Parliament and try for a more accommodating body at the polls, whilst the 'Clarendonians' strongly opposed any such move.[2] This second group seems to have acquired a more definite character after Clarendon himself had left the country. At some point in 1669 we find a number of them drawing up something very like a party programme:[3] they would revive the 1665 oath against attempting any change in Church or State; they would resist any proposal for toleration, and, on a more personal note, they would attempt to prosecute the Earl of Orrery, Buckingham's supporter and the great rival of Ormonde. Meanwhile Orrery himself had come to England to assist in Ormonde's ruin,[4] whilst other Buckinghamites had marked down an 'old cavalier' and friend of Arlington, Sir George Carteret, as an easy prey.[5] Lord Holles, a presbyterian, was preparing a book on the Skinner controversy which seemed certain to reopen old wounds,[6] and, lastly, several of the foreign ambassadors had

[1] B.M. Add. MSS. 36,916, ff. 112, 128, Starkey, Aug. 18, March 2.

[2] Ibid., ff. 103, 119, 120, 123, 126, 128, June 6, Nov. 18, Dec. 3, 22, 1668, Jan. 7, Feb. 16, March 2, 1669; H.M.C. 7th Rep., Verney MSS., p. 487, Dr Denton, April 14, 1669.

[3] F. E. Harris, Sandwich, ii. 311–12, 317, quoting Sandwich's MSS. journal.

[4] T. Carte, Ormonde, iv. 330–3, 336–41, 381–2.

[5] Harris, Sandwich, ii. 313, 315; Violet Barbour, Arlington, p. 163. He had exchanged his post as Treasurer of the Navy in June 1667 and was now Deputy Treasurer of Ireland, but his accounts had still not been officially cleared.

[6] B.M. Add. MSS. 36,916, ff. 143–4, Starkey, Oct. 5, 14; PRO 31/3/123, ff. 20, 26, 29, Colbert, Oct. 24, 31, Nov. 4.

been dabbling in parliamentary intrigue.[1] Under these un-
propitious circumstances Charles, who was busy concluding
an anti-Dutch treaty with France, chose to meet Parliament
to ask for money to check France and to assist our 'allies', the
Dutch.[2]

On more than one occasion Charles had told the Commons
that they might cease supporting him when they observed him
say one thing and do another.[3] That such a situation had now
arisen, the Commons had no means of knowing, but they were
certainly in a most uncooperative mood. They made no response
to Charles' plea for supply, ignored his request that they should
abandon past grievances, and instead plunged again into their
long inquest on the war.[4]

In the debates which followed, private vendettas merged
with genuine 'country' indignation. The main target for attack
was, as the Buckinghamites had planned, the sometime Treasurer of the Navy, Sir George Carteret, who had handled large
sums of money and whose accounts were not in order.[5] His
defence was that he had been forced to disregard parliamentary
appropriations, and other standing regulations, in order to
meet sudden emergencies, and this general question of how
much discretion could be allowed to the officials who handled
parliamentary grants was discussed at length during the debates. Cavaliers such as Finch, Henry Coventry, Duncombe,
now a Commissioner of the Treasury, and Philip Warwick,
sometime secretary to Lord Treasurer Southampton, argued
vigorously that attacks on Carteret were virtually attacks on

[1] So at least Arlington told Colbert, in what reads like an attempt to warn
him off, PRO 31/3/123, f. 5, Oct. 3.

[2] Lord Keeper Bridgeman was the actual spokesman on foreign affairs,
L.J. xii. 251, Oct. 19; Feiling, *British Foreign Policy*, pp. 289–96; Barbour,
Arlington, pp. 154–8, 164–5. The Venetian ambassador was sceptical of
Charles' professions at the time, *Cal. S.P. Ven. 1667–70*, pp. 124–5, Nov. 1.

[3] Supra, Chapters II, V.

[4] *C.J.* ix. 99–100. Tomkins led the call for a fresh report from the Commissioners of Accounts. The absence of applause for the King's speech was remarked upon by Colbert, PRO 31/3/123, f. 26–26v, Oct. 31.

[5] Chandaman, ii. 546. Professor Chandaman adds, however, that he had
probably spent the money on necessary expenses. Dr H. G. Roseveare takes
a more severe view of his conduct, op. cit., pp. 155–6. In fairness to Carteret
it should be added that a committee of the *Upper* House had accepted his
explanations, *H.M.C. 8th Rep.*, House of Lords, pp. 128–33, Oct. 26–Dec. 10.
See also Harris, *Sandwich*, ii. 315.

the King's prerogative.[1] Against them Lee, an increasingly
effective speaker and a true country backbencher, and Birch,
a presbyterian who had once been a Commissioner of the Navy,
returned a double charge: by Carteret's conduct acts of parliament had been violated; at the same time his manipulation of
funds, far from making it possible to meet sudden emergencies,
had left the seamen starving although money had been voted
specifically for their relief.[2] Seymour, Temple and Howard all
attacked Carteret, whose answers were hesitant and confused.[3]
Still the cavaliers hung on and it was not until the last day of
the session that Carteret's suspension from the House was
ordered, and then only by a majority of 100 to 97.[4]

In these debates on Carteret the cavaliers had served the
Crown and the Buckinghamites played to the country. In a
second series, on toleration, these roles were reversed. Since the
lapsing of the 1664 Conventicle Act the London meeting houses
had been full.[5] The undiminished anglicanism of the cavaliers
has already been noticed, and on November 3 they launched
a new conventicle bill.[6] Careless of royal displeasure Henry
Coventry, who was three years later to be made a Secretary of
State, denounced the insolence of the fanatics: was not treason,
he asked, at least as great a crime as 'cozening the King'?[7]
Finch, Sandys, and Sir Winston Churchill joined in; Seymour,
Littleton, and Temple opposed, but the cavaliers carried the
day.[8] Not only did the new conventicle bill get through two
readings[9] but the House accepted a resolution to 'adhere to the

----

[1] *Grey*, i. 158, 165–6, 170–3, 180, 203, 213–15, Nov. 8, 12, 17, 23, 24,
Dec. 3, 10.   [2] Ibid., i. 171, Nov. 17.

[3] Ibid., i. 157–9, 164, 171–2, 204, 214, Nov. 8, 11, 13, 17, Dec. 3, 10.
Both Sir Robert Carr (Arlington's brother-in-law) and Vaughan (a new
member) suggested that for anyone to defend Carteret was to reflect on the
integrity of the Commissioners of Accounts, ibid., i. 158, 169, Nov. 8, 13,
an argument not unlike that used in later years by Titus Oates.

[4] Ibid., i. 213–15, Dec. 10.

[5] Supra, Chapter VII. Charles had issued proclamations ordering them
to restrict their activities, but with little effect, B.M. Add. MSS. 36,916,
ff. 134, 137, 138, 140, Starkey, April 1, June 19, 29, Aug. 7, 1669.

[6] On Nov. 3, *C.J.* ix. 102; PRO 31/3/123, f. 41–41v, Colbert, Nov. 17.
[7] *Grey*, i. 174, Nov. 18.

[8] Ibid., i. 160–2, 174–5, Nov. 10, 18; B.M. Add. MSS. 36,916, f. 152,
Starkey, Nov. 16.

[9] *C.J.* ix. 102, 104, Nov, 3, 10. The debate of Nov. 18 referred to above
took place in committee.

King in maintaining Church and State as established by law'.[1]
The 1665 non-resistance test was itself not very far away.

Still in the realm of faction, rather than of a true court versus
country struggle, came an attempt to impeach the Earl of
Orrery. The occasion for this was that the Buckinghamites were
trying to impeach Ormonde: the cavaliers got wind of this and
resolved to get their blow in first.[2] In itself the impeachment was
of little importance. Like so many others it foundered on insufficient evidence,[3] and, having made a well organized defence,
Orrery soon had the satisfaction of seeing the charges transferred to King's Bench, where it seems to have been understood
that they would be dropped.[4] What is interesting is the way in
which the two sides lined up, Seymour, Howard, Temple, and
Clifford, defending the Earl, whilst Charlton, Atkins, and the
moderate presbyterian Swinfen, attacked him. Sir Thomas Lee
may have spoken for the central mass when he expressed the
hope that by the falling out of these great men the House might
learn much to its profit.[5] In fact the House learnt little, but
time was consumed which might otherwise have been given
to supply.

Still more trouble came from the old feud between the
Houses. Early in the session the Commons had introduced a
new bill intended to define the Lords' judicial powers.[6] This bill
reached the Lords on November 4, and on November 10 was
firmly rejected.[7] However, perhaps at Charles' instigation, the
Dukes of York and Buckingham formed a strange alliance in

[1] *C.J.* ix. 109, Nov. 18.

[2] T. Carte, *Ormonde*, iv. 370–82 and also supra. Colbert reported that it
was in fact Ormonde and not Orrery who was to be impeached, PRO
31/3/123, f. 49, Nov. 18, but this may be a reference to a petition presented
by the Earl of Meath to the Committee of Grievances. According to Sandwich, Buckingham disavowed this subsidiary attack, Harris, *Sandwich*, ii.
316.

[3] Starkey, as a supporter of Buckingham, writes scathingly of the prosecution's witnesses, B.M. Add. MSS. 36,916, f. 155, Nov. 30.

[4] *Grey*, i. 182–6, 195–201, Nov. 25, Dec. 1.

[5] Ibid., i. 184, Nov. 25. The vote of 182 to 144 declaring the charges to
be treason meant, as in the similar vote against Clarendon, that they would
amount to treason *if proved*, supra, Chapter VI.

[6] T. Howell, *State Trials* (1816), vi. 764. Some details of this bill are given
in a note by Sandwich, Harris, op. cit., ii. 313–15.

[7] *L.J.* xii. 260, 265, Nov. 4, 10; PRO 31/3/123, f. 43, Colbert, Nov. 11;
Cal. S.P. Ven. 1669–70, p. 133, Nov. 19; Marvell, ii. 88–90, Nov. 13, 20.

the cause of moderation, and a new, and it was thought conciliatory, bill was sent from the Lords to the Commons on
November 22.[1] When this bill was debated, not only backbenchers such as Carew, Lee, and Garraway, but also courtiers,
such as Clifford and Littleton, spoke against it.[2] The Lords in
exasperation revived their sentence upon Barnadiston;[3] the
Commons, at Temple's suggestion, proposed to tack a clause,
asserting their own claim, to a money bill, which had by then
begun its passage through the House.[4] Both Houses reaffirmed
their previous arguments, and although a conference was ordered
there seemed little hope of any agreement being reached.[5]

We have just mentioned that a money bill was in progress by
the beginning of December. This time it had been Arlington's
friend, Thomas Clifford, assisted by Downing, who had taken
the lead in requesting supply. This partnership was destined,
with the help of certain reinforcements, to secure remarkable
success in the near future,[6] but at this stage they found themselves attacked by not only the opposition, but even by members
of the court. When Clifford put forward, as an argument for a
grant, the need to pacify the 'mercenary' Swedes, his sometime
senior at the Stockholm embassy, Henry Coventry, jumped up
to dispute so disparaging a description of his former hosts.[7] In
the same debate Arlington's own brother-in-law, Sir Robert
Carr, opposed a grant, whilst Meres, for the opposition, asserted
that £1,000,000 of the war grants still remained unspent.[8] 'The
King it seems is in debt' added Carew, 'but how . . .? the
country is in debt also'.[9]

---

[1] Harris, op. cit., ii. 307–9; L.J. xii. 267–8, 271–2, Nov. 15, 16, 17, 22;
Cal. S.P. Ven. 1669–70, p. 131, Nov. 12.

[2] Grey, i. 189–95, Nov. 27.

[3] Howell, op. cit., vi. 765–6.

[4] Grey, i. 204–8, Dec. 4.

[5] Ibid., i. 209–10, Dec. 7.

[6] Infra, Chapter IX.

[7] Grey, i. 176–7, Nov. 19. Ironically it was Henry Coventry who was to be
dispatched in August 1671 to outbid the Dutch and buy a fresh alliance
with this 'unmercenary' nation, Feiling, British Foreign Policy, pp. 330–3.
A more immediate sequel was Henry's dismissal from his post as Gentleman
of the Bedchamber, Cal. S.P. Dom. 1670, pp. 1, 45, Jan. 1, 3, 1670; PRO
31/3/124, f. 96, Colbert, Dec. 29.

[8] Grey, i. 177, 186, Nov. 19, 26. Buckingham himself was blamed for
having started this rumour, Barbour, Arlington, p. 164.

[9] Ibid., i. 187, Nov. 26.

In the face of such opposition, and with the concurrent attack on Carteret providing apparent evidence of past wastage, the court were lucky to get a promise to provide £400,000.[1] After further argument it was agreed that this should be raised on wines, brandy, and French linen—an avowedly mercantilist and indeed anti-French proposal.[2] Garraway claimed that such a tax would yield £700,000, but in fact these commodities were already so heavily taxed that the chances of even raising credit on such a grant were considered extremely poor.[3] When Downing offered figures, the same figures which he was to use with much effect in the following year, the House refused to hear them.[4] Campaigning alone the Arlington faction had achieved little more than Buckingham's friends had done in 1668.

On December 11 Charles suddenly prorogued the House.[5] One current explanation of this was that they had been about to adjourn until after Christmas, keeping the session in being, the suspension of Carteret unrepealed, and making it impossible for a new supply bill to be introduced.[6] The French ambassador was much relieved since negotiations tended to hang fire whilst this troublesome assembly was sitting.[7] In Scotland Lauderdale persuaded a more docile House to promise him an army of 20,000 men, and more than one observer seems to have wondered if this might not be Charles' new answer to the intractable problem of supply.[8]

[1] C.J. ix. 113.

[2] C.J. ix. 115; Grey, i. 202. See also Colonel Sandys' speech of Dec. 10, Grey, i. 211; Chandaman, i. 73-4.

[3] Grey, i. 211, Dec. 9; B.M. Add. MSS. 36,916, f. 159, Starkey, Dec. 16, Chandaman, i. 80, points out that there were five separate duties on wines by 1670.

[4] Grey, i. 211, Dec. 9.

[5] L.J. xii. 285, Dec. 11. He sent Commissioners to make the announcement and there were no concluding speeches.

[6] They may also have feared a 'Christmas' majority for the court, supra, Chapter V. Comments on this adjournment and its possible causes can be found in B.M. Add. MSS. 36,916, f. 159, Starkey, Dec. 16; PRO 31/3/123, ff. 74-74v, Colbert, Dec. 13; Cal. S.P. Ven. 1669-70, p. 144, Dec. 17, Marvell, ii. 93, Dec. 12. Particularly interesting are the MSS. notes by Sandwich, printed in Harris, op. cit., ii. 311-17.

[7] PRO 31/3/123, ff. 9, 86, Sept. 30, Dec. 20.

[8] Verney MSS., Claydon, Sir Ralph Verney, Feb. 10; PRO 31/3/124, f. 131, Feb. 23; B.M. Add. MSS. 36,916, f. 165, Feb. 15; A. Marvell, ii. 299, March 21.

Yet although the long term implications of his new foreign policy could hardly be reconciled with a parliamentary form of government Charles was, at this time, about to make the most successful effort at 'management' in his whole reign. Exasperatingly the details remain obscure, but it is significant that in addition to consulting both Arlington and Buckingham, he was also in touch with Ormonde.[1] Either with Ormonde himself, or with his cavalier followers, a bargain was struck: Charles would accept new measures against nonconformists; he would hold off the attack on Carteret; and in return the cavaliers would rally to the court and provide a supply. During the recess Carteret surrendered his position as Deputy Treasurer of Ireland and was allowed to retire into comparative obscurity.[2] At the same time Charles attended meetings of the Commissioners of Accounts and, aided cheerfully by Pepys, turned the tables on this awesome body by subjecting them to vigorous cross-examination.[3] By the time the Houses reassembled the image of the Commission was considerably dimmed. It was now for the cavaliers to carry out their side of the bargain.

On the eve of the session Sir Robert Howard, still like Seymour and Temple 'ungratified', called a meeting of opposition members—their number was estimated at sixty but no names are known—and agreed to pursue Carteret as vigorously as ever and to work up indignation against Lauderdale's Scottish army.[4] The House then met, Charles asked for a supply, and they at once agreed to consider his request, rejecting a motion to postpone discussion by 137 to 130.[5] Three days later it was agreed by 175 to 138 that money should be given, in other words the court were gaining, not losing, as more members came up, and on February 18 the court carried two further divisions giving supply precedence over both accounts

[1] PRO 31/3/124, ff. 98, 101, 114, 118, Dec. 27, Jan. 18, 24, 31.

[2] B.M. Add. MSS. 36,916, f. 162, Jan. 25; *Cal. S.P. Ireland 1669-70*, p. 60, Jan. 11. He returned to office as a Commissioner for the Admiralty in 1673.

[3] B.M. Add. MSS. 36,916, ff. 162-3, Jan. 25, 29; A. Bryant, *Samuel Pepys: The Years of Peril* (1948), pp. 18-36 passim. Charles followed this up with a flat statement to Parliament that no money had gone astray, *C.J.* ix. 121, Feb. 14.

[4] PRO 31/3/124, f. 123, Colbert, Feb. 14. At this time Howard was alleged to be in the pay of Spain, Feiling, *British Foreign Policy*, p. 297.

[5] *C.J.* ix. 122, Feb. 14; B.M. Add. MSS. 36,916, f. 165, Feb. 15.

and inquiries into the war.[1] At this time some eighty members walked out in protest and the triumphant majority passed a vote continuing part of the 1668 wine tax for a further eight years.[2]

The eighty protesters were described in a news letter as 'country gentlemen'. Seeking a fuller explanation of their conduct we find the first serious accusation of court bribery in a well known pamphlet entitled 'The Alarum'.[3] If we set beside this Marvell's assertion that certain 'apostate patriots' had ratted to the court, and a rather imprecise reference by Bishop Burnet, we might suppose that the dark period of 'corruption' had already begun.[4] Yet there is reason to doubt if this is true. The writer of the news letter, John Starkey, was a strong opponent of the court, and got his information from the opposition diarist Anchitell Grey.[5] If indeed the eighty who withdrew were typical honest country gentlemen, others, equally uncorrupted, remained to join happily in the court programme.[6] The pamphlet attacking Clifford as 'bribe master general' names only members of the Arlington faction, and its ascribed period is one during which the court were enjoying no success at all; it could quite possibly have emanated not from an impartial country observer but from some rival courtier, very possibly a follower of Buckingham.[7] The apostate patriots denounced by Marvell and Burnet were Seymour, Garraway, Howard, and Temple, but all these remained in opposition until *after* the

[1] *C.J.* ix. 123, 124, Feb. 17, 18.

[2] *C.J.* ix. 124, Feb. 19; 22 Car. II, cap. 3; B.M. Add. MSS. 36,916, f. 167, Starkey, Feb. 22; Chandaman, i. 81.

[3] S.P. Charles II 266/152, printed in part by A. Browning, *English Historical Documents*, pp. 223–6.

[4] Marvell, ii. 303, 305, April 14, Nov. 28, 1670; G. Burnet, *History of my own Time*, ed. Airey, i. 486.

[5] Supra, p. 75 note 5. Grey's connection with Buckingham is noted by T. Carte, *Ormonde*, iv. 329. Starkey's later connection with the opposition is referred to in A. Browning, *Danby*, iii. 2. The gap in Grey's diary for this period suggests that he may well have been one of the seceders.

[6] Verney MSS., Claydon, Sir Ralph Verney, Feb. 23; Legh MSS., John Rylands Library, letter of Richard Legh, Feb. 22, quoted in part by Evelyn Legh (Lady Newton), *The House of Lyme*, p. 242; Hulton MSS., Lancashire Record Office, letter of William Jessop, Feb. 19; *H.M.C. Kenyon MSS.*, p. 84, G. Ayloffe, March 1.

[7] The MSS copy is dated Oct. 20, 1669. The pamphlet attacks only Arlington, Clifford and Littleton, with a side blow at Sandwich. The suggestion that it came from the Buckingham faction is also made by C. H. Hartmann, *Clifford*, p. 146.

H

summer recess, and the court's triumph seems to have been the cause rather than the consequence of their defection. Party lists were indeed compiled, but less with the aim of bribery than of finding which groups could be induced by natural interest to support the court, assuming always that their particular prejudices would be respected.[1] We have already seen that the dominant group in 1668 had been that of the cavaliers; Charles was now acting on the assumption that their dominance had survived and finding that this assumption was entirely correct.

With supply already agreed, and many opposition members sulkily withdrawn, Charles took another step to win the majority's goodwill. The Lords, rashly, had again revived the Skinner controversy. Charles now ordered them to remove all mention of it from their journals and records.[2] The Commons had to do likewise but in fact the only recorded *judgements* had been those of the Lords. If the whole case was razed, so also was the Lords claim to have had the right to consider it at all, and the Commons were as jubilant as the Lords were dejected. The Lords removed not merely all mention of the case but all record of this day's proceedings. The Commons, however, had the streets cleared, then marched two by two to Whitehall to offer profuse thanks to their genial Monarch, who in turn invited them down to his cellars to drink his royal health. The city was full of bonfires and it was many hours before the members staggered home to pen, next day, ecstatic tributes to the affability of their Prince.[3]

If more was needed to fill the cup of cavaliers like Richard Legh, it was Sir John Bramston's new bill against seditious conventicles.[4] True the tolerant minority remained as vocal as ever: 'Black Birch' declared that the bill would hinder trade, which was as 'the soul to the nation'; Sir Robert Howard talked of 'Alva and the Netherlands'; Waller observed that 'tops stand

---

[1] The best evidence for this is provided by the lists printed in A. Browning, *Danby*, iii. 31–44.

[2] *C.J.* ix. 126, Feb. 22.

[3] Verney MSS., Claydon, Sir Ralph Verney, Feb. 23; Evelyn Legh, *House of Lyme*, p. 242, Richard Legh, Feb. 22; B.M. Add. MSS. 36,916, f. 168, Starkey, Feb. 26; PRO 31/3/124, Colbert, Feb. 23.

[4] *C.J.* ix. 129, Feb. 27; Raines Transcripts, Chetham Library, 44, f. 6, Richard Legh, Feb. 26.

26560

up when whipped'.[1] To this Henry Coventry retorted that 'never was there a more merciful bill that punishes neither with blood or banishment a people that have punished us with both of these'.[2] The time for such retrospective arguments was passing, but for the moment enough veterans survived to carry the bill.

Having achieved the success which had eluded them in the two previous sessions the persecuting majority were prepared to make concessions. The Lords, ever more tolerant than the Commons, suggested several amendments to the bill, including a remarkable proviso which was reported to the Lower House on March 28. Nothing in the bill was to affect the King's

Supremacy in ecclesiastical affairs, or to destroy any of his Majesty's rights, powers, or prerogatives belonging to the imperial crown of this realm, or at any time exercised or enjoyed by himself or any of his royal predecessors, Kings or Queens of England.[3]

As it stood this was considered far too sweeping. Sergeant Maynard asked what trial any man had had before Magna Carta? William Coventry recalled the reign of Henry VIII, when protestants were burnt and papists hanged.[4] However, having removed the phrase beginning 'at any time enjoyed', the Commons accepted the reaffirmation of royal supremacy,[5] a natural enough decision from a house of cavaliers, but also a hopeful one for dissenters, when made in favour of an avowedly tolerant King.

All this time the wine tax bill was making steady progress, delayed only by rivalry between the London excise farmers and the merchant importers. The former, defended by Downing, Clifford, and Birch, wanted a retrospective increase in the rate on brandy of from 4*d.* to 8*d.* a gallon. The importers resisted, but after their counsel, the erratic John Ayliffe, had made rather a poor showing, three ungratified ex-Buckinghamites saw their chance to propose that the import of brandy should be stopped

[1] *Grey*, i. 220–1, March 2; *H.M.C. Kenyon MSS.*, p. 84, Sir Roger Bradshaigh, March 3. Bradshaigh asked his correspondent for instances of nonconformist insolence to quote in the House.

[2] *Grey*, i. 227, March 9.

[3] Ibid., i. 246; B.M. Add. MSS. 36,916, f. 172, Starkey, March 17.

[4] *Grey*, i. 246–50, March 28. Marvell described the proviso, which was presumably intended to help his co-religionists, as a 'compendious piece of absolute universal tyranny', ii. 305, April 14.

[5] *C.J.* ix. 148, March 28; 22 Car. II, cap. 1, clause 17.

Lincoln Christian College

altogether.[1] This suggestion carried strong overtones of both foreign policy and country grievance, since brandy accounted for part of our 'unfavourable trade balance' with France, and was also thought to have seduced 'the labouring mob' from their malt brewed English beer.[2] There followed a highly technical discussion on possible substitutes, especially for stocking ships at sea. Some speakers favoured whisky, some rum, whilst some alleged that anything distilled from corn tended to go 'ropey' south of the equator.[3] Eventually the excise farmers carried their point, it being thought that the higher rate they were demanding would in itself greatly lower consumption, and a bill authorizing the change passed at the end of the session.[4]

Meanwhile what had become of the once formidable Commissioners of Accounts? Deprived of their chairman,[5] browbeaten by the King, snubbed by Samuel Pepys,[6] they now found their revelations fell on inattentive ears. After much delay they did present one report, alleging fraudulence in the prize money fund, but even the word 'prizes' which had once elicited so lively a response, failed to produce action from the now quiescent House. In vain Seymour, Temple, and Howard pleaded for a full enquiry: a few days later one of the accused successfully repelled the charges and with that the Commissioners abandoned their task and scarcely met again.[7]

In the whole session one matter only fared doubtfully and that was one on which the court were themselves split. Years earlier Lord Roos, son of the Duke of Rutland, had, for very good reasons, separated from his wife.[8] Since then the lady had

---

[1] *Grey*, i. 215–19, March 1, especially speeches by Howard and Temple. Seymour joined in later, ibid., i. 241, March 21. This complicated wrangle has been clearly explained by Roseveare, pp. 159–61. On Ayliffe see infra, Chapter XI.

[2] Verney MSS., Claydon, Sir Ralph Verney, Feb. 23; Chandaman, i. 146, note 67. On the whole question of the unfavourable trade balance see the article by Margaret Priestly, *Econ. Hist. Rev.*, 2nd series, iv. (1951–2), pp. 38–52.

[3] *Grey*, i. 215–19, 225–6, 237, 240–2, March 1, 5, 19, 21.

[4] 22 Car. II, cap. 4; Roseveare, op. cit., p. 69.

[5] Sir Roger Brooke had been drowned in the previous year, B.M. Add. MSS. 36,916, f. 139, July 13, 1669.

[6] Supra.

[7] *C.J.* ix. 124, 128, 136, 141, Feb. 18, 26, March 10, 17; *Grey*, i. 233–5, March 17; B.M. Add. MSS. 36,916, ff. 171, 173, March 12, 26.

[8] Clarendon, *Life*, iii. 171–6.

born a son, tactfully christened Ignotus, of whom Roos was certainly not the father. By a private bill, passed in the session of 1666–7, this child had been declared illegitimate; Roos now desired a full divorce and the power to marry again. All this was very much a private matter but by this session the Roos' divorce had come to be regarded as a possible test case for a divorce by Charles himself.[1] Both the Bishops and the Duke of York were strongly against it—an odd alliance as things turned out—whilst Charles, perhaps for no more reason than a desire to tease his heavy witted brother, declared himself openly in its favour. On this occasion the Church of England party were defeated, perhaps the King's known wishes split their vote, and, after fierce debates in both Houses, the bill passed.[2] Roos got his divorce but Charles made no effort to follow his example.

On April 11 Parliament adjourned having heard a short speech of thanks from the King.[3] The only supply bill ready at this time was that for continuing the wine duty, though Charles was also grateful for a bill enabling him to sell off leases of crown lands.[4] Far more important than either of these bills was the amazing change in the general temper of debates. Andrew Marvell, revealing to his friend the bitterness he seems never to have expressed in the House, declared that Charles

was never since his coming in, nay all things considered no King since the conquest, so absolutely powerful at home as he is at present.[5]

Similar comments on the change in Parliament's attitude came from a minister, several backbenchers, and the French ambassador.[6] The last of these expressed some anxiety lest

[1] Marvell, ii. 301–2, March 21; Burnet, *History*, i. 471–2.

[2] For debates in the Commons see *Grey*, i. 251–3, 256–63, March 30, 31. For the Lords see Harris, *Sandwich*, ii. 318–33, and for general notices of the matter, Marvell, ii. 301–2, March 21; PRO 31/3/124, f. 146v, Colbert, March 12; B.M. Add. MSS. 36,916, ff. 170, 173, 175, March 8, 26, April 5.

[3] *L.J.* xii. 349.

[4] 22 Car. II, cap. 6; Chandaman, i. 324–8; Roseveare, pp. 158–9. For debates on this bill see *Grey*, i. 266–9, April 4, 5. These are notable for some very plain speaking on the Crown's debts by Downing and Clifford, and for unsuccessful opposition from Meres, Lee and the three future court converts, Seymour, Temple, and Howard.

[5] Marvell, ii. 301, March 21.

[6] *H.M.C. Various Collections*, ii. 134, Arlington, March 31; Raines Transcripts, Chetham Library, xxx, 40, ff. 4, 5, 6, Feb. 22, March 19, 26, letters

Charles should abandon his secret policy but his concern was needless. In the same week in which he took leave of Parliament Charles rode down to Dover and signed the treaty which had been talked of for so long.[1] By this he abandoned the Triple Alliance in favour of a new league with France. He agreed to make war on Holland; he agreed, in good time, to declare himself a catholic, quelling any possible disorder with the help of French troops. In return for this he was to get a subsidy, which would in fact work out at about £120,000 a year.[2]

Up to 1669 Charles might have been justified in wondering whether he could ever expect an adequate parliamentary supply. This spring session of 1670 had, however, showed how much a policy of resolute anglicanism could provide in the way of financial support. During the financial year from Michaelmas 1670 to Michaelmas 1671 Charles' ordinary revenue reached the figure of £1,165,000. In the next financial year it was to total £1,902,000, and from then onwards would remain steady at about £1,350,000.[3] The essential expenditure for government has been computed at about £1,250,000 a year.[4] These figures, and the record of divisions during 1670 and 1671, make the financial necessity of the new alliance very difficult to accept.[5]

---

of Richard Legh; *Calendar of Wynn Papers* (1926), p. 397, John Wynn, Feb. 28; PRO 31/3/124, ff. 130, 147, Colbert, Feb. 23, March 14.

[1] Ogg, op. cit., i. 344–6.
[2] Chandaman, i. 367–9.
[3] Ibid., ii. 506–7.
[4] Ibid., ii. 647–50.
[5] This is of course to take the long-term view. Charles' immediate financial position was extremely precarious, as was shown by his suspension of payments in 1672, but it must also be remembered that the French alliance brought him no escape from either short-term or long-term embarrassments, A. Browning, 'The Stop of the Exchequer', *History*, xiv (1929–30), p. 337.

CHAPTER IX

THE DOMINANCE OF THE COURT

THE adjourned spring session was reopened on October 24, 1670. The debates of the next seven months are well recorded; Grey's diary is supplemented and often clarified by the diary of a courtier, Sir Edward Dering. Yet though it is possible to follow the course of business in some detail it must be admitted that there is a marked lack of tension, for although a vestigial opposition survived the court's dominance was scarcely ever theatened. What these debates do illustrate are the difficulties of pushing complicated financial proposals through a House which, however co-operative, contained a large number of self-opinionated and ill-informed members, each of whom was prepared to argue over technicalities which he did not really understand. This was one of the chores of parliamentary government, and a very wearisome one at times, but it was far better than that of coping with the gloomy resentment of the period immediately following the second Dutch war, or the downright hostility of the years after 1673.

'All run, who can run fastest into the court party.'[1] So wrote one correspondent, and his words were certainly true of that seasoned trio of debaters, Seymour, Temple, and Howard. Joining three other some-time 'country' spokesmen, Clifford, Littleton, and Osborne, with Downing as formidable seventh to their number, they showed that they could still play a prominent part in debates when they spoke from the government side. Against them remained Lee and Carew, neither of them to hold office in this reign,[2] Garraway and Meres, the one to be commissioner of customs and the other a court candidate for Speaker,[3] and Sir William Coventry, often credited with the desire to make a 'come back', but in fact having ended all

---

[1] Verney MSS., Claydon, Dr Denton, Nov. 3, 1670.

[2] Lee was an Admiralty Commissioner from 1689 to 1691.

[3] Garraway was appointed a Commissioner of Customs, at a salary of £2,000, in September 1671, *Cal. Treasury Books 1669–72*, ii. 935, Sept. 24. For Meres' candidature as Speaker see A. Browning, *Danby*, i. 318–20 and infra, Chapter X.

connection with the administration.[1] In terms of speakers the sides were not too unfairly matched but when it came to votes the court won time and time again.

The first debate with which we deal, however, was not one in which 'court' and 'country', or 'government' and 'opposition', were the right terms to employ. In or out of office Temple, Seymour, and Sir William Coventry spoke for toleration, whilst Duncombe and Finch opposed it, and the same was true of Lee on the one hand, and Meres on the other, as representatives of the country. This well-worn topic was revived, early in the autumn session, following a lawsuit brought by two dissenters, Jekyll and Hayes, against Sir Solomon Sterling, Lord Mayor of London. Whilst Charles had been away at Dover wild rumours had spread through the city that ten thousand fanatics were planning an assembly. Sterling and his fellow magistrates had therefore arrested several leading dissenters and ordered them to enter recognizances for good behaviour. Hayes and Jekyll refused, were committed to Newgate, and at once sued for writs of Habeas Corpus. Released, they were brought before the Privy Council who upheld the Lord Mayor but allowed the two men bail. They then brought suits for wrongful arrest and Sterling, in exasperation, laid the whole case before the House of Commons.[2]

Both Sterling and the Aldermen appeared at the Bar and told their stories, after which there was a long rambling debate.[3] All the arguments for and against severity were brought out once again. Marvell, Love, Hampden, Birch, Temple, and Carew spoke for leniency, whilst a group of 'old cavaliers' indignantly defended the Lord Mayor.[4] Hayes had made a

[1] Sir William Coventry's position is discussed more fully in D. T. Witcombe, 'The Parliamentary Career of Sir William and Mr Henry Coventry', Oxford B.Litt. thesis, 1954, pp. 64–5, 108–9.

[2] B.M. Add. MSS. 36,916, ff. 182, 183, 184, 186, Starkey, May 28, June 11, 21; *The Parliamentary Diary of Sir Edward Dering*, ed. B. Henning (1940), p. 4, Nov. 21. This was the same period as the famous trial of Penn and Mead, Add. MSS. 36,916, f. 191, Sept. 10. The situation was further complicated by the fact that Charles was heavily indebted to the London nonconformists, whose assistance had made possible the completion of a recent government loan, Add. MSS. 36,916, ff. 190, 192, Aug., Sept. 22. See also Marvell, ii. 304, Nov. 28.

[3] *Dering*, pp. 4–7; *Grey*, i. 294–300, Nov. 21.

[4] These included Henry Coventry, Birkenhead, and Churchill, *Grey*, i. 294–7.

poor impression on the House and eventually Sterling was not only excused, but thanked, for committing him. Jekyll had put his case better, and although Sterling was again excused this committal was not thought worthy of thanks.[1]

In some ways this leniency towards Jekyll did his cause little good, for he was merely encouraged to continue his suit for wrongful arrest. Since the Commons had declared the arrest to have been lawful Jekyll was defying their ruling, and in a fury they ordered the arrest of not only Jekyll himself but also of his attorney and counsel.[2] Before the Sergeant could find them they all three surrendered, submitting themselves to the justice of the House. The Speaker, perhaps by an oversight, did not order them to kneel, and although polite they did not appear particularly cowed. Their behaviour infuriated the cavaliers, who insisted that it reflected on the dignity of the House, and demanded some further sentence. At this point, however, William Coventry, displaying the good sense that more than once enabled him to dominate a confused debate, reminded his colleagues that they were coming perilously near to acting as a court of law, which might easily involve them in a losing battle with the Lords. At this even so good a churchman as Sir Edward Dering saw that it was time to call a halt; Jekyll agreed to drop his action and, by 105 to 79, the incident was declared to be closed.[3]

This debate apart, the eight weeks before Christmas were given entirely to supply. At the opening ceremony Lord Keeper Bridgeman had discoursed, 'in all innocency', on the King's plans to maintain a balance of power, and to support the Triple League.[4] Three days later the members had agreed, *nem. con.*, to grant a supply proportionate to the King's present occasions[5] and, as in 1661 and 1663, they were again prepared to hear official figures from the court. Clifford, Downing, and

---

[1] *Dering*, p. 7.

[2] *Dering*, pp. 9–10; *Grey*, i. 303–7, Nov. 23.

[3] *Dering*, pp. 10–12; *Grey*, i. 307–10, Nov. 24. Compare infra, p. 119, for a similar example of the Commons' new scrupulousness in judicial matters.

[4] *L.J.* xii. 352–3, Oct. 24. Spain and Holland were said to have been reassured by this speech, *Cal. S.P. Ven. 1669–70*, p. 295, Nov. 7; on the other hand Arlington, feeling apparently that Bridgeman had really gone too far, made unsuccessful efforts to prevent the speech being printed, Marvell, ii. 108–9, 304–5, both letters dated Nov. 1.

[5] *C.J.* ix. 159, Oct. 27.

Littleton then declared that the King's debts already totalled £1,300,000, that a further £800,000 was needed to set out a fleet, and that the grants of 1668 had proved quite insufficient for the navy's needs.[1] These statements were, it seems, allowed to pass without any of the protests which had been heard less than twelve months earlier.

After a detailed list of debts had been produced the first definite proposal was made, on November 3, when Sir Thomas Dolman suggested an excise on beer.[2] Horrified, Meres protested that such a tax should be the last extremity, and Carew added that a decline in the demand for malt would hardly help restore declining rents.[3] Before anything could be settled the debate had drifted on to the iniquities of the Bankers. These men had already been defended by Clifford, who had pointed out that it was better to borrow, even at 10 per cent, than to buy goods on credit, paying 40 per cent interest.[4] Though sound, such arguments made no great impression on an assembly packed with debtors; the cry of 'interest up, land down' was heard, and Garraway advanced the theory that Bankers were by nature 'commonwealthsmen', and enemies to both the gentry and the King.[5] Amid all this the original purpose of the debate was forgotten and the day passed without any decision being reached.

On November 4 a new proposal was made, this time for a rate on a wide range of imported commodities.[6] Though this would, of course, have brought in money, its prime purpose was protective: many of the imports to be taxed were French, most were manufactures, and the rates were set so high that the duties would have been almost prohibitive.[7] Since the ministers had recently concluded a trade treaty with France, to say noth-

---

[1] *Grey*, i. 270-1, Oct. 27. These demands had been anticipated in two debates on April 4, 5, *Grey*, i. 266-9.

[2] *Grey*, i. 271-5, Oct. 31, Nov. 3. On Oct. 31 Seymour made his first speech in support of supply, though even then he covered his change of front by attacking Clarendon and the bankers.

[3] *Grey*, i. 273.

[4] *Grey*, i. 270-1, Oct. 27.

[5] *Grey*, i. 272-5, Nov. 3. Birch was also prominent in these attacks. On the number of debtors in the House see Dr Denton's letter of April 16, 1668, in Verney MSS., Claydon.

[6] *C.J.* ix. 160; *Grey*, i. 275-7.

[7] Chandaman, i. 73-5.

ing of Charles' political treaty of April, this can hardly have delighted the court and even the protectionist courtier Downing questioned its value.[1] Debates on this topic took place over several months and eventually a bill was drafted and put through the Commons, only to lapse by reason of an inter-House dispute.[2]

So far the court party had maintained its new ascendency, but there was still the danger that faction might again deplete its strength. Progress so far had been the work of Arlington's friends; now Sir Robert Howard, half 'country' and half Buckinghamite, decided to claim a share of credit for himself. On November 7 the House heard, with some surprise, an offer by Howard to farm all new taxes for between £400,000 and £600,000.[3] Clifford and Downing do not seem to have been warned of this and showed considerable scepticism, only to learn a few days later that Howard's scheme had already received the approval of the King.[4] During the first uncomfortable period when he was being attacked from all sides Howard found an ally in the ever hopeful Temple.[5] Though this particular scheme fell through the chance of both these worthy patriots had come, and by the next session both would be found among the office-holders of the court.[6]

Clifford and Downing, Howard and Temple, had at least reasonably coherent schemes to lay before the House. Others of both court and country had their own list of taxable commodities, ranging from periwigs to playhouses, and all this took up valuable time.[7] Recurrent prejudices were revived, more was heard of the unfavourable trade balance with France,[8] whilst a

---

[1] *Grey*, i. 276-7, Nov. 4. On the trade treaty see Ogg, op. cit., i. 336-7, and note.

[2] *Infra*. [3] *Grey*, i. 278-9; Roseveare, pp. 167-70.

[4] *Grey*, i. 280-4, Nov. 10, 11. [5] *Grey*, i. 281, Nov. 10.

[6] Howard replaced Downing as Secretary to the Treasury Commissioners in Oct. 1671, and later became Auditor of the Exchequer, *Cal. Treasury Books 1669-72*, ii. 939, *1672-3*, p. 83, March 11, 1673. Temple became a Commissioner of Trade and Plantations, and later of Customs, G. Davies, *Hunt. Lib. Quart*. iv. 1940-1, pp. 58-9.

[7] *Dering*, pp. 8-9, 20, 23, Nov. 23, Dec. 2, 6.

[8] *Grey*, i. 293, 310-11; *Dering*, p. 13, Nov. 18, 25, 28. See also PRO 31/3/125, f. 304, Colbert, Dec. 2; Marvell, ii. 116, Nov. 29; *Cal. S.P. Ven. 1671-2*, p. 5, Jan. 9, 1671; Margaret Priestley, 'Anglo-French Trade . . . 1660-1685', *Econ. Hist. Rev*., 2nd series, iv (1951-2), pp. 37-40, 52.

proposal to tax Irish salt, though manifestly unfair, was accepted because no-one dared to speak for that unfortunate dominion.[1] Despite all the delays the court held together, helped by the latest of their recruits, Edward Seymour, who had become Chairman of the Committee of Ways and Means. When, on one occasion this committee rejected a rate of 2s. 6d. per hundredweight on imported copper plates, Seymour then allowed a proposal to be put for a rate of 5s. and put the question that all who did *not* agree should say 'aye'. Baffled by this the opposition found themselves voting for the higher rate; Dering, though a courtier, was shocked at such sharp practice but, however lamentable, it had secured one more source of income for the crown.[2]

By the beginning of December there were three supply bills under way: the imports tax, the excise on beer, and a tax on legal documents, which had been slipped in without much comment and which was eventually to bring in £18,000 a year.[3] Still there was need for more, and on December 1 Clifford led off with a long speech, adding to the old story of the King's debts an immediate threat that the recent death of one of the wealthiest bankers would shake the credit of all.[4] He ended his speech with a request for a further supply bill, but did not specify what form this should take. Before any other court speaker could rise, Sir William Coventry cut in with a denunciation of land tax, a levy which he said only created enmity between subjects and their King. Possibly Coventry remembered Clarendon's tactics of 1664: possibly Clifford had remembered them too, for immediately after Coventry's interruption, a motion for land tax was put. Temple chose this debate to make his debut for the court; Finch joined him, as one who might carry weight with the old cavaliers, but for once the opposition found themselves in greater strength. Garraway opposed the land tax and Carew added several sharp references to the waste of earlier grants, and to the new fortunes made by men who had once been glad to ride to town on a padnag. As

---

[1] *Dering*, pp. 14–17, Nov. 26.

[2] Ibid., pp. 14–17, Nov. 26.

[3] It was first proposed by Howard on Nov. 25, *Dering*, p. 14. Estimates of its yield varied from Howard's £50,000 to Dowdeswell's £150,000, *Dering*, p. 20, Dec. 5. For the true figure see Chandaman, i. 346.

[4] *Grey*, i. 314–15.

it became clear that there was a majority against the tax Clifford himself prepared the way for surrender, asking only that the House should take care to find the money elsewhere.[1] After the formal rejection,[2] the country noted with relief that no further motion for land tax could be put in that session; Charles twitted his ministers with having been too confident,[3] but in fact the court were far from having exhausted their strength.

By an earlier vote it had been resolved that no new propositions for supply should be considered after December 3.[4] The first need was to reverse this, since the court's chances would increase with the approach of Christmas and the probable departure of the countrymen to their homes. The vote was rescinded, apparently without a struggle, and the House then asked for an estimate of how much would be provided by the three half-completed bills, after which the amount still required would be reckoned by subtraction.[5] On December 9 Clifford proposed that the existing bills should be reckoned as worth £400,000 a year. Howard, Duncombe and others spoke in support, arguing that if anything this estimate was over-generous since the consumption of beer would be reduced by a new excise and the import tax would stop many commodities coming in at all. Counter statistics were offered by Sir William Coventry, Boscowen, Lee, and Meres, but after some argument the House accepted the claims of the court.[6]

Following these successes Charles himself decided to lend a hand. On December 10 he summoned the House to Whitehall and told them of a message he had just received from Louis.[7] The latter had explained that although he would be visiting Dunkirk in the following summer with a force of forty thousand this was purely a routine inspection and should cause the English no alarm. Most disingenuously Charles now asked the

[1] Ibid., i. 315–17, Dec. 1. For an example of country feeling against Land Tax see the letter of J. Fisher, *H.M.C. 6th Rep.*, pt. 1, p. 369, Nov. 1, 1670.

[2] By 152–109, *Dering*, p. 19.

[3] B.M. Add. MSS. 35,916, f. 199, Starkey, Dec. 6; Verney MSS., Claydon, letter of Dr Denton, Dec. 8.

[4] *Dering*, p. 20, Dec. 3; Marvell, ii. 117, Dec. 8.

[5] *Dering*, pp. 20–4; *Grey*, i. 319–21, Dec. 3, 5, 6, 7, 8, 9.

[6] *Dering*, pp. 24–7, Dec. 9.

[7] Ibid., p. 27.

Commons if it was proper for the King of England to have to rely on such assurances of another monarch's good will, or whether it would not be more consistent with our dignity to have a fleet so strong that no movements of troops or ships could cause us alarm. He ended by requesting a further £800,000 for defence and so sent them back to continue their debate.

On the whole the Commons reacted to this supposed threat from France with what the court, or at least those in the full secret, may have thought somewhat ominous vigour.[1] If one of the new proposals for a tax was just a device to waste time[2] several others were made in good faith and a useful vote seemed likely to be achieved.

Finding things going against them the opposition tried one more time-honoured tactic, insisting that before any figure should be named all proposals should be fully examined in a Committee of the Whole House. The court knew well enough what opportunities this might provide for delay, and suggested that before the House went into committee it should agree on 'instructions' to its other self. Having carried this they tried to name a figure, but another old argument was revived, namely that the only way to raise a predetermined sum was by monthly assessment and that to fix the yield would thus be to determine the method of the supply. Since 'land tax' had already been ruled out the court were willing to retreat, asking only that some indication of the sum should be given, and so it was agreed that the committee should find a way of raising 'about £800,000'.[3]

Even after this the opposition did not quite give up and they were soon helped by a stupid blunder of Downing's. In his

---

[1] *Dering*, p. 20, Dec. 10. There may be some significance in the fact that both Coventrys spoke strongly for the repayment of a debt owed by Charles to his nephew, William of Orange. This debt was later provided for by an addition to one of the money bills, *Dering*, p. 97, March 17, 1671; Marvell, ii. 135–6, April 13; *Cal. S.P. Dom. 1671*, p. 179, April 8.

[2] *Dering*, p. 27, Dec. 9. The time wasting proposal was made by Carew and 'Mr Williams, alias Cromwell', member for Huntingdon. They tried to revive the idea of a tax on new buildings within the boundaries of London, on which the House had already spent some time, *Grey*, i. 301–2, Nov. 22; *Dering*, p. 10, Nov. 23.

[3] *Dering*, pp. 28–30, Dec. 10. This debate lasted to 5 p.m., *Calendar of Wynn Papers*, p. 401, John Wynn, Dec. 10.

efforts to deny the old opposition story that £1,000,000 remained unspent from previous grants, Downing remarked that considerable sums of money were in fact still owed to the King by members of the Lower House.[1] At once there was an outcry, the Speaker resumed the chair, and Downing was ordered to substantiate his charge. He duly named four members, the Accounts Commission, brought back to life for one brief moment, produced a few more names, and later Downing added to his original list. The whole affair, however, proved trivial; the sums owed were small and in some cases were held as security for debts of the King. Downing had to apologize for his reflections and was lucky to escape without some more severe censure.[2]

In earlier or later sessions such an incident might have led to a delay of several weeks. All that it produced at this time was a resolution that no future taxes should be handled by members of the Commons, a check to 'gratifications' but one which the court were later able to rescind.[3] After this the House went back to discussing possible taxes[4] and at last, on December 12, agreed that there should be a pound rate on the true yearly value of all lands and offices, and a further rate upon ready money and goods.[5] This 'New Subsidy' formed the fourth and last supply bill, and if the word subsidy did not arouse much confidence,[6] the court had their chance in committee to do everything possible to ensure that it would produce a reasonable yield.

One week was left before the Christmas recess. Attendance fell sharply,[7] but the opposition did what they could and were at least able to enjoy themselves at the expense of the Bankers.

---

[1] *Dering*, pp. 30–1, Dec. 12.

[2] Ibid., pp. 31–4; *Grey*, i. 322–3, Dec. 12, 13.

[3] *Dering*, p. 34. The debate ended with a discussion of how best to collect arrears of taxes. Reference was made to the high collector for Ipswich, who had absconded with £5,000, and it was suggested that the Commissioners who had appointed him should make up the sum from their own pockets. Eventually the matter was referred to a committee, but there is no mention of any further report, ibid., p. 35.

[4] For example, a tax on Jews, *Dering*, p. 32, Dec. 12.

[5] Ibid.

[6] Supra, Chapter II.

[7] B.M. Add. MSS. 36,916, f. 201, Starkey, Dec. 20. On Dec. 19 a division of 41–36 was recorded, *C.J.* ix. 186.

All ready cash was first charged at the high rate of 10s. per £100. Then money held by the Bankers was raised to 15s. per £100. Finally a proposal was approved to allow the King to borrow at 7 per cent on the security of this new tax. Since the Bankers borrowed at 6 per cent and lent to the King at 10 per cent, this would, it was hoped, induce private investors to transfer their money from the banks to the Treasury, whilst at the same time the Bankers might be persuaded, or forced, to accept the new 7 per cent security on existing loans, thus saving the King an immediate 3 per cent.[1]

Merchants and office-holders were dealt with next[2] and then the main contest took place over the rate on lands. Garraway had secured the postponement of this until the last possible moment,[3] presumably in the hope that reinforcements might appear, and certainly the division figures showed a marked rise when this topic came under debate. The committee had already spent much time arguing over the acreage of taxable land in England—estimates ranging from seventy-six, to twenty-four millions had been put forward—and one member had proposed to settle the matter by consulting the Domesday Book to find the number of Knights Fees.[4] Other attempts to reckon the value of land had proved little more successful and thus the whole debate took place without anyone being sure what sums were involved. The argument resolved itself into whether the rate should be 1s. or 8d. per £1; Garraway was for the lower figure, Dering, Howard and Osborne for the higher, and at last they carried it by 103 to 97.[5] Reckoning up, Dering hoped for £160,000 from stock in trade, offices and ready cash, and £600,000 from land; perhaps the court's defeat over the land tax had not been so decisive after all.[6]

With a little wrangling over tax-free covenants,[7] the first half

---

[1] *C.J.* ix. 185, Dec. 17; *Dering*, pp. 37–8; *Grey*, i. 325, Dec. 14. This matter is dealt with at some length by Dr Roseveare, op. cit., pp. 172–4.

[2] Merchants had their stock in trade rated at 6s. per £100 while office holders paid 2s. per £ of the yearly value of their place, *Dering*, pp. 38–9; *Grey*, i. 325–6, Dec. 14, 15.

[3] *Dering*, pp. 36–7, Dec. 14.

[4] Ibid., pp. 36, 38 and note; *Grey*, i. 323–5, Dec. 14. The correct figure seems to have been about 27 million acres, *Dering*, p. 59, note.

[5] *Dering*, p. 40; *Grey*, i. 327, Dec. 15.　　　　[6] *Dering*, loc. cit.

[7] *Grey*, i. 328–31, Dec. 16. Temple seized an opportunity to get in an attack on the anglican clergy, see infra.

of the session came to an end. On December 20 the House adjourned, at the King's request, for nine days, adding a last order for a roll call on January 9 with double assessment of the subsidy for any absentees.[1] Apart from minor matters there were only four bills depending, and all were measures of supply.

This success makes it the more extraordinary that a band of courtiers should have been foolish enough to endanger the harmony that others had worked so long to achieve. During a debate on a possible theatre tax a courtier had remarked that 'the players' had often given pleasure to the King.[2] Sir John Coventry, a young and somewhat erratic nephew of Henry and Sir William, at once asked if this service had been performed more by the men or by the women players, a rather clumsy witticism which annoyed some bravos among the royal guards. A few days after the adjournment they ambushed Sir John as he was returning to his home, knocked him down, and slit his nose to the bone.[3]

The Commons had been angry in the past when a member's servant had been arrested for debt. To assault, not merely arrest, a member and not merely a servant, was to send the House almost hysterical with rage. Parallels eluded them, the atrocities of Marius or Sulla were the best they could find, and their anger was soon expressed in the sombre form of an attainder.[4] Yet the most noteworthy feature of the whole affair was the restraint with which they used their most powerful weapon, the withholding of supply. When they first reassembled they ignored the attack. Instead they read the Subsidy bill and then postponed its further consideration for a week. On the following day they read the Import Duties bill and then postponed that eight days. On January 5 they read the bill for the Excise on beer and postponed that a fortnight. Before they turned to seek redress for their grievances they thus gave pledges that, if such redress were granted, there would be no permanent loss of revenue to the crown.[5]

---

[1] *C.J.* ix. 187, Dec. 20.
[2] *Grey*, i. 332, note, Dec. 17.
[3] The story is summarized in *Dering*, pp. 43–5. See also B.M. Add. MSS. 36,916, f. 202, Starkey, Dec. 24; Marvell, ii. 307–8, Jan, 1671.
[4] *Dering*, pp. 44–7; *Grey*, i. 333–41, Jan. 10.
[5] *Dering*, p. 41, Jan. 3, 4, 5.

I

Once the debates on the attack began there came, as we have already suggested, a torrent of invective and reproach. Underlying this, however, was the real contest between the opposition diehards and the court. The courtiers did not defend the assault, to have done so would only have been to add fuel to the flames, but they did oppose the suggestion that all other business should stop until the bill attainting the criminals should have passed both their own House and the Lords.[1] In favour of some such sanction were Carew, Boscowen, Whorwood, and Birch, together with Cavendish, first coming into prominence, and the merchants Jones and Knight.[2] Against it were Duncombe, Finch, Clifford and Downing, with those valued recruits, Seymour, Temple, Littleton and Howard; also against was Henry Coventry, who approved of the attainder but was not prepared to let family feeling carry him too far, whilst even Sir William, who had drafted the bill,[3] was not in favour of holding up supply. Eventually it was agreed to continue with the money bills but not to send them to the Lords until the Coventry bill had been passed. Again there was a dispute, whether this should mean passed by both Houses or only by the Commons, and again after a division the second and more moderate definition was accepted.[4]

The terms of the bill were not unlike those offered to Clarendon: the criminals were offered the chance to escape attainder if they would surrender and stand trial.[5] During a discussion in committee Meres added the sensible suggestion that more general safeguards might be written into the bill, and eventually it was extended to impose the penalties for felony on any person trying to maim or disfigure another, whether a member of the House or not.[6] Further argument took place on whether the King should be debarred from granting pardons—a cavalier was quick to remark that he had already been allowed to pardon his own father's death[7]—but on this occasion he was only

[1] *Dering*, pp. 45–6; *Grey*, i. 335–41, Jan. 10.

[2] Representing Bristol and London they had cause to welcome delay in the Import Duties bill.

[3] His rough draft is in Coventry MSS., Longleat, 101, f. 64.

[4] *Dering*, pp. 46–7, Jan. 10. Over three hundred members had come up by the time of this debate, B.M. Add. MSS. 36,916, f. 204, Jan. 10.

[5] 22 & 23 Car. II, cap. 1.

[6] Ibid., clause 6; *Dering*, pp. 47–8, Jan. 12.

[7] Colonel Kirkby, *Grey*, i. 342, Jan. 13.

empowered to make such a grant if it was confirmed by a further Act of Parliament.[1] When the bill reached the Lords they made some minor amendments; several conferences took place, and eventually the bill became law on January 24, though it does not appear that any of the assailants were ever brought to justice.[2]

Had the opposition succeeded in delaying all other business, then supply would certainly have fallen far behind. As things were good progress was still made, though at one point the subsidy bill had to weather a determined attempt to destroy it altogether. On January 16 Jones, Meres and Garraway formally proposed that the bill should be abandoned but they could return no answer when Henry Coventry asked for their alternative suggestions, and their attempt failed by 170 to 109.[3] It was now time to get back to detailed discussion, and the first clauses to be considered were those relating to the new rates of interest and the Bankers.

The essence of these clauses, it will be recalled, was the Crown's unwillingness to go on paying the Bankers 10 per cent on money which the latter had themselves borrowed at only 6 per cent.[4] By borrowing direct from private investors at 7 per cent the Crown hoped to attract money away from the Bankers and at the same time reduce the interest it had previously been forced to pay. One pertinent point that no one seemed willing to consider was whether the New Subsidy, earmarked for the new repayments at 7 per cent, would in fact produce a sufficient yield. This was passed over but much other argument was heard without any conclusion being reached.[5]

These weeks of January and February saw the delays caused by sheer stupidity and pedantry at their worst. On one occasion, in the midst of all the wrangling over percentages, the Committee of the Whole House decided to appoint a sub-committee. The latter could not be ordered to report back on the following day because its instructions came from the main committee and

[1] 22 & 23 Car. II, cap. 1, clause 4.
[2] *L.J.* xii. 412. The assailants were excepted from the general amnesty issued in 1673.
[3] *Dering*, p. 49; *Grey*, i. 349–50, Jan. 16; B.M. Add MSS. 36,916, f. 206, Starkey, Jan. 19.
[4] Supra.
[5] *Dering*, pp. 50–2; *Grey*, i. 350–3, 355–7, Jan. 16, 17, 18, 19.

the main committee had officially no knowledge of when the House would sit again. If the Speaker were to return to his chair, and the House were thus to be restored, then they could still not instruct the sub-committee since until the main committee had made its report the House had no official knowledge of the sub-committee's existence.[1] Between the percentages of the financiers and the law books of the constitutionalists it was not surprising that Starkey was able to report that out of one hundred and five clauses of the subsidy bill a single one had occupied an entire day.[2]

Other sections of the bill did not, however, present such difficulties. On stock-in-trade a duty of 6s. per £100 was retained, despite the impassioned arguments of Gould and Birch, the latter declaring that it would mean ruin for men to disclose how much stock they held.[3] When it came to 'corn in the barn', the country lobby secured a victory, but the yield from this would possibly have not been very great.[4] Taxes on offices produced another exchange in which Birch was prominent: he had revived a proposal, first made in 1668, to charge 'the dignified clergy', and at once had Birkenhead, Crouch, Meres, and other anglicans accusing him of bitterness over his lost church lands. As usual the Colonel showed little embarrassment at this reference to his past—after all he could claim to have been imprisoned twenty-three times for the sake of the King—but he eventually lost his point, and the clergy were spared.[5]

On January 21 the opposition, or perhaps it would be fair on this occasion to say the country, made one last effort to reduce the rate on land. They had, it will be remembered, originally proposed 8d. in the £1, but the House had agreed on 1s. Now they framed a motion that land owners should be entitled to a rebate of one third for expenses, a concession granted to office holders earlier in the day. Unfortunately the country had now fallen into the careless habits which had earlier been characteristic of the court: though more than two hundred country

[1] *Dering*, pp. 50–1, Jan. 17.

[2] B.M Add. MSS. 36,916, f. 206, Jan. 19.

[3] *Grey*, i. 357–60; *Dering*, pp. 56–7, Jan. 20.

[4] *Grey, Dering*, loc. cit.

[5] *Grey*, i. 361–2; *Dering*, p. 57, Jan. 21. On Birch's Crown lands see *Cal. S.P. Dom. 1660–1*, p. 461, 1660, and on his various imprisonments his speech on Feb. 20, 1673, *Grey*, ii. 46–7.

members were said to be in town, half of these failed to sit
through the debate, and the proposed concession was lost by
124 to 114.[1]

With this, discussion of the subsidy bill was almost at an end.
After mines of coal, tin, lead, but not for some reason iron, had
been charged,[2] it remained only to settle the Bankers' fate.
After much argument and several changes of fortune the proposals to transfer the crown's debt were abandoned. Though
charged at 15s. per £100 on cash in hand the Bankers were
allowed to pass on 10s. of this to their own creditors, whilst
commissioners for the act were refused, by 94 to 67, permission
to inspect ledgers as a check on fraudulent returns.[3] Another
group granted a late reprieve were the absentee members, who
had been threatened with a double assessment.[4] Some unnamed
member pointed out that this would be, in effect, to fine them,
in other words to act as a court of law. With memories of the
Skinner dispute still fresh the court were quick to see the
danger; the clause was removed, and on February 18 the bill
was sent up to the Lords.[5]

The completion of this complicated bill, at a time when the
Coventry outrage had aroused great bitterness against the
court, was a measure of the latter's strong position. Further
evidence of court strength came with the passage of the second
supply bill, for an Excise on beer and ale. On one minor point
the old hatred of excisemen still showed itself. Since it was
proposed to tax private brewing it would be necessary for
officers to enter private houses and check that no one was evad-
ing the tax. This proposal was denounced as a return to the
worst days of the Long Parliament; Clifford, as court spokesman, realized that to make a fight on this point might be to
imperil the whole bill, and the offending clause was withdrawn.[6] To balance this the court secured the removal of an

[1] *Grey*, i. 362–3; *Dering*, pp. 57–60, Jan. 21; B.M. Add. MSS. 36,916, f.
207, Jan. 24.

[2] *Dering*, pp. 60–2; *Grey*, i. 365–8, Jan. 23.

[3] *Dering*, pp. 73, 75, 77–9, Feb. 7, 10, 15; B.M. Add. MSS. 36,916, f.
210, Feb. 14.

[4] Marvell, ii. 120, Dec. 20. For an example of the alarm caused by this
see *Calendar of Wynn Papers*, p. 402, Sir Roger Mostyn, Jan. 9.

[5] *Dering*, pp. 79–80; *Grey*, i. 390–4, Feb. 16; B.M. Add. MSS. 36,916, f.
211, Feb. 21.

[6] *Grey*, i. 395–9, Feb. 22; Marvell, ii. 109–10, Nov. 8.

appropriation clause from the preamble, and on February 28 the bill was engrossed.[1]

In return for these money bills the court were being asked to concede very little. Certainly the country had measures of their own—at the end of the session twenty-seven public and thirty private bills received the royal assent—but none of these could be described as damaging to the crown. Legal delays, short measure in corn and salt, frauds in Smithfield market, embezzlement of the poor rate, or of the money granted for the relief of indigent cavalier officers, were all proceeded against.[2] So too were the poaching of game and coney catching, rick burning, tobacco planting, thefts of naval stores, delivering up merchant ships to pirates in return for a part of the loot—the equivalent it would seem of modern insurance frauds—and the too harsh treatment of prisoners for debt.[3] Despite some weighting in favour of the landlord class many of these bills show great good sense and even charity; they did credit to the House which passed them and at the same time, in marked contrast to the course of other sessions, were never allowed to impede progress in supply.

All this was very satisfactory. One rather less pleasing feature, so far at least as Charles was concerned, was the cavaliers' insistence on the other side of their bargain—the right to enforce by penal sanctions adherence to the anglican church. Rather foolishly critics of the establishment had worked in several side blows during earlier debates;[4] in return the anglicans had collected evidence of the 'insolence of the fanatics' and as early as December had carried two readings of a new conventicle bill.[5] Thereafter its progress had been slow, but on March 22 and 30 it reached its final stages in the Lower House.[6]

---

[1] *Dering*, pp. 84–5, Feb. 25; ibid., pp. 76–7, Feb. 13; *Grey*, i. 394–5, Feb. 16. The proposal for appropriation, made by Sir John Cotton and Lee, was to tie the money to the support of the Triple League. Surprisingly it was Garraway who opposed this, on the grounds that to express approval of any foreign policy might be to incur further obligations, as had been the case in 1664.   [2] 22 & 23 Car. II, caps. 4, 12, 16, 19, 21.

[3] Ibid., caps. 25, 7, 26, 23, 11.

[4] *Grey*, i. 319–20, 328–30, 361–2; *Dering*, p. 21, Dec. 3, Jan. 21.

[5] *C.J.* ix. 178–80, Dec. 7, 8. Information about nonconformists' activities was sent to Colonel Sandys, for him to use in debates, *Cal. S.P. Dom. 1671*, pp. 20–1, Jan. 13.

[6] *Grey*, i. 406, 412–15, March 22, 30. According to Dr Denton the bill

For the persecutors Colonel Titus, sometime exile and future exclusionist, proposed to debar nonconformists from celebrating baptisms, marriages and funerals, the same limitations that Louis was applying to the Huguenots in France; for the tolerant party Cavendish made an unsuccessful attempt to secure the repeal of the clause demanding 'assent and consent' to every article in the prayer book. When Waller talked of the need for protestants to unite Bramston replied that he did not hold men to be christians unless they worshipped in the way which Christ had prescribed, apparently believing this to be that laid down in the prayer book of 1662. On April 5 a final argument took place over a clause indemnifying zealous Justices of the Peace from actions such as had been brought by Hayes and Jekyll. Temple, Howard, Lee, and Birch opposed this, but in vain, and the completed bill was approved by the Commons.[1]

The majority for the bill, 74 to 53, was the last in favour of prosecuting protestants to be recorded in this reign.[2] Two years later the same House of Commons would approve a bill for limited toleration.[3] Far different was the case of the catholics, who had so far escaped with more or less routine votes of censure but who were soon to feel the full strength of a hostile Protestant front. On February 6 Mr Crouch of Cambridge, a pillar of the anglican church, remarked upon the alleged increase in the number of recusants.[4] On February 17 Sir Trevor Williams, whose persecuting activities spanned the reign, added a lurid account of jesuit activity, especially around the private chapels near the court of St. James.[5] Some catholics were said to have even been buying up advowsons, and so gaining control

---

was nearly thrown out during the first of these debates, *H.M.C. 6th Rep.*, Verney MSS., p. 489, March 23.

[1] *C.J.* ix. 230; *Grey*, i. 417–23.

[2] The First and Second Test Acts may have caused hardship to a few nonconformists but they were aimed entirely at Catholics, and the first was linked to a toleration bill, infra, Chapter X.

[3] Infra, Chapter X.

[4] *Dering*, pp. 70–1, Feb. 6.

[5] Ibid., pp. 80–1, Feb. 17. Williams had come forward as an Anglican champion as early as 1660, *Parliamentary History*, xxii. 374, July 9. He pursued this role at least up to 1678, *H.M.C. 12th Rep.* ix. 68, letter of the Marquess of Worcester, April 27, 1678. For a comment by Colbert see PRO 31/3/126, f. 27, Feb. 20.

over preferment in the anglican church; others had defied the
law and sent their children to be educated overseas. Talk of
catholic activity led naturally enough to fear of Irish massacres,
and the House added bitter criticism of the alleged leniency
shown to catholics in Ireland, making particular mention of the
defiant attitude of Talbot and Plunket, titular Archbishops of
Dublin and of all Ireland.

Seeking remedies for this grave state of affairs, the Commons
considered, among other suggestions, a much stricter check to
prevent papists holding any office, military or civil. Significantly this close anticipation of the 1673 Test Act was soon
embodied in a bill;[1] the House was no longer content for the
King to issue a proclamation to which no one would pay the
least attention. First read on March 1 the bill was through the
Lower House by March 11.[2] In the Lords it met some opposition, a clause against presbyterians was tacked on in an attempt
to split the anti-catholic vote,[3] and eventually it lapsed by reason
of the prorogation. Some weeks earlier Charles had told Colbert
that Parliament's feeling against catholics was dying down, but
a truer indication of their views and those of a wide section of
the public was to be drawn from the alarm and indignation
excited that April by rumours that a priest had visited the
death-bed of Ann Hyde, Duchess of York.[4]

However unwelcome, these bills were still part of the main
bargain and at least the Commons showed themselves quite
prepared to observe their own side. The third supply bill, for a
tax on various imports, occupied much time during March and
seemed to be going very well. On March 4 transference of the
duty to the custom house not only pleased the enemies of
excise but also halved the cost of collection; it was said that the
merchants agreed to this believing that their less affluent com-
petitors, unrepresented in the House, would be unable to pay
the duty and be driven out of business.[5]

[1] This bill, which was not completed, is summarized in *H.M.C. 9th Rep.*
ii, app., p. 2, March 13.
[2] *C.J.* ix. 210–11, 217.
[3] PRO 31/3/126, f. 40, Colbert, March 24.
[4] PRO 31/3/126, ff. 28, 45–6, March 9, April 3; B.M. Add. MSS.
36,916, f. 217, Starkey, April 4. According to Sir Ralph Verney, the Duchess
died a staunch anglican. Her last words, so he reported, were 'Duke, Duke,
death is horrible, death is very horrible', Verney MSS., April 6, 1671.
[5] *Dering*, pp. 87–8.

Naturally, however, the court could not always count on the merchants' interests being the same as the King's—'What's good for trade is bad for money', Downing had remarked earlier in this session[1]—and many importers whose wares were now threatened by the new tax tried their luck with petitions, perhaps backed by arguments from counsel.[2] Among these petitions was one from certain refiners of white sugar, resident in Barbados, who asked for the duty to be removed or at least reduced. Naturally the home refiners objected, since it was in their interests to reduce the import of sugar that had already been refined, and it seems that, possibly with the aid of bribes, they secured the petition's rejection.[3] This was only one of many such incidents, but the bill still made progress and at last, on March 24, it was sent to the Lords.[4]

It now appeared that the Barbados sugar refiners had not accepted defeat. They had in fact tried next the Council of Trade and Plantations, which had referred them back to Parliament. Possibly Sandwich, who sympathized with them and on whose account we depend for most of our information, may have suggested that they should next put their case to the Lords.[5] The motives of the Upper House are far from clear: certainly there had already been some independent criticism from them of the Commons' freedom in granting supply[6] but it

[1] *Grey*, i. 276, Nov. 4.
[2] For examples of such petitions see *Cal. S.P. Dom. 1671*, p. 96, Feb. 23; Marvell, ii. 134, March 25; *H.M.C. 9th Rep.*, Part ii. pp. 10–15, March–April. The commodities concerned included tobacco, linen, brandy and silk. The court at one point objected that to make such a petition implied a knowledge on the part of outsiders of what was being discussed in the House, but Sir William Coventry stoutly defended the right of a member to inform his constituents of matters which might concern them, *Grey*, i. 401–4, dated March 1 in error for March 4. It is clear from his Hull correspondence that Marvell took a similar view, *Poems and Letters*, ii. 1–236, *passim*.
[3] F. R. Harris, *Sandwich*, ii. 335–6. Sandwich was not only President of the Council of Trade but also played a leading part in the Lords' debates on this matter, so that his own MSS. notes are of great value. See also *Grey*, i. 401–4, March 1 (for 4th).
[4] *C.J.* ix. 223, March 24.
[5] Harris, *Sandwich*, ii. 335–6.
[6] Notably in the famous speech by Lord Lucas, W. Cobbett, *Parliamentary Debates*, iv. 473–5. This speech was widely circulated in MSS. form and became a favourite source of quotation for the opposition. The Lords, however, took exception to such undignified procedure and ordered a copy to be burnt, *L.J.* xii. 469, March 24.

is quite possible that the refiners' petition was considered purely on its merits. The Lords decided that there were grounds for a reduction in the duty and altered it from one penny per pound to 'a halfpenny half farthing'.[1] This trifling change was going to cost the court the entire yield of the bill.

Already, when the Lords made their amendment, there was friction between them and the Lower House. After minor arguments over the Coventry bill, the New Subsidy, and a proposed embargo on brandy,[2] they had quarrelled over a procedural point connected with a joint address to the King. A messenger from the Lords had asked the Commons for a conference on an unspecified subject. The Commons had replied that they would return an answer 'by messengers of their own'. The Lords objected that the Commons' reply was 'unparliamentary'[3] and at this point the new issue of the Lords' amendment to the supply bill was added to the dispute. On the whole both Houses seem to have closed their ranks: Lee, for the tolerant country, Meres for the country anglicans, Temple and Clifford for the tolerant court, Finch and Henry Coventry for the anglican court, were all united in denouncing the arrogance of the Upper House.[4] Sandwich suggests that all these, even Temple, could now be classified as friends of Arlington, and thus as anxious to discredit Buckingham, who was now urging on the Upper House.[5] How far any member was genuinely indignant, how far playing a part, will never be known. The dispute became more and more tangled, a wealth of precedents were exchanged, but no compromise was reached. At quite an early stage the Commons passed their most important, and lasting, resolution, that 'in all aids given to the King, the rate of tax ought not to be altered by the Lords'.[6] The Upper House were,

---

[1] *L.J.* xii. 482, 486–7, April 8, 12; Harris, *Sandwich* ii. 333.

[2] For the dispute over the Coventry Bill see *Grey*, i. 368–70, 372–83, 387–90, Jan. 25, Feb. 4, 6, 9. For the New Subsidy see *Dering*, pp. 86–7, March 1, 2, 3. For the brandy embargo see *Dering*, pp. 97, 101–3, March 17, 20; *L.J.* xii. 460, 472, 482, March 17, 29, April 8; Marvell, ii. 133–5, March 16, 23, April 6.

[3] *C.J.* ix. 233–4, April 10, 11, 12; *L.J.* xii. 484–6, April 11, 12; *Grey*, i. 424–35, April 10, 11, 12.

[4] The arguments on this began on April 13, and were continued on April 14, 15, 22, *Grey*, i. 435–45, 463–7.

[5] Harris, *Sandwich*, ii. 334–5.

[6] *C.J.* ix. 235, April 13.

in time, to admit this, but it was not to be expected that they would do so in this session.[1] By good fortune the tax on Legal Proceedings had somehow passed both Houses despite the continuing dispute,[2] and with that, the new subsidy, and the excise on beer, already completed, Charles decided to prorogue Parliament, even if this meant losing the Import Duties Bill.[3]

Charles was certainly disappointed, for two weeks he was even angry with Buckingham,[4] but on reflection he might have found much for which to be thankful. The bill he had lost had been less a revenue measure than an attempt to extend Protection, especially against the French.[5] Lost with it had been a conventicle bill, and a bill against catholics, neither of which Charles can have viewed with much approval.[6] On the other hand he had added to his ordinary revenue an eight year rate on wines, a six year excise, and a nine year tax on legal papers. These would produce, on average, another £160,000 a year, bringing his ordinary revenue up to £1,300,000 a year.[7] In addition to this he had the new subsidy, not indeed to provide the £800,000 the court had asked, but at least yielding the useful lump sum of £350,000.[8] This was by far the richest harvest since the revenue had first been established at the beginning of the reign.

Still more satisfying than the actual money bills was the change in the whole character of the debates. From the first walkout of the opposition, in February 1670, the court had dominated the House; the contrast with the sessions of 1668 and 1669 could not have been more sharp. If this state of affairs could be maintained, perhaps for one more session, Charles might secure a permanent 'ordinary' revenue sufficient to free him from ever having to meet Parliament again. Had Sir

[1] Indeed they expressly denied it on April 17, *L.J.* ix. 498, and see also the conference on April 22, *L.J.* ix. 510–13.

[2] It passed the Commons on April 10 and the Lords on April 12, *C.J.* ix. 233, *L.J.* xii. 488. This was despite a petition presented to the Lords by the officers of the Court of King's Bench, *L.J.* xii. 490, April 13.

[3] The prorogation took place on April 24. Charles seems from his speech to have concealed his annoyance, *L.J.* xii. 515–16.

[4] B.M. Add. MSS. 36,916, ff. 221–2, Starkey, May 2, 9.

[5] Harris, *Sandwich*, ii. 335; Chandaman, i. 74–5.

[6] Marvell, ii. 136–8, April 18, 22.

[7] Chandaman, i. 114, 218, 346; ii. 506.

[8] Ibid., ii. 476–8.

Thomas Osborne been chief minister at this time, instead of having to wait another four years for power, his policy of 'Church and King' could almost certainly have been successful. Unfortunately the accent would still have had to lie more heavily on the 'Church'; when Charles tried to base an appeal on loyalty to the 'King' alone, he found that all his gains could be as quickly swept away.

CHAPTER X

THE COURT IN DECLINE

SURRENDER ON RELIGION

THE session of 1670–1 had given Charles the long-term prospect of solvency, but it had left his immediate financial position insecure. The drain on the Treasury produced by Downing's new system of repaying loans 'in course', and the expense of preparations for a new Dutch war, produced a temporary bankruptcy from which the King was forced to extricate himself by the Stop of the Exchequer.[1] More serious than this was the fact that the new war failed to pay for itself, and the French subsidy proved poor compensation for the lack of extraordinary parliamentary grants. By the middle of 1672 it was clear that the King would soon have to face his tiresome 'company of fellows' once again.[2]

What policy should Charles now lay before Parliament? The previous session had given generous financial endorsement to the Triple Alliance, and to the Second Conventicle Act. Since then we had not merely abandoned the United Provinces, but declared war on them, whilst the 'fanatics', who should have been cowering in terror at the conventicle act, were instead basking in the comfort of Charles' Declaration of Indulgence.[3] Could the King go back to his earlier programme? So far as foreign policy was concerned, he could not; now, and until the end of his reign, he was in the hands of an astute and remorseless blackmailer, in other words his royal cousin of France. Regarding religion, however, events were to show that Louis cared less for English catholics than for the English alliance, whilst the nonconformists could offer Charles little except some short-term financial aid.[4] Charles stayed firm to his French alliance by necessity, but his determination to uphold his

[1] Ogg, op. cit., ii. 448–9; A. Browning, 'The Stop of the Exchequer', *History*, xiv (1929–30), pp. 333–7.

[2] The Council's discussions of this problem are recorded in a minute book of the Committee of Foreign Affairs, PRO, SP 104/177, ff. 57–101.

[3] This had been issued in March 1672, Ogg, op. cit., i. 354–5.

[4] For an earlier example of such assistance see supra, p. 106, note 2.

Declaration must be attributed to both royal pride and a very real desire to establish limited toleration.

Some minor concessions could be made to parliamentary prejudice. In May 1672 Charles appointed Henry Coventry Secretary of State, securing the support of a diehard cavalier who seems to have commanded more respect and affection than any other member of the court.[1] Finch was now Attorney-General, Duncombe was Chancellor of the Exchequer, Osborne was a Privy Councillor,[2] and, after long discussion in which the names of Seymour, Meres and Howard were mentioned, the staunchly anglican, if physically feeble, Sir Job Charlton was selected as the official candidate for the Speaker's Chair.[3] The anglicans had thus a strong representation amongst the second rank of ministers. Above them, however, were the tolerant protestants, Buckingham and Shaftesbury, together with the catholic or crypto-catholic conspirators, Clifford, Arlington, the Duke of York, and finally the King.

With so marked a change of policy to justify, and without even much in the way of military or naval success to present,[4] it was not surprising that the council several times recommended the postponement of a proposed new parliamentary session.[5] Eventually, shortage of money made a meeting imperative and the date was fixed as February 4. Arlington, who had been talking wildly to the Venetian ambassador of subduing the assembly by the use of troops,[6] pulled himself together and called a group of members to an eve of session meeting at his house,[7] whilst Charles himself issued a new declaration reaffirm-

[1] Charles' own friendly letter confirming this appointment is in Coventry MSS., Longleat, appendix volume, f. 18, May 31. For an account of Coventry's parliamentary career see my thesis on this subject, Oxford B.Litt. 1954, especially pp. 16–18.

[2] A. Browning, *Danby*, i. 90. Osborne had ousted his colleague Littleton in 1671 and was now sole Treasurer of the Navy, ibid., i. 86–7.

[3] For these discussions see PRO, SP 104/177, ff. 101–9. Meres was Charles' own choice, whilst Seymour's claims were also acknowledged, 'if he would behave'.

[4] The main event had been the drawn battle of Sole Bay, Ogg, op. cit., i. 357–61. Before this we had launched an unsuccessful surprise attack on a Dutch convoy and had been forced to follow this up with a tardy and shame-faced declaration of war, ibid., i. 355–6.

[5] PRO, SP 104/177, ff. 78–85, Aug. 18, Sept. 15, 16, 1672.

[6] *Cal. S.P. Ven. 1673–5*, pp. 9–11, Feb. 10.

[7] PRO 31/3/128, f. 2, Colbert, Dec. 23.

ing his devotion to the Established Church.[1] Calling on even
the most doubtful of their friends to help them,[2] the court
prepared to make yet another bid for supply.

From the very first, things went badly, for a stupid gesture by
Shaftesbury allowed the initiative to pass immediately from the
hands of the court. During the recess some thirty members had
died. In the normal way their seats would have remained un-
filled until the opening of the new session, when the Speaker
would have instructed the clerks of Chancery to send out bye-
election writs. This time however Shaftesbury, taking his stand
on good though somewhat ancient precedents,[3] sent out the
writs himself, and when members assembled many of the elections had already taken place. Of these elections six had fallen
in the county of Dorset, where Shaftesbury had his family
estates. Rivals for parliamentary dominance in that county
were the family of Strangeways, on the other side during the
Civil War, and now represented by a leading cavalier backbencher, Colonel Giles Strangeways, member for Dorset.[4]
Believing, rightly or wrongly, that Shaftesbury was using his
official position to assist him in a local feud, Strangeways stood
up on the first morning to 'spy strangers', in other words the
new members elected on the controversial writs.[5]

Before Charles had had a chance to make his appeal, before
even the new Speaker had been chosen, the court had been
thrown on to the defensive. Three court cavaliers, Henry
Coventry, Finch, and Birkenhead, were able, however, to secure
the postponement of an enquiry until after the Speaker's election,
and this election went through smoothly enough.[6] Charlton
then led the members to hear Charles make a vigorous defence

---

[1] Thynne MSS., Longleat, 16, f. 54, Thomas Thynne, Jan 2.

[2] Sir William Coventry could hardly be considered a courtier at this
time, yet he received from a nephew, then in the household of the Duke of
York, a clear indication that his presence at debates would be welcomed,
Thynne MSS. 16, ff. 53, 54, Thomas Thynne, Jan. 1, 2. Thynne was later
to join Sir William and another of the family, Halifax, in moderate opposition, but at this time his letters are impeccably orthodox.

[3] On the precedents for and against Shaftesbury see *Dering*, pp. 108–10.

[4] PRO, SP 104/177, f. 127; B.M. Stowe MSS. 201, f. 107, Godolphin,
Jan. 25; W. A. Christie, *Shaftesbury*, ii. 112–13, 121–6. Strangeways' father
had had his house burnt by Shaftesbury during the Civil War.

[5] *Dering*, pp. 104–5; B.M. Stowe MSS. 201, f. 139, Aungier, Feb. 4.

[6] *Dering*, pp. 103–5, Feb. 4; *C.J.* ix. 245.

both of the war and of the Declaration of Indulgence, with particular stress on his determination that the latter should not be
withdrawn.[1] Shaftesbury added a long blustery attack on the
Dutch, a word for those creditors of the King who had been hurt
by the 'Stop', and perhaps significantly a repudiation of suggestions that Charles had been won over to Rome.[2] The members
then trooped back to their own chamber to consider what they
had heard.

The strong appeals put forward by King and Chancellor
should, apparently, have been followed by a motion from two
backbenchers, Sir Charles Musgrave and Sir John Bramston.
Before they could begin, however, Meres, who might by now
have been occupying the Speaker's Chair, rose to revive the
vexed question of the Chancellor's writs.[3] Seymour and Howard
returned briefly to the ranks of the opposition, there was a
rather confused debate, and eventually the new members, none
of whom were in fact now present, were officially ordered to
withdraw. Only then was Musgrave able to propose a vote of
thanks for the King's speech. Whilst the clerks were penning
this motion, Bramston tried to throw in a clause promising
support against the King's enemies. Such tactics might have
worked well enough two years earlier but now the atmosphere
had changed. Lee demanded a vote on 'candles'; this was taken
and the motion to bring them was rejected. Desperately the
court hung on, arguing for four hours by the light of the one
candle at the Clerk's desk, but they could not persuade the
House to commit themselves to a supply. At last, Thomas
Osborne, making one of his rare interventions, suggested that
they should compromise for the time on a simple vote of thanks
but bind themselves to debate supply within two days, and with
this the House at last adjourned.[4]

On February 7 the contest was renewed.[5] Sir Thomas Dolman opened for the court, proposing a supply of £1,260,000,
only to be answered by a critical speech from Meres, who asked

[1] *C.J.* ix. 246, Feb. 5.

[2] *C.J.* ix. 246–8. This was the famous 'Delenda est Carthago' oration.

[3] *Dering*, pp. 105–8. It was notable that Birch and Swinfen spoke for the
opposition; few of the 'presbyterian' members seem to have shown much
gratitude for Charles' grant of Indulgence.

[4] Ibid., p. 107.

[5] Ibid., pp. 111–12. For hopes of supply before the session opened see
Godolphin's letter of Jan. 25, B.M. Stowe MSS., 201, f. 107.

why Charles had embarked on this war without consulting Parliament. This was a fair question considering that an entirely different foreign policy had been made the ground for the previous appeal for supply, yet at the same time it implied a radical claim for the Commons to have a voice in foreign affairs.[1] Henry Coventry was prepared to be conciliatory—he was indeed prepared to offer an explanation for the change in foreign policy—but before doing so he could not resist drawing attention to, and firmly rejecting, Meres' claim. He followed this rejection with a long, well argued, and almost certainly sincere defence of the war, stressing the need for England to secure her trade, and making capital out of the capture of the two Dutch 'spies', who had been arrested a few days earlier.[2] This speech may well have impressed the House, but in fact Henry could apparently have spared his breath. When he sat down, instead of further opposition Garraway, Strangeways, and Meres rose to approve a sum almost identical with that first suggested by Dolman. Within an hour the whole matter was settled, the supply was agreed, and when Sir John Holland began his almost traditional plea for a reduction in his county's share the House refused to hear him, so zealous were they that nothing should obstruct the passage of the vote.[3]

Henry Coventry's speech had, as we have said, been an able one, but it is hard to believe that the three opposition stalwarts had been converted by it alone. An alternative explanation is offered by Burnet, who may have had his story from Littleton, and who declares that on the previous evening Garraway and Lee had been offered large bribes to support supply.[4] This fails to account for Strangeways and Meres, Lee does not seem to have spoken in this debate, and Garraway, though now a Commissioner of the Customs,[5] was soon to revert to sharp criticism of the court. A more credible explanation, though one unsupported by evidence, is that the opposition, whether as a 'party' or, more probably, in unco-ordinated groups, were carrying

---

[1] See supra, Chapter IX, and infra, Chapter XIII.

[2] K. D. Haley, *William of Orange and the English Opposition 1672–4*, pp. 71, 76–84.

[3] *Dering*, p. 112. See also B.M. Stowe MSS. 201, f. 147, Aungier, Feb. 8.

[4] G. Burnet, *History of my own Time*, ed. Airey, ii. 15–16. For Burnet's friendship with Littleton, ibid., ii. 92.

[5] Supra, p. 105, note 3.

K

out a policy predicted by one of Du Moulin's English correspondents some months earlier.[1] Its aim was the removal of the Declaration of Indulgence: to achieve this Charles was to be coerced or tempted, by the refusal or promise of war supply. The events of the next few weeks tally with this hypothesis, and it is possible that Burnet merely misinterpreted some unofficial discussion on these lines.

Following this debate, the Commons began to alternate progress on supply with measures designed to safeguard protestantism. On February 8 Mr Crouch suggested that, having dealt with one part of the King's speech in debating supply, the House should now turn to the part dealing with the Declaration of Indulgence.[2] The court staved off a full debate for two days, but on February 10 the matter was raised again. For a time no one was anxious to speak and an attempt was made to pass to other business, but Meres and Lee quickly protested.[3] After this the King's Declaration was read, followed by the resolution passed by the Commons against a similar proposal in 1663. Speeches now came thick and fast. Seymour and Howard, consistent friends of toleration, returned to the court, whilst Finch and Henry Coventry, both of whom showed their detestation of dissenters on many earlier and later occasions, found themselves forced to defend on principle the King's discretionary power. Against them, however, were not merely the intolerant country, like Strangeways, but others, like Thomas Lee and William Coventry, who were usually opposed to persecution; what Mr Ogg has called the 'bogle of popery' was turning Charles' natural allies into enemies. Though the speeches, as recorded by Grey, seem evenly divided, it apparently became clear that some gesture would be made against the Declaration. The court now tried to limit this to an address, allowing the King to make a graceful withdrawal, whilst the more extreme opposition wanted rejection by a formal vote. After much argument this second party triumphed, by 168 to 116, and the

---

[1] Haley, op. cit., p. 68, letter of John Ayliffe, Oct. 10, 1672. Ayliffe had once appeared as counsel for the wine merchants, supra, Chapter VIII, and later became famous for an anti-French gesture during the autumn session, infra, p. 143, note 6.

[2] *Dering*, p. 113.

[3] Ibid., pp. 114–18; *Grey*, ii. 12–26, Feb. 10. A one folio note on this debate, adding a few names and comments, is quoted from the original in Legh MSS., John Rylands Library, by Evelyn Legh, *Lyme Letters*, p. 52.

House recorded a *nem. con.* resolution 'that penal statutes in matters ecclesiastical cannot be suspended but by an act of Parliament.'[1] Only then was a committee appointed to draft an address.

The King would be disappointed, wrote loyal Richard Legh, but members could have done no less without being unfaithful to their church.[2] A committee packed with courtiers felt unable —some members of it were probably unwilling—to tone down the Commons' vote, and the address they drew up left Charles no loophole for escape.[3] At the beginning of the session he had committed himself unequivocally to the defence of his Declaration. Now he would have to accept the humiliation of surrender, or lose all hope of a supply. In the council Henry Coventry and Rupert urged him to give way, Clifford, Shaftesbury and the Duke of York wished to stand firm,[4] but the deciding arguments probably came from Ambassador Colbert and his colleague Mlle. de Querouaille. When help for English catholics meant the loss of an ally Louis XIV put national interests before religion; whether presented in the council or the bed chamber, the arguments of France were for surrender and supply.[5]

Charles liked his ease, but he was also conscious of his royal dignity. Moreover his continued efforts to establish some form of toleration suggest that this was a cause for which he felt very strongly indeed. He tried a change of Speaker, the anglican Charlton succumbing to a politic illness and being replaced by the tolerant Seymour[6]—office at last for this resolute campaigner—and, following this, a deceptively polite reply was sent to the Commons' address. When, however, Sir Philip Warwick tried to secure thanks for this reply, Sir William Coventry pointed out that, for all its assurances on religion and property it still left the Declaration unrepealed.[7] Thanks were voted but

---

[1] *C.J.* ix. 251.

[2] Letter of Feb. 11 quoted by Legh, *Lyme Letters*, p. 53.

[3] *C.J.* ix. 252, Feb. 14. The committee included Attorney General Finch, Osborne, Seymour, Temple, and Secretary Coventry, ibid., ix. 251, Feb. 10.

[4] PRO, SP 104/177, f. 143v–144v, notes on Council meetings, Feb. 12, 14.

[5] PRO 31/3/128, ff. 33, 37–8, 39–40, Colbert, Feb. 24, 28, March 6, 10.

[6] *Dering*, pp. 120–1; *Grey*, ii. 37; SP 104/177, f. 146v. Charlton had in fact complained of ill health before the session began, Coventry MSS., Longleat, 4, f. 68, Dec., 1672.

[7] *C.J.* ix. 256; *Dering*, pp. 131–3; *Grey*. ii. 54–60.

only for the 'gracious expressions' contained in the message; on February 27 a second address was sent, requesting politely that the Declaration be withdrawn.[1]

Whilst all this was going on, the supply bill had been given two readings.[2] There had been little opposition, but it was clear that its completion was unlikely until the religious question was settled.[3] Meanwhile the changed attitude of a majority of the Commons was made apparent by the introduction of two further bills. Catholics were now the enemy; the 'fanatics', however misguided, were no longer past rebels, but future allies against Rome. The Commons were thus prepared to ease protestant dissenters, though by statute rather than by proclamation, whilst at the same time they were eager to ban catholics from any position of trust.

In the debate on the first of these bills, the one to ease the condition of protestant dissenters, the grouping was quite different from that on the King's declaration. Since no question of prerogative was involved court cavaliers, like Henry Coventry and Duncombe, felt free to join Meres and Strangeways in opposing the bill, whilst the tolerant opposition, for example Garraway and William Coventry, joined courtiers like Temple and Howard in giving it their support. During a series of debates it became clear that, perhaps as the result of the long series of bye-elections, the tolerant party were at last in a majority.[4] The House heard with respect a restrained and moving plea from Alderman Love,[5] and by the end of February there seemed every chance that the dissenters would obtain some measure of relief.

Very different was the case of Roman catholics. During the debates on the bill of ease, Sir Robert Carr, Arlington's brother-in-law, had tried to put in a word for them, recalling their

---

[1] *C.J.* ix. 257, Feb. 26; B.M. Stowe MSS., 201, f. 207, Aungier, Feb. 25.

[2] *C.J.* ix. 251, 254, Feb. 13, 18.

[3] B.M. Stowe MSS. 201, ff. 178, 184, 188, 217, 229, 231, Henry Coventry, Feb. 21, Robert Southwell, Feb. 22, Aungier, Feb. 22, March 14, Godolphin, March 4.

[4] Debates took place on Feb. 14, 19, 20, 27, *Dering*, pp. 122–4, 125–6; *Grey*, ii. 26–36, 38–48, 69–74; B.M. Stowe MSS. 201, f. 188, Aungier, Feb. 22.

[5] *Dering*, pp. 123–4; *Grey*, ii. 40, Feb. 19. Years earlier Love had been censured by the House for failing to attend Corporate Communion, *C.J.* viii. 289, July 3, 1661.

loyalty in the Civil War, only for Clarges, Monck's brother-in-law, to reply that in fact their treachery had lost Charles I the battle of Edgehill.[1] Without pursuing this unlikely assertion, Garraway, Swinfen, William Coventry, and Strangeways, all made it plain that they would have no 'romanists' in the bill.[2] In the previous session a bill to bar them from office in Church or State had only failed by reason of the inter-House dispute.[3] Since then there had been the rumour of the Duchess of York's catholic deathbed, and although her husband's conversion seems not to have been widely known there was already much fear of catholic influence at court. All this was summed up in a new bill presented by a new member on February 28. The bill was to become the First Test Act: the member, William Sacheverell, was to compete with Thomas Aquinas and the Devil for the variously regarded title of 'First Whig'.[4]

Before Sacheverell's bill could receive full discussion Charles made his decision on the Commons' address. His last hope had been that the Upper House might support him[5]—he may have regretted his snub to them in February 1670[6]—but although generally tolerant, and despite the presence of Clifford, Shaftesbury, and the Duke of York himself, the peers refused to intervene.[7] Charles' maternal grandfather had been Henry IV of France: perhaps supply was, after all, worth the surrender of a Mass. On March 8 Charles summoned the Commons to announce the issuing of a new proclamation against priests and

[1] *Grey*, ii. 32–5, Feb. 14.

[2] *Grey*, ii. 31–6; *Dering*, pp. 119–20, Feb. 18; letter of Richard Legh, quoted from Legh MSS. by Legh, *The House of Lyme*, p. 252.

[3] Supra, Chapter VIII.

[4] *Grey*, ii. 74–8. Sacheverell was awarded his title by his descendant, Sir George Sitwell in *The First Whig* (privately printed, one copy in Bodleian Library). Many of Sir George's arguments are exaggerated but it is true that Sacheverell was by far the most extreme member of the opposition, and that his appearance as an active debater in this session—he had been elected in 1670—heralds a general sharpening of the debates.

[5] For the King's appeal to the Lords see B.M. Stowe MSS. 201, ff. 215–216, 217, Ranelagh, March 1, Godolphin, March 1. See also *L.J.* xii. 539–40, March 1.

[6] Supra, Chapter VII.

[7] The Lords replied, with exasperating politeness, that Charles had done well to refer the matter to Parliament, and that he would be wise to exchange his Declaration for a Bill, *L.J.* xii. 543, March 4; B.M. Stowe MSS. 201, f. 229, Aungier, March 4.

jesuits; his Declaration was withdrawn, the great seal torn away, nothing in it was to serve as any kind of precedent for the future.[1]

This has sometimes been seen as a surrender by Charles, perhaps the most striking ever made by a member of his House. In a sense it was so, but it was a surrender not to his enemies but to his friends. The joy expressed at his announcement came above all from men like Henry Coventry, Robert Southwell, and Richard Legh.[2] These were the men who had rallied delightedly to the anglican policy of 1670, and who had been both shocked by its abandonment, and horrified to find themselves forced into something like opposition to the crown. Now they could show their gratitude by hurrying on the supply bill and this they were happy to do, so that in three weeks the King was giving it his consent.[3] In this sense Charles had merely reverted to the bargain of 1670–1.

What, however, these delighted anglicans could not know, was that their whole position had been undermined. As part of the bargain the Test Act was also pushed forward,[4] and although Henry Coventry and others objected to certain of its terms—an oath denying transubstantiation offended their high anglican views, and they disliked, very understandably making men's private beliefs the subject of a political test[5]—they found the act as a whole quite proper. When it seemed likely to embarrass the Queen they tried to avoid giving her any offence:[6] they were yet to learn that this act threatened not merely the Queen Consort, but the Heir Presumptive himself.

After some discussion in the Commons, the Test Bill went to the Lords on March 12.[7] There Clifford attacked it with rash

---

[1] *C.J.* ix. 266; *Grey*, ii. 91–2; *Dering*, pp. 134–5.

[2] Coventry MSS., Longleat, 83. f. 3, Henry Coventry, March 10; B.M. Stowe MSS. 201, ff. 237, 239, 241, 243, 245, Arlington, Aungier, Southwell, Godolphin, Henry Coventry, March 8; Richard Legh, quoted Legh, *The House of Lyme*, p. 252; Verney MSS., Claydon, Sir Ralph Verney, March 10. For rejoicing outside London see Thynne MSS. 16, f. 98, Sir William Coventry, March 22; *Cal. S.P. Dom. 1673*, pp. 36–41, March 12–13.

[3] On March 29, *L.J.* xii. 584.

[4] *Dering*, pp. 135–7; *Grey*, ii. 78–89, 97, 100; *C.J.* ix. 261–8, March 3, 5, 6, 10, 12.

[5] *Grey*, ii. 78–82, 97–100, March 3, 12.

[6] *Grey*, ii. 140–4, 157–9, March 21, 25; *Dering*, pp. 146–7, March 21.

[7] *C.J.* ix. 268.

vehemence and it was returned to the Commons, much amended, on March 21.[1] Sacheverell and Mallet seized the chance to denounce Clifford as, at best, a known friend to popery—they may possibly have guessed at his conversion—and to ask whether he was a fit person to hold office as Lord Treasurer, and so handle money given by the Commons to the King.[2] Even more serious was an attempted extension, by Mallet, of this attack to the Duke of York, but this seems to have shocked even some of the opposition and the House ignored his intervention.[3] They dismissed too Mallet's attempt to indict Clifford on Common Fame—forgetting perhaps how this had been considered as a basis for attacking the Chancellor.[4] On the other hand when a courtier tried to oppose restrictions on the Queen's household, saying that this might spoil some future marriage project, Birch declared that having previously opposed the restrictions he would now support them, in the hope that there might be no more catholic brides for members of our royal House.[5] Again there was a threat for the future: in less than a year the Duke of York was to contract a catholic marriage, and by that to arouse the most bitter protests from the House.

The Test Act passed, with most of the Lords' amendments withdrawn;[6] as a time bomb it would explode within three months and blow the ministry apart. Scarcely more pleasing to Charles can have been the bill to ease protestant dissenters, for with this in force all excuse for a general indulgence would be lost, and he would only be able to help catholics by coming out openly as their friend. Debates on this were at least more bitterly contested than those on the Test Act, for the cavalier courtiers, Finch, Duncombe, and Henry Coventry, seized the liberty accorded them by the withdrawal of the Indulgence to rage forth against men who they still regarded as at least as dangerous as the catholics.[7] A proposal to remove or modify the oath against the Covenant aroused violent protests, and

---

[1] C. H. Hartmann, *Clifford of the Cabal*, pp. 261–6; *C.J.* ix. 271–2.
[2] *Dering*, pp. 148–9, March 22; *Grey*, ii. 152–4, March 22.
[3] *Grey*, ii. 143, March 21.
[4] Supra, Chapter VI.
[5] *Dering*, pp. 147–8; *Grey*, ii. 144, March 21.
[6] 25 Car. II, cap. 2.
[7] *Grey*, ii. 89–96, 100–6, 116–18, 132–5; *Dering*, 133–42, March, 7, 10, 13, 17, 19.

Henry Coventry closed ranks with Strangeways, arguing that even a beleaguered garrison would not be helped by taking in recruits infected with the plague.[1] When these arguments failed, Strangeways proposed that dissenters should at least be barred, like catholics, from membership of the Commons, and after much argument this was, in principle, agreed.[2] A clause was not, however, tacked to the bill of ease, as Duncombe had wished, but a new bill was ordered, drafted by Meres, and eventually abandoned.[3] The main bill passed the House on March 19 and was sent up to the Lords.[4]

The Commons had thus shown themselves ready to grant terms similar to those eventually conceded in 1689. The Lords had generally been the more tolerant House, and the non-conformists might have thought their worst trials were at an end. Unfortunately, in their eagerness to advance toleration, the Lords incorporated as an amendment, a clause allowing Charles to dispense with penal status during a recess.[5] The Commons saw in this a rejection of the principle which they had been at such pains to establish. Strangeways accused ministers of a design to raise revenue by selling dispensations —a charge denied a little too quickly by Sir Robert Carr— and Garraway made it clear that, though in favour of *parliamentary* toleration, he would not have even protestants indulged by prerogative powers. Attacks on the prerogative brought Henry Coventry round to defend the proposal aided by Littleton and Howard; Seymour, from the Chair, remarked that laws existed only by permission of the King—one wonders if he was merely trying to prolong the debate for he can hardly have expected such a sally to be well received—and

---

[1] *Grey*, ii. 43, Feb. 20. Compare his savage comment some weeks later: 'he could never receive the blood of his Saviour from his hands that . . . was guilty of his Sovereign's blood', *Grey*, ii. 104, March 13.

[2] *Grey*, ii. 89–90, 92–6; *Dering*, 133–5, March 7, 10.

[3] *Dering*, p. 135; *Grey*, ii. 96, March 7, 10. Meres' draft was reported on March 17, *C.J.* ix. 270, after which no more was heard of it.

[4] *C.J.* ix. 271.

[5] *C.J.* ix. 279; *Grey*, ii. 163–9, 171–3, March 28. This was no doubt the product of a committee set up by the Lords some weeks earlier, before Charles had finally recalled his Declaration, *H.M.C. 9th Rep.*, pt. ii. House of Lords MSS., p. 25, March 6. Both Sir John Hobart and Sir William Coventry had feared that the Lords might spoil the bill, Tanner MSS., Bodleian Library, 42, f. 1, March 26; Thynne MSS., Longleat, 16, f. 102, 'Easter Eve'.

the wrangle continued into a second day, only to be interrupted by Black Rod, and the end of the session.[1]

Catholics were to be persecuted; protestants were not to be indulged; the King was to have a grant of supply: all this was a return to the pattern of 1670–1. There was, however, another side to the debates of these last weeks. On March 17 Sir John Coventry, careless of further damage to his features, rose to suggest that a day be set aside for 'Grievances'.[2] Rather foolishly the new Solicitor General, Francis North, asked why he had made no specific complaint. Coventry, Sir Thomas Lee, Mr Holt, and Sir Richard Everard, at once produced instances of money being levied by prerogative rather than by statute; Powle, Birch, and St John complained of martial law, billeting, and pressing men for the fleet;[3] Sir Trevor Williams and an anonymous colleague attacked the alleged favouritism shown to catholics in Ireland, and in particular to the brothers Peter and Richard Talbot.[4]

'Popery and arbitrary power': this would have been a fair summary of these assorted complaints, which thus anticipated the main concern of the Commons during the remainder of Charles' reign. If this was diagnosed as the danger, then the remedy must lie in constitutional amendment and eventually in Exclusion. A new element had entered the Commons, a new note was being sounded in these debates. Yet for the time the complaints remained unco-ordinated. Sir William Coventry left London, as disgusted with the spitefulness of the 'gentlemen of the corner' as he had earlier been with the arbitrary attitude of the court.[5] Whether other moderates followed his example is not known, but the new table of grievances produced only a few addresses to which Charles promised to give attention at his leisure.[6]

On March 26 the supply bill passed the Lower House:[7]

[1] *Grey*, ii. 163–9, 177–81, March 28, 29.

[2] *Dering*, p. 142, March 17.

[3] Nine years earlier the same House had been considering how to make the Press Gang more effective, *C.J.* viii. 570. Dec. 2, 1664.

[4] *Dering*, pp. 142–5; *Grey*, ii. 118–32, March 17–18.

[5] Thynne MSS. 16, ff. 98–106, March 22, 26, 31.

[6] *Dering*, 143–5; *Grey*, ii. 118–32, 159–63, March 17, 18, 25; *C.J.* ix. 270; *Essex Papers*, ed. O. Airey (Camden Soc., 1890), p. 61, Godolphin, March 18.

[7] *C.J.* ix. 278. For attempts to delay supply until redress of grievances had been granted see *Grey*, ii. 108–15, 137–9, March 15, 21.

so too without apparent debate, did an 'Act of Grace' under which one minister at least was to shelter for several years.[1] The opposition, seeing their hopes fade, proposed in a fury to print the addresses which they had sent to the King.[2] Henry Coventry told them sharply that to do this would be to break the law, and after an angry debate the votes were found to be tied. Speaker Seymour thereupon remarked that he wanted his lunch, and so adjourned; late that evening the session was itself adjourned.[3]

Had the session been a failure? In terms of results the King could balance a supply worth £1,180,000[4] against the cancellation of the Declaration and the passage of the First Test Act. In terms of mood the opening weeks had shown almost the whole House united against the policy of toleration, but once Charles had given way on that point the opposition had been unable to delay supply further, even when they had genuine and serious grievances to present. The arrival of Sacheverell in the House marked the beginning of a new form of opposition, impervious to bribes—or at least to bribes from the court[5]—and destined to challenge the whole basis of royal authority. On the other hand his party, even when helped by the revelation of York's conversion and by suspicion of Charles' dealings with France, was never to win the unqualified support of this Parliament. Even though the old basis of agreement between King and cavaliers was soon to be shattered[6] the Cavalier Parliament would never abandon its ultimate loyalty to the King. Eventually, in 1681, this trust was to be endorsed by a majority of the nation, but before that both King and court were to suffer much discouragement and alarm.

---

[1] 25 Car. II, cap. 5. This bill seems to have originated in the Lords and to have been read once only by the Commons, L.J. xii. 576; C.J. ix. 280. According to Aungier it passed the Commons by only 12 votes, B.M. Stowe MSS. 201, f. 305, March 29. A similar act had been expected in 1671, Cal. S.P. Ven. 1671–2, pp. 40–1, April 14, 1671. The minister who found it so useful a shield was Lauderdale, infra, Chapter IX.

[2] Grey, ii. 175–7; C.J. ix. 281, March 29.

[3] Grey, ii. 180–1; L.J. xii, 585.

[4] Chandaman, ii. 443.

[5] Their acceptance of bribes from France is notorious, but there is no reason to suppose that these affected their conduct, infra, Conclusion.

[6] On the hopelessness of Danby's struggle to rebuild it see infra, Chapter IX.

CHAPTER XI

DEADLOCK ON FOREIGN POLICY

FIRST HINTS OF EXCLUSION

SOON after the spring session was over the Venetian resident told his superiors that he had discovered a great secret: the Parliament had been won over by bribes.[1] If this quite unsupported piece of gossip was true then Charles got little value for his money. Far more effective than any bribes, English, Dutch, Spanish or French, in influencing the Commons was the brilliant new pamphlet, prepared by Peter du Moulin and entitled '*England's Appeal*'.[2] Copies of this were poured into the country during the spring of 1673[3] and were soon supported by a series of most unfortunate events.

Du Moulin's main contention was that the new foreign and domestic policies were closely linked. England was tied to catholic France abroad in order to secure her subjection to autocracy, and probably to catholicism, at home. As long as we maintained the French alliance, indeed as long as we failed to ally ourselves with the Dutch, then our ministers should be looked on as suspect: Parliament should therefore challenge both our foreign and domestic policy. Reinforcing this pamphlet came news of how, in the main naval battle of the summer, the French had 'stood off', leaving Rupert to bear the brunt of the battle.[4] At the same time our failure to secure naval superiority stranded 8,000 troops, many of whom were catholic Irish, on the Norfolk coast, awaiting convoy to

---

[1] *Cal. S.P. Ven. 1673–5*, p. 33, April 6.

[2] The full text of this can be found in *State Tracts* (1693), pp. 1–25.

[3] K. D. Haley, *William of Orange and the English Opposiiton*, pp. 97–107. Du Moulin also sent letters to individual but unfortunately anonymous members of the Commons.

[4] *Letters to Sir Joseph Williamson* ed. W. D. Christie (Camden Soc. 1874), i. 73, 120, 162, 168, H. Ball, R. Yard, W. Bridgeman, R. Southwell, June 27, July 18, Aug. 15, 17; Essex Papers (Camden Soc. 1890), p. 121, William Temple, Sept. 10; *Cal. S.P. Ven. 1673–5*, p. 100, Sept. 1. It was later alleged in the Commons that the French had lost only two men in this war, and one of those died from 'an unfortunate disease', *Grey*, ii. 212, Oct. 31; and compare the speeches during the remainder of that debate, ibid., ii. 198–213.

the Continent.[1] Martial law and billeting, already complained of, became a necessity;[2] even the choice as commander in chief of so good a protestant as Marshal Schomberg was criticized.[3] As it became more probable that Spain would become involved in the war, merchants feared the loss of a valuable market;[4] such a loss might itself offset any gains we could make by destroying the Dutch. To crown all, after the resignations of Clifford and the Duke of York had shown how far catholicism had spread,[5] the latter insisted on carrying through his marriage with a princess who was commonly believed to be the daughter of the Pope.[6]

All this meant that Parliament would again be difficult to manage. This time, however, the administration approached the session without any settled plan. Clifford had resigned, Shaftesbury was unreliable, Buckingham and Arlington hated each other more bitterly than ever. Charles hoped to stay in the war and, having agreed to the Test Act, was prepared to offer further measures against catholics in return for money. What he would not accept was any measure by which his prerogative was, or seemed to be, impaired.

[1] Ogg, op. cit., i. 373–4, 379.

[2] Supra, Chapter X. Thynne MSS., Longleat, 16, f. 142, William Coventry, July 7; Letters to Williamson, i. 42, 116, 153, 158, H. Ball, R. Yard, June 26, July 18, Aug. 9, 11. The ingenious Sir Samuel Morland was in great anxiety about his share in having the Articles of War printed, ibid., i. 148, H. Ball. Aug. 8.

[3] Cal. S.P. Ven. 1673–5, p. 76, July 21; Letters to Williamson, i. 67, H. Ball, June 26.

[4] Cal. S.P. Ven. 1673–5, pp. 143–5, Oct. 20; Letters to Williamson, i. 88, ii. 44, 47, H. Ball, R. Yard, July 4, Oct. 17. Even at the beginning of this reign Clarendon had thought it necessary to couple with his announcement of Charles' Portuguese marriage an apology for any possible breach with Spain, L.J. xi. 244, May 8, 1661; Cal. S.P. Ven. 1661–4, p. 14. For Spanish boasts of their influence over Parliament see Letters to Williamson, i. 116, H. Ball, July 18, and compare Cal. S.P. Ven. 1673–5, p. 9, Jan. 27.

[5] Clifford resigned on June 19 and soon afterwards died, perhaps by his own hand, C. H. Hartmann, Clifford, pp. 276, 296. James resigned his post as Lord High Admiral in the same month of June, D. Ogg, op. cit., i. 370.

[6] Letters to Williamson, ii. 27, 48, Sir Nicholas Armourer, Oct. 2, R. Yard, Oct. 17; Hatton Correspondence (Camden Soc. 1878), i. 108–10, Charles Hatton, June 26. A good example of divided loyalty is found in Sir William Coventry's letter to his brother, the Secretary, where, distressed at what he heard of his past employer, he could only fall back on 'Derby's prayer, God bless the King, God bless the Duke', Coventry MSS., Longleat, 4, ff. 123–5, June 23.

The spring debates had been ended only by an adjournment.[1] The session was thus still in being, and so was a resolution against accepting any further proposals for supply.[2]
Charles, therefore, explained to Shaftesbury and Seymour,
Speakers of the Houses, that he wanted an immediate prorogation, followed a few days later by a new session in which
money could be obtained.[3] Shaftesbury's motives at this
time are obscure, but for whatever reason he dallied over
routine business in the Lords and thus allowed the opposition
time to take action in the Commons.[4] The men of 'the old
corner' yelled Seymour to the Chair;[5] his proposal to read
prayers was pushed aside and various speakers, including
not only Birch and Powle but also the place-holding Howard,
bitterly attacked the proxy marriage between Mary of Modena
and the Duke of York. Friends of the Duke were shouted
down and the House approved, without a recorded division,
an address demanding that this marriage be repudiated. Only
after this did Shaftesbury summon the Commons and the prorogation take place.[6]

The decision to direct an attack against the Duke's marriage
suggests that some at least among the opposition were already
moving towards a policy of 'limitations' on a catholic successor.
The approval of their address, and of a second one a few
days later, further suggests that others besides this extreme
opposition were considering the Duke's position with alarm.

[1] *L.J.* xii. 585.
[2] *C.J.* ix. 278, March 27; *Letters to Williamson*, ii. 51, Musgrave, Oct. 20.
[3] Ibid.; Louise Brown, *Shaftesbury*, p. 215.
[4] W. D. Christie, *Shaftesbury*, ii. 151–3; *L.J.* xii. 586, Oct. 20. The routine
business included the admission of three new peers, one of whom was Sir
Robert Paston, Viscount Yarmouth, and another Sir Thomas Osborne,
Viscount Latimer.
[5] *Letters to Williamson*, ii. 51–2, Musgrave, Oct. 20. References to 'the
corner' and, more specifically, 'the south east corner' are quite frequent at
this time; clearly some members of the opposition were anticipating the
'Mountain' of 1792.
[6] *Letters to Williamson*, loc. cit.; *C.J.* ix. 281–2, Oct. 20; B.M. Stowe MSS.
203, ff. 107, 147, Bridgeman, Oct. 21, Aungier, Oct. 28; *Dering*, pp. 149–
151; *Cal. S.P. Ven. 1673–5*, p. 161, Oct. 24; Verney MSS., Claydon, letter of
Dr Denton, Oct. 23. It was on this occasion that the erratic John Ayliffe
placed a French sabot under the Speaker's Chair: he was possibly acting
on du Moulin's orders but escaped censure on the grounds of insanity,
Hatton Correspondence, i. 118; Charles Hatton, Oct. 28; *Cal. S.P. Ven. 1673–5*,
p. 168, Oct. 31, and many other accounts.

Nevertheless the address was at best impolite, at worst a monstrous invasion of royal privacy, and Charles, however much he might himself regret his brother's tactlessness, would never accept dictation of this kind. With this address we move into a period in which even moderate members were to make demands which Charles could only refuse. Looking forward we find that the next session was to produce a series of bills described by Secretary Coventry as grave invasions of the prerogative, but by the no less loyal Sir Ralph Verney as 'very necessary measures for the defence of liberty and the Church'.[1]

The political scene now became one of utter confusion. Party groupings changed, or were thought to have changed, every day. The promotion some months earlier of Sir Thomas Osborne to the Lord Treasurership offered the promise of a new court leadership more purposeful, if not more successful, than any in the reign, but among so many changes and rumours of changes this had attracted little attention.[2] To strengthen outside influence on the Commons, Ruvigny, son of the ambassador of 1667 and a kinsman to the opposition stalwart Russell, was sent with official congratulations on the Duke's marriage and an unofficial bag of guineas to be employed as he thought most fit.[3] Fresno and Salinas continued their efforts on behalf of Spain, Dutch agents were as busy as ever,[4] whilst party groups, if not parties, were meeting to concert their tactics.[5] Unpromising though this situation was, the

---

[1] Coventry MSS., Longleat, 83, f. 35, Henry Coventry, Feb. 23, 1674; Verney MSS., Claydon, Sir Ralph Verney, Jan. 26, Feb. 16, 26, 1674. Compare also *Letters to Williamson*, ii. 142, Southwell, Feb. 6, and B.M. Stowe MSS. 204, f. 175, Conway, Feb. 10.

[2] A. Browning, *Danby*, i. 99–102. Sir William Coventry was one of the first to discern Osborne's (or Danby's) true ability, Thynne MSS., Longleat, 16, f. 142, July 7. For a less accurate estimate see *Letters to Williamson*, i. 99, H. Ball, July 11.

[3] PRO 31/3/129, f. 49, instructions sent to Ruvigny, Oct. 25. On Nov. 7 Ruvigny referred to Russell as his nephew, ibid., f. 77.

[4] PRO 31/3/129, f. 36, Colbert, Sept. 25; *Cal. S.P. Ven. 1673–5*, p. 175, Nov. 17; Haley, op. cit., pp. 127–30, 140–1; B.M. Add. MSS. 25,122, f. 158, Henry Coventry, Oct. 8.

[5] *Letters to Williamson*, ii. 55, Sir Thomas Player, Nov. 3; *Cal. S.P. Ven. 1673–5*, p. 68, June 30. *Essex Papers*, i. 130–1, prints a letter by Sir William Temple, dated Oct. 25, which gives a very detailed account of party groupings. Temple distinguishes four different objectives; annulment of the Duke's marriage; peace with the Dutch; peace coupled with safeguards for religion and property; and all these with a change of ministers. These seem

King had to have money, and on October 27 the members reassembled to hear the official speeches at the opening of the new session.[1]

Charles spoke firmly of his need for supply, stressing that the continuance of the war was due entirely to the obstinacy of the Dutch. He reaffirmed support for the established church and threw in a reference to the money still owing from the 'Stop' of 1672. Shaftesbury, making one last return to orthodoxy, added a few rhetorical flourishes, and the Lords dutifully voted thanks and ordered the speeches of both King and Chancellor to be printed. In the Commons, however, thanks even for the 'gracious expressions contained in the speech' were refused.[2] Instead, proceedings opened with an attack on Speaker Seymour, pushed forward not by the usual opposition leaders but by members of Arlington's faction, notably Littleton, Howe, and William Harbord.[3] Garraway, half opposition member, half a follower of Osborne, defended Seymour, as did cavaliers of court and country, among them Strangeways, Birkenhead, and Finch. Neither acceptance of a Privy Councillorship nor having danced naked when in drink were held to be a disqualification for the Chair,[4] and Seymour survived for eight years to be removed eventually at the behest not of the House, but of Danby and the King.

On the following day Henry Coventry presented Charles' reply to the address against his brother's marriage. This contained the brief statement that it was too late to interfere, with

---

probable enough but the men he names did not play quite the roles he ascribes to them. (Sir William Coventry's 'brother' should almost certainly read 'nephew', i.e. Sir John, Coventry MSS., Longleat, 5, f. 63. May 3, 1673.) On this question of parties see infra, Conclusion.

[1] *L.J.* xii. 588–9, Oct. 27.

[2] Ibid., vii. 590; *C.J.* ix. 282, *Dering*, p. 152.

[3] This attack had been predicted before the session began, Thynne MSS., Longleat, 16, f. 108, William Coventry, April 12; *Letters to Williamson*, i. 34, Southwell, June 13. His three main accusers were all prominent in Arlington's defence early in the following year, infra, Chapter XII. Seymour, though about to join forces with Danby, was still reckoned a Buckinghamite, PRO 31/3/129, f. 59, Ruvigny, Nov. 9; *Essex Papers*, p. 146, Conway, Nov. 29.

[4] *Dering*, pp. 152–4; *Grey*, ii. 186–8, Oct. 27. One last attempt to discredit Seymour was made by arranging for a 'mean whore' to deposit a bastard on his doorstep, watched by five hundred spectators. He seems to have taken this in his stride, *Letters to Williamson*, ii. 70, Talbot, Nov. 13.

a comment that catholic marriages, Charles' own included, had aroused no hostility in the past.[1] After one of the 'long silences' often recorded at this time the presbyterian, Birch, joined the anglican, Meres, in proposing an immediate new address. Henry Coventry then admitted that a protestant match might indeed have been 'more chusable', but suggested that all that could now result from breaking off the match would be bigamy by the Duke and a confused succession. Neither this nor an appeal to support the King's honour moved the House—the coronation oath, it was said, came before any promises made to foreign powers—and a new address was approved by 186 to 88.[2] Garraway then proposed a new test bill, extending the oath to members of both Houses;[3] Sacheverell secured the withdrawal of a new member elected by the royally enfranchised borough of Newark,[4] and with these two blows the House adjourned.

The next day, October 31, was that appointed to consider supply. The opposition began by getting an adjournment into Committee—for the rest of this Parliament's existence the court did better in the House, where silent voters carried more weight —and the Lords Russell and Cavendish then launched a ferocious attack on the whole idea of a war against the Dutch.[5] Parliament had not been consulted, our ally had let us down; these points were made by several members in what was virtually a paraphrase of Du Moulin's pamphlet. Even if the war had to be continued it was claimed that there was ample money remaining from the previous session's vote.

Henry Coventry had the advantage of genuinely approving the war. To those who objected to France as a catholic ally he put the question as to when Austria or Spain had become pillars of the reformed religion. A direct negative to supply would be like the Long Parliament's 'vote of no addresses',

[1] *C.J.* ix. 283, Oct. 30.

[2] *Dering*, pp. 155–6; *Grey*, ii. 189–96, Oct. 30.

[3] *Dering*, p. 156; *Grey*, ii. 196–7; *C.J.* ix. 284, Oct. 30.

[4] *Dering*, pp. 156–7; *Grey*, ii. 196–7. See also *Grey*, ii. 368–72, Jan. 31; *C.J.* ix. 388–9, Feb. 26, 1677; *Savile Correspondence* (Camden Soc. 1858) pp. 43–8, H. Savile, April 11, 16, 21, May 8, 1677; E. Hallam, *The Constitutional History of England* (1872), iii. 40.

[5] *Dering*, pp. 157–8; *Grey*, ii. 197–215, Oct. 31; PRO 31/3/129, ff. 62–3. Cavendish had spoken once or twice in previous sessions but this was the first time that he and Russell had come forward as leaders in a debate.

and as fatal in its results. Joined by fellow anglicans, Finch and Duncombe, but not by the friends of Arlington or Buckingham, Coventry went some way to winning back the centre of the House. That his efforts failed was due very largely to his brother, Sir William, who now put into effect a plan he had sketched out earlier in the summer.[1] The King should be offered a supply, but only if he could show that the Dutch had refused reasonable terms; otherwise the assessments of the previous March should run their course, whilst negotiations were continued for a peace. This conditional proposal, made late in the debate, won the support of a majority.[2] The King was advised to negotiate before asking for more money and the House turned back to approve the new address against the Duke's marriage, with its exclusionist amendment hoping that the Commons might yet have the pleasure of congratulating Charles himself on a son.[3]

This firm refusal of supply meant that the session's life was now strictly limited. One more debate did take place on November 3, and dealt with the inconvenience, if not illegality, of keeping up the so-called 'standing army'.[4] Birch had paved the way for this with a proposal that we should encourage trade by allowing more foreigners to apply for naturalization; Meres took the cue, and declared that a better way to improve trade would be to remove such unprofitable employment as service in the army. Birch abandoned his original theme with suspicious readiness—it is at least possible that the whole introduction was a put-up job[5]—and was joined by Sir Henry Capel, brother to the Lord Lieutenant of Ireland, in a violent attack upon the religious principles and general conduct of

---

[1] Thynne MSS., Longleat, 16, f. 147, July 13. The series of letters written by William Coventry to his nephew, Thomas Thynne, between March and September 1673, Thynne MSS., 16, ff. 98–168, well illustrates the former's hardening attitude towards the French alliance. Sir William nowhere mentions *England's Appeal*, of which he was for a time supposed to have been the author, Haley, op. cit., p. 107, but his letters and subsequent speeches read like close paraphrases, and it seems almost certain that he saw the pamphlet. Comparison with other private letters would be most instructive but it does not appear that any similar series has survived.

[2] *Letters to Williamson*, ii. 69, Talbot, Nov. 13.

[3] *C.J.* ix. 285, Oct. 31; *Dering*, p. 158.

[4] *Dering*, pp. 159–61; *Grey*, ii. 215–22, Nov. 3.

[5] Though similar bills had been used as a device for advocating toleration, supra, Chapter VI, and to this Meres had always been opposed.

Schomberg's troops. Henry Coventry, Temple, and Howard urged the usefulness of keeping up these forces—the last two may have been encouraged by Buckingham who had hoped for the command[1]— but their quite reasonable arguments produced only three negatives to a resolution declaring that a standing army was a 'grievance'. As this was being penned Sacheverell amended it to '*the*' standing army, and in this more forceful form it was carried *nem. con.*[2]

On the following day Sir Robert Thomas had planned to move to a more personal attack. His victim was to have been Lauderdale,[3] but before the debate had got very far Black Rod called the House to attend the King.[4] Charles spoke bitterly of Dutch delight at Parliament's recalcitrance. Despite it he would fit out a fleet and maintain our essential interests; no less would be his care in providing for the security of the established Church. He would meet Parliament again on January 7, by which time he hoped to find members more ready to concentrate on the essentials of national security. Meanwhile they could return to their homes.[5]

The court party in the House was now led by Henry Coventry, aided by Duncombe, Seymour, Temple, and Howard.[6] None of these could be relied on to oppose a further test act; the last three showed little dislike for 'limitations' on a future catholic King. At the other extreme were those whose political future, and indeed personal security, already hinged on some form of Exclusion. If James were to succeed, then Sacheverell,

---

[1] *Letters to Williamson*, i. 67, H. Ball, June 26.

[2] *Dering*, pp. 160–1, Nov. 3; *C.J.* ix. 286. Lee, Powle, and Carew were also prominent in this debate.

[3] Who had prudently retired to Scotland, clutching his copy of the previous session's Act of Grace, *Letters to Williamson*, ii. 35–6, H. Ball, Oct. 10. Sir Robert Thomas had been considered a follower of Buckingham in 1669, Browning, *Danby*, iii. 39. He had first appeared for the opposition in March 1673, *Grey*, ii. 175, March 29, and was now among the most violent of the court's opponents, *Letters to Williamson*, ii. 24, 27, 51–2, Armourer, Oct. 2, 6, Musgrave, Oct. 20, though I can find no evidence to support Sir Arthur Bryant's description of him as 'one of Shaftesbury's lieutenants', *Pepys: The Years of Peril* (1948), p. 110.

[4] *C.J.* ix. 285, Nov. 4; *Grey*, ii. 222–3.

[5] *L.J.* xii. 593, Nov. 4.

[6] Finch went to the Lords when, immediately after this session, he took the Seals from Shaftesbury and became Lord Keeper, W. D. Christie, *Shaftesbury*, ii. 154–5.

Russell, Mallet, and others, who had pushed on the Test Act and the addresses against a catholic marriage, might find themselves only too well 'remembered'. Fear of what James might do, fear even of what Charles might do if once released from his financial shackles, was to become the main motive of such men, uniting them eventually with Louis in a common desire to frustrate all reconciliation between Parliament and King. Midway between these two extremes came a third group, perhaps the largest in the House. These were men such as William Coventry, Powle, Littleton, and Capel,[1] in other words those whose willingness to trust Charles had been damped but not destroyed. Such men would oppose Exclusion; they would even grant supply, upon conditions. Unfortunately their conditions were such as Charles, hamstrung by his secret promises to Louis, would never be in a position to concede.

[1] Feiling, *History of the Tory Party*, app. i, pp. 494–5.

CHAPTER XII

SURRENDER ON FOREIGN POLICY

A NEW COUNTRY PROGRAMME

PARLIAMENT was due to meet on January 7, 1674, but no one, not even Charles himself, was sure whether this particular Parliament would ever meet again.[1] Much discussion took place among the great men of the court, but in the last event the deciding voice lay with the new Lord Treasurer. Without either peace or a parliamentary supply Latimer—it would perhaps be better to anticipate and call him Danby—saw no chance of balancing his accounts.[2] French ambassadors might argue vigorously against a session but they lacked the funds which alone would have given weight to such arguments. It was at last agreed that Parliament should meet.

Once this was agreed Arlington and Buckingham had one overriding interest, to protect themselves and, if possible, to secure the destruction of their rivals.[3] The King's business came a long way behind. Such plans as were made seem to have been the work of Henry Coventry and Finch, aided perhaps by Danby and Seymour.[4] After discussing matters with Ruvigny Charles agreed to show Parliament the open clauses of the Dover Treaty, a decision pleasing to those of his ministers who did not know that other clauses existed. At the same time he put on a show of severity against catholics and emphasized his devotion to the Church.[5]

[1] K. D. Haley, *William of Orange and the English Opposition*, pp. 156–7; *Letters to Williamson*, ii. 75, William Bridgeman, Nov. 17; PRO 31/3/129, ff. 63, 74, Ruvigny, Nov. 3, 17; *Essex Papers*, pp. 153–6, Conway, Dec. 20, Sir William Temple, Dec. 20 (25); B.M. Stowe MSS., 203, f. 163, Arlington, Nov. 4; Coventry MSS., Longleat, 83, f. 29, Henry Coventry, Dec. 27; *Cal. S.P. Ven. 1673–5*, p. 176, Nov. 14.

[2] A. Browning, *Danby*, i. 113, 120–1.

[3] See once again the Venetian ambassador's comment, supra, p. 38, note 2.

[4] Accounts of party groupings at this time are confused in the extreme. For a typical set of comments see Conway's letters of Nov. 8, (15), 22, 29, Dec. 6, 13, 20, *Essex Papers*, 140–2, 146, 150, 152, 153.

[5] Coventry MSS., Longleat, 83, ff. 24, 27, Henry Coventry, Nov. 14,

At the opening, on January 7, the King and Lord Keeper Finch made much of these measures, but laid even greater stress on the mulish obstinacy of the Dutch.[1] The Commons had refused supply unless the Dutch should make peace impossible; Charles suggested that this situation had now arisen.

Ages to come will celebrate your memory as the truest physicians, the wisest councillors, the noblest patriots, and the best session of the best Parliament that ever King or Kingdom met with.

Thus Heneage Finch ended his oration, in a panegyric ironically similar to those which had been exchanged between King and Commons in the first years of the reign. The Commons, however, paused only to set up their usual committees and then adjourned to January 12.[2] There was to be no quick vote of supply pushed through a thin House.

During the interval the Dutch distributed more propaganda while the House of Lords initiated new measures against catholics.[3] On January 12 the Commons reassembled, four hundred strong, to give further consideration to the King's speech.[4] Henry Coventry now came forward as the supporter of a peace, provided only that it was on honourable terms. He pointed out, however, the need to keep up our strength whilst negotiations were proceeding; 1667 had shown the danger of reducing our forces too soon. Even in the event of a peace being agreed there would still be the need for a navy to guard our plantations; he therefore proposed an immediate grant.[5]

Dec. 27; *Cal. S.P. Ven. 1673–5*, p. 183, Nov. 28. It was feared, however, by Ruvigny that suspicion that there were other secret articles was already widespread, PRO 31/3/130, f. 18, Dec. 29, and it was unfortunate that Charles, when he was denying that such articles existed, stumbled badly over his words, *Essex Papers*, pp. 160–1, Conway, Jan. 10.

[1] *L.J.* xii. 594–8, Jan. 7.

[2] *C.J.* ix. 290–1, Jan. 7. Lord Ranelagh thought that the House was in an angry mood, B.M. Stowe MSS., 204, f. 25, Jan. 10, though Ruvigny reported an unusual amount of applause for Charles' speech, PRO 31/3/130, f. 31v, Jan. 8.

[3] *L.J.* xii. 601, Jan. 7; Coventry MSS., Longleat, 83, f. 31, Henry Coventry, Jan. 7; B.M. Stowe MSS., 204, ff. 19–20, Bridgeman, Jan. 10. The Lords also heard a petition against Buckingham, *Letters to Williamson*, ii. 107, J. Richards, Jan. 9; *Essex Papers*, pp. 159–61, Conway, Jan. 10; PRO 31/3/130, f. 34, Ruvigny, Feb. 11.

[4] *Letters to Williamson*, ii. 108, Col. Whitley, Jan. 12; *C.J.* ix. 291.

[5] *Grey*, ii. 227–35, Jan. 12.

Having established the court 'line', Henry would, we presume, have looked round for some of his colleagues to come forward in support. Not one of them did so: in the whole of this session, that is in a period of rather more than six weeks, there was only one further speech made in favour of supply, and that too was by the Secretary.[1] On this occasion the opposition ignored his remarks, Birch denounced the war, Cavendish and Clarges extended this denunciation to those counsellors who had supported recent policy, and the House eventually resolved that before proceeding any further on the royal speech they would first

have grievances redressed, Protestantism, liberty and property established, (and) catholics and dangerous councillors removed from positions of trust.

Having delivered this broadside they did agree, on Howard's motion, to offer thanks for 'gracious expressions' contained in the King's speech.[2]

The next week contained the most dramatic events of the session. First Lauderdale, then Buckingham, then Arlington, were subjected to bitter personal attack. Over Lauderdale, though several courtiers put up a formal defence,[3] there was really no battle. Without much time being lost it was agreed to ask for his dismissal as a man dangerous and obnoxious to the State.[4] Arlington and Buckingham, however, still had powerful factions in the House, and even before the session had begun these had been spoiling for a fight.[5] As in 1667 and 1669 it was hard to distinguish 'the Grand Inquest of the Nation' from a list in which great barons carried on their private jousts.[6]

---

[1] *Grey*, ii. 352, Jan. 27. For comments on the court's dependence on Coventry, and lack of other effective speakers see *Letters to Williamson*, ii. 129, Southwell, Jan. 23, and William Temple, *Essex Papers*, p. 132, Oct. 25, 1673.

[2] *C.J.* ix. 292. The division figures on the motion for 'thanks' were 191 to 139, St John and Cavendish telling for the losers.

[3] These included Henry Coventry and Duncombe, but Temple was active for the prosecution, *Grey*, ii. 236–44, Jan. 13, Conway, on Jan. 17 and Feb. 10, commented on Lauderdale's lack of friends in the House, B.M. Stowe MSS., 204, ff. 73, 175.

[4] *C.J.* ix. 292, Jan. 13.

[5] *Letters to Williamson*, ii. 105, Sir Gilbert Talbot, Jan. 2.

[6] See the Venetian ambassador's comment of Oct. 27, 1673, *Cal. S.P. Ven. 1673–5*, p. 155.

Buckingham's original aim had been to prevent Parliament meeting at all. Once a meeting had been agreed upon, however, he had deserted the French ambassador and rushed back to his old allies the Presbyterians.[1] Neither this, nor attendance at Church on Christmas Day, prevented the relatives of his murdered victim, Shrewsbury, presenting a petition against him to the House of Lords, where it was received with sympathy.[2] Faced now with further attacks in the Commons the Duke resolved to make a personal appearance there, but forgot to ask permission from either his fellow peers or the King. Clutching 'a scribbled ragged paper' he spoke twice from the bar, alternating a modest defence of his own conduct with the frank admission of his colleagues' guilt. After he had answered several questions put to him by the Speaker he withdrew, leaving his defence in the hands of his supporters.[3]

More interesting than these rather contemptible manœuvres was the way in which, as in the earlier attack upon Orrery,[4] the latent factions reappeared. For Buckingham there was Speaker Seymour, Robert Howard, Birch and Swinfen, and, astonishingly, Duncombe and Sir John Birkenhead. Against him were Russell, Lee, Meres, Strangeways, and both Coventrys—Henry had been shocked by his violation of a councillor's oath—whilst Cornbury, Clarendon's son, gladly seized this opportunity to pay off some old scores.[5] Voting figures would be interesting, but none have been recorded; after fierce argument the King was asked to remove Buckingham from all posts held during pleasure—respect for the sacred right of property was strong enough to spare his freehold, as Master of the Horse[6]—and from the royal presence and

---

[1] *Essex Papers*, pp. 158–61, Conway, Dec. 30, Jan. 10; PRO 31/3/130, f. lv, Ruvigny, Dec. 22.

[2] *L.J.* xii. 599; B.M. Stowe MSS., ff. 19–20, Bridgeman, Aungier, Jan. 10. This petition was said to have received support from both Ormonde and Buckingham's future ally, Shaftesbury, PRO 31/3/130, f. 32, Ruvigny, Jan. 8; Verney MSS., Claydon, Sir Ralph Verney, Jan. 8. For the subject of the petition see supra, p. 84 and note.

[3] *Grey*, ii. 244, 249–51, 260–3, Jan. 13, 14; B.M. Stowe MSS., 204, ff. 38–9, 40–1, Aungier, Orrery, Jan. 13; Verney MSS., Sir Ralph Verney, Jan. 15; *Essex Papers*, pp. 162–4, Aungier, Jan. 17.

[4] Supra, Chapter VIII.   [5] *Grey*, ii. 244–70, Jan. 13, 14.

[6] This point was made by Buckingham's enemy, William Coventry, *Grey*, ii. 267, Jan. 14, and see Tanner MSS., Bodleian Library, 42, f. 74, Hobart, Jan. 15.

councils for ever.[1] Even after this the Duke's friends managed to hold up the presentation of the address—on February 5 they lost by only 142 to 124 a motion to request the Lords' concurrence, which might have produced further delay—but at last, on February 7, it was delivered.[2] Charles was furious with Buckingham and removed him from all offices;[3] nevertheless the attraction of the Duke's conversation was such that not even open opposition could procure his banishment from the King's presence for any length of time.[4]

Buckingham's turn had come first, but Arlington knew that his would soon follow. Unlike his rival he prepared himself by asking both Charles and the Upper House for permission to give evidence before the Commons, and on January 15 he too stood at their Bar.[5] Sacheverell, one of Arlington's enemies, urged the House not to make this Lord accuse himself.[6] Such unusual tender-heartedness suggests that he may have anticipated the strength of Arlington's defence. In the event both friends and enemies were astonished at the firmness and skill with which the Secretary parried every question; when he withdrew he left a very different impression from that which Buckingham had produced on the previous day.[7]

Debates on Buckingham had occupied two days; those on Arlington took five.[8] Against him were Sacheverell, Garraway, and Birch, joined by Strangeways for the cavaliers, and once again Cornbury, avenging his father. For him, however, there were not only his own friends like Littleton and Holt, but also the Essex faction, notably Capel and William Harbord, both of whom had, in the previous session, been opponents of supply, Duncombe and Henry Coventry for the cavalier court, and,

---

[1] C.J. ix. 293, Jan. 14.

[2] Ibid., ix. 303, 305, Feb. 5, 7.

[3] B.M. Stowe MSS., 204, f. 175, Conway, Feb. 10; Cal. S.P. Dom. 1673–5, p. 147, Feb. 12.

[4] Feiling, History of the Tory Party, p. 156.

[5] L.J. xii. 608, Jan. 15; Violet Barbour, Arlington, p. 230; Grey, ii. 274–5, Jan. 15.

[6] Grey, ii. 275, Jan. 15.

[7] Ibid., ii. 275–80, Jan. 15. A fuller text of Arlington's reply is noted in Cal. S.P. Dom. 1673–5, pp. 103–6, and for tributes to his bearing see Letters to Williamson, ii. 112, 114–15, 118, Bridgeman, Musgrave, Talbot, Jan. 16; B.M. Stowe MSS., 204, ff. 61, 67, 73, Southwell, Ormonde, Conway, Jan. 17; Essex Papers, pp. 162–4, Aungier, Jan. 17.

[8] Grey, ii. 280–301, 303–29, Jan. 15, 16, 17, 19, 20.

perhaps as valuable as any, the Earl of Ossory, Ormonde's son, who stood in the lobby soliciting votes on Arlington's behalf.[1] As in other attempted impeachments a witness failed to appear,[2] specific charges proved impossible to sustain, and on January 19 the prosecution had to rush through an adjournment in order to prevent the whole affair being dropped.[3] Arlington's friends, now confident of an acquittal, decided to press for a formal impeachment, and staving off a last attempt to proceed by way of an address achieved their aim by 166 to 127.[4] Their assumption proved well founded; despite one or two reminders the managers of the impeachment were to make little headway, and Arlington was able to retire, uncensured, to the less influential but safer post of Lord Chamberlain.[5]

Private battles though these impeachments were, in one important aspect they were very different from the earlier attack upon Clarendon. The Chancellor had been accused of failing to carry out royal policy efficiently; with Arlington and Buckingham it was the policy itself that formed the basis of the charge. Who advised the shutting up of the Exchequer? Who promoted the Dutch war? Who backed the Declaration of Indulgence?[6] The Commons were determined to fix responsibility for these actions and when Henry Coventry talked of his councillor's oath of secrecy Meres told him sharply that the

---

[1] Ibid., ii. 280, note. For Arlington's acknowledgement of the help given him by Capel and Harbord see his letter of Feb. 5, B.M. Stowe MSS., 204, ff. 156–7.

[2] *Grey*, ii. 290, Jan. 17. This man, a Captain Paulden, was described as a 'menial servant of Buckingham' by Aungier, *Essex Papers*, pp. 162–4, Jan. 17, and as a false rogue by no less an authority than Thomas Blood, *Letters to Williamson*, ii. 120, Jan. 19. For similar situations in 1669 and 1675 see *Grey*, i. 201, iii. 51–2, Dec. 1, 1669, April 29, 1675

[3] *C.J.* ix. 295, Jan. 19; *Grey*, ii. 317. The voting figures were 197 to 97. See also *Letters to Williamson*, ii. 119, Talbot, Jan. 16, and, for presbyterian support for Arlington, Verney MSS., Claydon, Sir Ralph Verney, Jan. 19.

[4] *C.J.* ix. 296, Jan. 20; B.M. Stowe MSS., 240, ff. 82, 86, 90, 92, Aungier, Harbord, Orrery, Jan. 20, Temple, Jan. 21; *Letters to Williamson*, ii. 125, Fairfax, Jan. 20.

[5] *C.J.* ix. 302, 311, Feb. 3, 17; *Essex Papers*, pp. 173, Aungier, Feb. 7; *Letters to Williamson*, ii. 135, 138–9, Talbot, Jan. 30, Derham, Feb. 6; B.M. Stowe MSS., 204, f. 114, Conway, Jan. 27; Violet Barbour, *Arlington*, p. 243. Buckingham and Lauderdale are said to have regretted that they too had not tried for an impeachment, *Cal. S.P. Ven. 1673–5*, p. 205, Feb. 2.

[6] *Grey*, ii. 260–3, 275–80, Jan. 14, 15.

House was competent to question both councils and cabals.[1]
One charge against Arlington was that he had supplied naval
stores, not to the Dutch, but to our allies, the French.[2] It was
less the war's failure that was being criticized than the government's choice of sides. Throughout the debates no member
suggested that he was anxious to do more than prevent evil
councillors leading the King astray, yet from the interrogations
of Arlington and Buckingham it was not so long a journey to
the impeachment of a minister for a letter written at the direct
command of the King.[3]

Coupled with these attacks on past policy came a full, and
possibly concerted, programme of bills designed to meet the
threat presented by a catholic heir.[4] There were nine of these,
divided into three main groups: bills to preserve liberty, bills to
preserve property, and bills to preserve the anglican establishment. The first group was headed by a Habeas Corpus bill,
drafted by Lord St John, and first read on January 20. Though
opposed by the Attorney General, and by Secretary Coventry,
this had received two readings when the session closed.[5]
Coupled with it was a bill to check the transportation of
prisoners, which not only reached the Lords but was only one
reading short of its completion when the session ended.[6] To
measures dealing with prisoners before and after trial was
added a third, to make judges' patents run 'quam diu se bene
gesserint' and not, as hitherto, during the King's good pleasure.
The lions under the throne were to be given their freedom;
despite protests against creating a new set of overlords, this bill
too was committed.[7]

[1] *Grey*, ii. 258, Jan. 14.

[2] Ibid., ii. 304, Jan. 19. For Pepys' reluctance to help the French see
A. Bryant, *Pepys: Years of Peril* (1948), pp. 108–9 and also PRO 31/3/129,
f. 83, Ruvigny, Nov. 27.

[3] This was the fate that threatened Danby in 1678–9, A. Browning,
Danby, i. 300–10.

[4] B.M. Stowe MSS., 204, f. 175, Conway, Feb. 10; *Letters to Williamson*, ii.
156, Talbot, Feb. 28. The problem of how far this programme was concerted
is merged into the whole question of the existence of parties and is discussed
infra, Conclusion.

[5] *C.J.* ix. 296, 298, 313, Jan. 20, 23, Feb. 23; *Grey*, ii. 433–5, Feb. 17;
H.M.C. 9th Rep., pt. ii, app., House of Lords, p. 46, Feb. 23.

[6] *C.J.* ix. 299, 303, 305, Jan. 26, Feb. 3, 7; *Cal. S.P. Dom. 1673–5*, p. 119,
Jan. 26; *L.J.* xii. 640, Feb. 17, *H.M.C. 9th Rep.*, pt. ii, p. 42, Feb. 9.

[7] *C.J.* ix. 305, 308, Feb. 9, 12; *Grey*, ii. 415–20, Feb. 13. Harbord, Chur-

Subjects would, if these bills had been passed, have been assured of a trial, and possibly of that trial's fairness. Also in the section dealing with the liberty of the subject, may be placed two bills designed to increase the effectiveness of Parliament itself, and in particular of the House of Commons. A bill to secure a better attendance of members was presumably a check on rushing legislation through a thin House.[1] Birch proposed to add a clause against the appointment of any member to an office of profit whilst Parliament was sitting—it is not quite clear whether he was ready to surrender his own place in the Excise—but whether or not his clause was accepted this bill too was checked by the prorogation.[2] Last in the group came a bill to regulate elections[3] and this must in turn be linked with a definite attempt by the opposition to turn by-elections against the court.

The best example of this new interest in elections is the dispute over Pepys' return for the borough of Castle Rising. Pepys had already given good service to the court by his testimony before various committees enquiring into the alleged defects of the administration during the Second Dutch War.[4] This had not made him popular, nevertheless the court, desperately short of able speakers, were eager to have him as a fully qualified member of their ranks. Not without opposition his election had been secured[5] and he had quickly taken his part in debates, defending the loan of anchors to the French and

---

chill, and Howard warned the House not to put too much power into the hands of these new overlords, the last recalling, with justice, the recent conduct of Lord Justice Keeling, on which see supra, Chapter VI. A further point suggested by the supporters of the bill was that the patents should not be terminated by the King's death, *Letters to Williamson*, ii. 148, Talbot, Feb. 13.

[1] *C.J.* ix. 301, 311, Jan. 31, Feb. 18.

[2] *Grey*, ii. 435, Feb. 18. This was extended in the following year into a full Place Bill of which the original is quoted from Coventry MSS., Longleat, 8, ff. 168–86, in my thesis on the Coventrys, Oxford B.Litt. 1954. See also the article by G. E. Aylmer in *Transactions of the Royal Historical Society*, 5th series, xv, 1965.

[3] *C.J.* ix. 297, 308, 310, Jan. 22, Feb. 12, 16; *Grey*, ii. 425–6, Feb. 16. One feature of these bills was the attempt to revive the residence qualification first suggested in 1666, supra, Chapter V. *Letters to Williamson*, ii. 130, Southwell, Jan. 23; *Cal. S.P. Dom. 1673–5*, p. 113, Jan. 23.

[4] Supra, Chapters V and VII.

[5] A. Bryant, *Pepys: Years of Peril*, pp. 87, 105–7.

pointing out the necessity of using a press gang if the fleet was to be manned.[1] Meanwhile his defeated opponent, Mr Offley, had presented a petition to the Committee of Elections alleging bribery and influence, and throwing in a hint that Pepys was a catholic or at least a friend to Rome. This broader charge was taken up by the opposition and on February 10 Sir Robert Thomas, a renegade courtier, rose to make it good.[2]

The ensuing debates on February 10, 13, and 16 showed the more violent opposition at its worst.[3] In lieu of evidence a series of vague charges were produced: Pepys had been rude to the Committee of Accounts; he had given too much help to our French allies; he had been seen kneeling before a crucifix in his house.[4] Henry Coventry remarked at this that Sir John Byron had once been under a similar accusation when the 'crucifix' had proved to be his periwig resting on a stand; the House was shocked at this levity, though in fact the cases were not so very different. More valuable for Pepys, in fact perhaps the main reason for his eventual escape, was the friendship of Henry's brother Sir William; no one could accuse him of any sympathy towards catholics but he knew Pepys too well to doubt the latter's protestantism, and he persistently demanded proper witnesses or some degree of proof. Ordered to name his informants Thomas named Shaftesbury, Sir John Banks, and Littleton, the last of whom was of course a member of the House. Littleton flatly refused to confirm the charge and one of Thomas' supporters turned on him, but Garraway and Powle somehow got him excused.[5]

After some argument a committee was sent to visit Shaftesbury. With some difficulty Sir William Coventry got Pepys permission to go with them, and three days later they reported that the Earl's memory had failed him and he was unable to confirm or deny whether the crucifix had existed.[6] On February 16 the prosecution's last witness, Banks, came to the bar and flatly denied any knowledge of the affair, after which

---

[1] *Grey*, ii. 304, 330–1, Jan. 19, 21.

[2] *Grey*, ii. 407, Feb. 10; Bryant, op. cit., pp. 109–16; B.M. Stowe MSS., 204, f. 61, Southwell, Jan. 17.

[3] *Grey*, ii. 407–13, 420–1, 426–33, Feb. 10, 13, 16.

[4] Ibid., ii. 407–11, Feb. 10.

[5] Ibid., ii. 411–13.

[6] Ibid., ii. 420–1.

Pepys rose to make a fervent speech of self-defence.[1] Thomas
rashly declared that he would avow on oath that Shaftesbury
had told him of the crucifix; further efforts were made to force
the reluctant Littleton to speak and at last he was ordered to do
so by the House. He retaliated by naming St John as a witness
but St John said nothing; Thomas named Child and Child
could remember nothing.[2] By this time Meres, Lee, and Swinfen
were all showing strong sympathy for Pepys;[3] the prosecution
had lost heart, but despite a protest from the Speaker they
managed to adjourn the enquiry for a fortnight and so leave it
unsettled when the session ended.[4] Less fortunate than Pepys
was Sir Edward Spragge, whose election for Dover was quashed
on the grounds of undue 'influence' exerted by the court,[5]
and the member for Newark whose right to sit remained
unrecognized.[6]

Having taken these steps to safeguard the Liberties of the
subject, members turned their attention to the preservation of
Property. Committees were set up to review the Hearth Tax
and Sealed Paper Tax and a bill was ordered for the 'explanation' of the second,[7] whilst a more important check was provided by a bill against all 'illegal exactions'.[8] Not only did this
produce a new 'parliamentary' treason, to levy money without
the authority of Parliament,[9] but it also contained a proviso
that on Charles' death the right of the Crown to the Customs
should end. Any successor would thus be forced to meet
Parliament very early in his reign.[10]

---

[1] Ibid., ii. 426–8; Bryant, op. cit., pp. 114–16.

[2] *Grey*, ii. 428–32, Feb. 16. This recalls the wriggling of witnesses during
the attempt to impeach Clarendon, supra, Chapter VI.

[3] Sir Arthur Bryant does rather less than justice to the way in which these
less violent members of the opposition were prepared, however reluctantly,
to accept the evidence of Pepys' innocence.

[4] *C.J.* ix. 310, Feb. 16. Offley renewed his attack in 1675 but Pepys retained the seat, Bryant, op. cit., p. 146.

[5] *C.J.* ix. 294, Jan. 16.

[6] *C.J.* ix. 301, Jan. 31; *Grey*, ii. 317, 368–71, Jan. 20, 31, and see supra,
p. 146, and note.

[7] *C.J.* ix. 296, 298, 302, 306, 313, Jan. 20, 24, Feb. 3, 10, 23; E. Hughes,
'English Stamp Duties, 1664–1764', *Eng. Hist. Rev.* lvi (1941), p. 240.

[8] *C.J.* ix. 304, 305, 313, Feb. 6, 9, 21.

[9] *Grey*, ii. 404–7, Feb. 9.

[10] *Cal. S.P. Ven. 1673–5*, p. 220, Feb. 23; *Letters to Williamson*, ii. 147,
Talbot, Feb. 13; PRO 31/3/130, f. 71v, Ruvigny, Feb. 19.

As for the defence of Anglicanism, this was restricted to a revised test bill which would have extended the oath against transubstantiation to members of the Lower House.[1] One reason for the comparative lack of activity may have been the measures already under discussion in the Upper House, which included a bill for educating the children of catholic princes by protestant divines, and the compelling of James himself to take the Oath of Allegiance, in company with the remainder of the peers.[2] The request for a proclamation against priests and Jesuits was made and granted as before and with this the protestant zealots appear to have been satisfied.[3]

Still linked with this programme of safeguards were three further investigations by the Commons. The first concerned their own members: it was alleged during one debate that a member had received a bribe.[4] The Commons at once demanded an enquiry and eventually it was proposed that every member should purge himself by oath.[5] So far as the records show this was never done: the Venetian ambassador's explanation was that Ruvigny had at once threatened to publish, first the names of the Dutch pensioners, and then those of France, if this dangerous suggestion was not killed.[6] Ruvigny, however, makes no mention of this in his letters to Louis, and since the Venetian ambassador was generally hostile to the Commons, his story may well be untrue.[7] True or not, the currency of

---

[1] *C.J.* ix. 296, 300, 312, 314, Jan. 21, 29, Feb. 5, 6, 20, 23; *Grey*, ii. 446, Feb. 22; *Cal. S.P. Dom. 1673–5*, p. 136; Verney MSS., Claydon, Sir Ralph Verney, Jan. 22.

[2] *L.J.* xii, 604, 618, 626, Jan. 12, 24, Feb. 3; *Cal. S.P. Ven. 1673–5*, p. 232, Feb. 28; *H.M.C. 9th Rep.*, pt. ii, House of Lords, pp. 45–6, Feb. 21; *Letters to Williamson*, ii. 136, Talbot, Jan. 30; Verney MSS., Claydon, Sir Ralph Verney, Jan. 15, 26.

[3] *C.J.* ix. 292, Jan. 12; *Cal. S.P. Dom. 1673–5*, p. 102, Jan. 14; *Cal. S.P. Ven. 1673–5*, p. 183, Nov. 28.

[4] *Grey*, ii. 374–5, Jan. 31; *C.J.* ix. 301. The sum named was £5,000. The accusation was made in the middle of an attempt to hasten Buckingham's dismissal and the accused member was Howe, who had been prominent in Arlington's defence. Could this have been yet another private feud?

[5] *C.J.* ix. 301–2, Jan. 31; *Cal. S.P. Dom. 1673–5*, p. 142, Feb. 6.

[6] *Cal. S.P. Ven. 1673–5*, p. 215, Feb. 16.

[7] For the Venetian envoy's attitude to the Commons see *Cal. S.P. Ven. 1673–5*, p. 206, Jan. 23. This allegation seems to have escaped the many letter writers who comment on this session.

such a rumour is itself a pointer to the development of 'corruption' in the next few years.[1]

The other two enquiries concerned the standing army, and the condition of Ireland. On February 7 the Committee of Grievances called for the army's disbandment. On February 11 their complaint was extended to include the troops raised by Lauderdale in Scotland.[2] In vain Henry Coventry spoke of the need to preserve public order, recalling the apprentices' riot of 1668.[3] Lee urged the King to find his best defence in the hearts of his subjects; Birch doubted the value of existing garrisons; Holt spoke of 'Praetorians and janissaries', who might end by turning against their master.[4] Charles eventually agreed to disband his army and to order the Irish troops back to their home country;[5] he forbore to mention that one contingent would continue to fight for Louis as 'volunteers', a decision which was to cause much trouble in the future.[6]

Sending the Irish troops home was a welcome gesture, but one that served also to direct members' attention to that kingdom. At the same time Lords Aungier, Orrery, and O'Brien seem to have launched a private vendetta against Viscount Ranelagh, who was both Chancellor of the Irish Exchequer and Farmer of the entire revenue of that country.[7]

Accusations of peculation were soon extended into renewed complaints against favour shown towards catholics in Ireland. This involved the Lord Lieutenant, Essex, together with his predecessors, Berkely, Robartes, and of course Ormonde, whilst it also provided another chance to embarrass Arlington who,

---

[1] Accusations of bribery had, of course, been made on several occasions, supra, Chapters VI, VIII, X, XI. The court at least took Dutch bribes seriously enough to institute a long, though unsuccessful, search for lists of members who had received them, *Cal. S.P. Dom. 1673-5*, pp. 264-306, May 26-July 14, 1674, passim, and see Haley, op. cit., p. 198.

[2] *Grey*, ii. 390-9, 413-14, Feb. 7, 11; *C.J.* ix. 305, 307.

[3] *Grey*, ii. 392, Feb. 7. For the riot in question see B.M. Add. MSS. 36,916, f. 89, Starkey, March 28, 1668; B.M. Egerton MSS. 2539, f. 180, Nicholas, March 24.

[4] *Grey*, ii. 395, 397, Feb. 7.

[5] *C.J.* ix. 307, Feb. 11.

[6] Haley, op. cit., p. 183, and infra, Chapter XIII.

[7] T. Carte, *Ormonde*, iv. 501, gives Ranelagh a very poor character. A year earlier Aungier had been accused by Ranelagh himself of using general attacks on the Irish administration as a cover for a private feud, *Cal. S.P. Dom. 1673*, pp. 100-1, March 29.

as Secretary for the northern province, had given the King's representatives their instructions.[1] In addition to these attacks there was apparently a concurrent attempt to lift the embargo on Irish Cattle.[2] With so many interests involved charges and countercharges were scattered wildly; several of the leading actors rushed off letters to Essex excusing their own behaviour and blaming that of everyone else,[3] and after two days the House wearily set up committees to examine the revenue, militia, armed forces and religion of Ireland.[4] To these committees at least the prorogation may have proved a welcome release from the task of compiling a report.

The opposition had thus put forward attacks on several leading ministers, a series of bills restricting the prerogative, and a new batch of enquiries likely to cause trouble in the near future. Whilst they had pursued their programme Charles had been trying to bring the House back to the topic of supply. On January 24, a day on which the House had arranged to debate the 'grievances of the nation', Charles had suddenly released the text of new proposals made by the Dutch, which he himself considered to be 'in a more decent style' than those which they had previously presented.[5] These proposals came in reply to overtures made by Arlington, but the idea of showing them to the Parliament, as 'a bone' to set one party, or one House, against the other, seems to have come from Danby.[6] If Charles hoped to gain a supply through them he was to be disappointed, but he certainly did succeed in opening a split in the opposition ranks.

The King had offered his information on a Saturday. Unfortunately Henry Coventry's health had given way—he had throughout this session been sustaining almost single-handed the

[1] *Grey*, ii. 435–40, 441–5, Feb. 18, 20.

[2] *Cal. S.P. Ven. 1673–5*, p. 229, Feb. 20; *Cal. S.P. Dom. 1673–5*, pp. 166–9, Feb. 1673; B.M. Stowe MSS. 204, p. 116, Harbord, Jan. 27; Verney MSS., Claydon, Sir Ralph Verney, Jan. 22; *Essex Papers*, p. 167, Aungier, Jan. 27.

[3] *Essex Papers*, pp. 177–9, Orrery, Feb. 21; B.M. Stowe MSS. 204, f. 218, 220, Aungier, Ranelagh, Feb. 21.

[4] *C.J.* ix. 312, Feb. 20.

[5] *L.J.* xii. 616–18; B.M. Stowe MSS. 204, f. 100, Southwell, Jan. 24.

[6] *Essex Papers*, pp. 167–8, Conway, Jan. 27; Barbour, *Arlington*, p. 236. Earlier Talbot had been trying to produce a more amenable attitude in the Commons by passing on news sent from Williamson, who was attending the peace negotiations at Nimwegen, *Letters to Williamson*, ii. 126, Talbot, Jan. 23.

duties of the court[1]—and Garraway was able to secure an adjournment.[2] On the Sunday several members are believed to have discussed the new terms with agents of the Dutch.[3] Then, on January 26 and 27, the main debates took place.[4] In Grey's rather confused report two main groups can be distinguished. The first, which included William Coventry, Holland, Clarges, Birch, Powle, Capel, Harbord, Howard, and Seymour, was ready to approve, and even to take responsibility for, a peace on the new terms. The second, which included Sacheverell, Hampden, Lee, Cavendish, and, rather surprisingly, Littleton,[5] wanted at the least to insist on a 'separate' peace—in other words to emphasize our desertion of France—whilst some would have refused all advice and thus left Charles to extricate himself from a situation for which they considered him entirely responsible. On the first day the debate was adjourned; on the second it was agreed that the King should be advised to make a 'speedy', but neither an 'honourable' nor a 'separate', peace.[6] After another short delay, caused by a threatened quarrel with the Lords, both Houses addressed the King in these terms.[7]

During these discussions Henry Coventry had shown himself sufficiently recovered to make one last plea for a supply.[8] At the same time Ruvigny had himself drafted an address which deplored the desertion of an ally, and had tried to get this adopted by the Lords.[9] Neither Coventry nor Ruvigny met with any success and on February 11 Charles told Parliament that

[1] *Letters to Williamson*, ii.129, Southwell, Jan. 23.

[2] *Grey*, ii. 338–41, Jan. 24; B.M. Stowe MSS. 204, f. 102, Harbord, Jan. 26. The House were said to have been pleased but rather dazed by the news, *Letters to Williamson*, ii. 129, Southwell, Jan. 23.

[3] Haley, op. cit., p. 179.

[4] *Grey*, ii. 343–9, 350–7, Jan. 26, 27; *Cal. S.P. Dom. 1673–5*, p. 125, Aungier, Jan. 30.

[5] Who seems to have been running against the policy of his patron, Arlington.

[6] *Grey*, ii. 363–4, 375–7, Jan. 29, Feb. 3; *C.J.* ix. 300, Jan. 29; *L.J.* xii. 622–3, 625, Jan. 28, 29, Feb. 3; *Letters to Williamson*, ii. 134, Talbot, Jan. 30; Verney MSS., Claydon, Sir Ralph Verney, Jan. 28.

[7] *C.J.* ix. 302, Feb. 3; *L.J.* xii. 625, Feb. 3.

[8] *Grey*, ii. 352, Jan. 27. He gave as his reason the need to supply the Navy.

[9] *Cal. S.P. Ven. 1673–5*, p. 211, Jan. 31; *H.M.C. 9th Rep.*, pt. ii, House of Lords MSS., p. 40, Jan. 29.

M

he had, in accordance with their advice, concluded a peace.[1] Still no supply was forthcoming;[2] on the other hand, as we have already seen, a number of unwelcome bills were nearing the point at which Charles might be asked to give them his approval. Without consulting his cabinet council, Charles came suddenly to the Parliament on February 24 and, neither blaming nor thanking its members, declared the session at an end.[3]

The immediate result of the prorogation was to unnerve the opposition. Showing a foretaste of the panic which was to ruin them in 1681, leading speakers burnt their papers, cancelled a 'party' dinner, and dispersed hurriedly to their homes.[4] In an open contest with the prerogative the odds were still against them though if their programme for the session had been completed the balance might well have been more favourable. So far as exercising control over the King's ministers was concerned the Commons had still been able only to damage those who, like Buckingham or Clarendon, had first forfeited the support of the King. Arlington had retired at his own wish and Lauderdale, the most hated of all, remained in office secure in his master's protection.[5] On policy the opposition had enjoyed far greater success: within a year Charles had been forced to abandon both toleration and the French alliance. Granted this change in policy some, like Danby and Henry Coventry, saw no reason why harmony between King and Parliament should not be restored.[6] The debates on the proposal for a peace, and indeed

[1] *C.J.* ix. 307.

[2] The House voted their thanks and returned at once to a discussion of grievances, *Grey*, ii. 413, Feb. 11; *C.J.* ix. 307.

[3] For comments on this prorogation see *Letters to Williamson*, ii. 155, 156, Aungier, Talbot, Feb. 24, 28; B.M. Stowe MSS. 204, ff. 228, 230, 237, 273, Bridgeman, Aungier, Feb. 24, Harbord, Feb. 26, Ormonde, March 3; Tanner MSS., Bodleian Library, 42, f. 87, Hobart, Feb. 24; Coventry MSS., Longleat, 83, f. 36, Henry Coventry, Feb. 24; Verney MSS., Claydon, Sir Ralph Verney, Feb. 26, March 2; *Essex Papers*, pp. 179–80, Conway, Feb. 24; *Cal. S.P. Ven. 1673–5*, p. 232, Feb. 28. Ormonde and Henry Coventry stress that it came as a surprise to the Council; Verney and Hobart were angry; Conway sardonically amused.

[4] *Letters to Williamson*, ii. 157, Talbot, Feb. 28; Haley, op. cit., p. 191.

[5] He eventually gave up his posts between 1680 and 1682, apparently on account of declining health, having previously survived a long series of addresses demanding his removal.

[6] Browning, *Danby*, i. 146–9; Coventry MSS., Longleat, 83., f. 40v, March 13, and other letters quoted in my thesis on the Coventrys, Oxford

on the impeachments, had shown that there was still a very real division between the extreme and moderate opponents of the court. Two major obstacles, however, remained: our peace with the Dutch did not mean the end of Charles' obligations to, or hopes from, Louis XIV, and, in the long run still more serious, it was unlikely that even the most loyal cavaliers would be prepared to oppose limitations on the prerogative if these were presented as safeguards against a catholic successor.

B.Litt., 1954, pp. 123–5. Danby's optimism was such that he had even sent overtures to Sacheverell, *Essex Papers*, pp. 159–61, Conway, Jan. 10.

CHAPTER XIII

DANBY'S HOPELESS QUEST

FOR ten years Charles and his ministers had groped their way towards control of the Lower House. Now, after the debacle of Charles' 'secret policy', Danby had to begin all over again. In some ways his position was more fortunate than had been that of Clarendon. Though Arlington retained his place at court[1] and Charles still visited Buckingham,[2] Danby, as Lord Treasurer, was undisputed head of the ministry in a way which Clarendon had seldom been. Moreover the lessons of 1670–71 had not been lost on him. A cavalier parliament needed a cavalier policy: at the same time a few 'gratifications', both to loyal supporters and to trouble-makers, would smooth any manager's path.[3] Nevertheless Danby not only failed to re-establish control over the Commons but in fact never came near to success. In the first ten years the demands of the central mass of members, as distinct from the professional trouble-makers, had been irritating to the King but had not seriously challenged his prerogative. Even the trouble-makers had been ready to serve the King, provided that they could do it with some profit to themselves. Now the central mass were coming to demand complete neutrality in the Franco-Dutch conflict, if not actual intervention on the side of the Dutch,[4] whilst in home policy their programme of safeguards against a catholic successor, expressed in the bills of 1674, called for concessions by the crown almost as far-reaching as those eventually extorted by the revolution of 1688. As for the new trouble-makers, they were no longer merely seeking office. Without submitting their demands and policies to more detailed scrutiny it is not safe to hazard more than an opinion, but at first sight at least it would seem that Shaftesbury, Sacheverell, Russell, and their comparatively small band of followers, were aiming at something nearer a republic than a parliamentary monarchy.[5]

---

[1] Barbour, *Arlington*, pp. 243, 249–52.
[2] Browning, *Danby*, i. 240; Feiling, *History of the Tory Party*, p. 156.
[3] Browning, op. cit., i. 146–9; Feiling, op. cit., pp. 154, 157–9.   [4] Infra.
[5] Betty Behrens, 'The Whig theory of the Constitution in the Reign of

With the aspirations of these extremists Danby had no sympathy whatever. The aims of the centre block were, however, a very different matter. However much he might distribute from the Excise, however many places he might find for faithful friends, Danby could not get Charles the money he demanded without the support of at least a large section of the uncommitted centre.[1] With their demands, moreover, he very largely concurred: he wanted greater hostility towards France, and as for the problem of the catholic succession his famous proposal for an oath against any change in the established government of Church or State[2] was as powerful a weapon against Catholicism as against Whiggery, a fact which James perhaps recognized when he attempted to amend it in the House of Lords.[3] Unlike Clarendon, Danby was thus in sympathy with the desires of a majority of the Lower House, yet he was never able to express this sympathy in action. The need to retain the King's favour caused him to appear as the supporter of a policy he detested and his enemies, who were at least as much involved in French intrigues as he was, were able to use his own letters, quoted out of context, to destroy him.[4]

Glancing quickly over the remaining sessions of this Cavalier Parliament we find a long series of misunderstandings between Danby and the Commons. In 1675, after he had put forward a Bill to revive the 1665 oath against changes in the establishment of Church or State,[5] he tried hard to coax the Lower House into granting a supply. When Arlington's friends launched one of the factious impeachments so common in this reign, Danby had the satisfaction of finding not only his own paid followers but also several independent members ready to recognize the

---

Charles II', *Cambridge Hist. Journal*, vii (1941), especially pp. 42–3, 63–7; F. S. Ronalds, *The Attempted Whig Revolution of 1678–1681* (1937), pp. 77–8; E. S. de Beer, 'The Development of Political Parties during the ministry of Danby', London M.A. thesis, 1923, especially pp. 1–15. This view was also advanced by the Warden of St Anthony's College, Oxford, in a course of lectures given in 1953 and may be reinforced by a study of William Sacheverell's speeches, of which a list will be found in *The First Whig* by Sir George Sitwell (privately printed 1894), p. 205.

[1] Browning, op. cit., i. 171, 221, iii. 61–2, 94, 120–1.
[2] Infra.
[3] Browning, op. cit., i. 154 and compare Feiling, op. cit., p. 156.
[4] Infra.
[5] Browning, op. cit., i. 152–4; Feiling, op. cit., pp. 160–1.

evident inadequacy of the charges, and the matter was quickly dropped.[1] When, however, it was urged that Lauderdale, whom Charles still retained in office, should be removed,[2] or that the English troops left in French service after the Treaty of 1674 should be recalled,[3] the voting went the other way,[4] and on these points Danby could not get Charles' permission to yield. Thus when a very reasonable proposal to give money for the navy was put before the Commons it was considered, not on its merits, but in the light of the administration's refusal to grant requests which seemed to many loyal members both reasonable and moderate. Pepys' carefully compiled accounts never got a hearing,[5] and even before the session had been snarled up by another dispute between Commons and Lords,[6] the former had passed a resolution barring any further motion for supply.[7]

In the autumn of 1675 the story was much the same. Charles was asked to recall the troops serving with the French—a bill was drafted which might possibly have convicted the future Duke of Marlborough of treason[8]—and several of the bills of 1674 were again revived.[9] This time Danby rallied his pen-

[1] *C.J.* ix. 324-9, April 26–May 4; *Grey*, iii. 40-7, 49-53, 58-96, April 26–30, May 3; Browning, op. cit., i. 155-60.

[2] *C.J.* ix. 316-17, 322, 331-2, 348, April 14, 15, 23, May 6, 7, 31; *Grey*, iii. 24-33, 17-112, April 23, May 7.

[3] *C.J.* ix. 319, 330, 333-5, 343, 351, April 19, May 5, 8, 10, 11, 20, June 2; *Grey*, iii. 3-9, 103-4, 116-39, April 19, May 5, 10, 11; Browning. op. cit., i. 160-1.

[4] For votes against Lauderdale see *C.J.* ix. 322, 330, 348, April 23, May 5, 31: So far as the English troops were concerned the court won a division on May 11 but the opposition seem to have carried the other resolutions *nem. con.*

[5] *Grey*, iii. 34-40, 96-102, April 24, May 4; A. Bryant, *Samuel Pepys: The Years of Peril* (1948), pp. 145-7.

[6] *C.J.* ix. 329, 333, 335-57, May 4, 8 and May 12–June 9, passim; *Grey*, iii. 112-15, 139-389, May 12–June 9, passim; T. Howell, *State Trials*, vi.15 1122-70; Feiling, op. cit., p. 160.

[7] *C.J.* ix. 340, May 17. They agreed, by 169 to 121 to accept no new bills except from the Lords, and bills from the Lords could not refer to money. This resolution did not, however, prevent the progress of Danby's anglican test bill, indeed it positively encouraged its prosecution. See also *Grey*, iii. 156-66, May 17.

[8] *C.J.* ix. 363, Oct. 23; *Grey*, iii. 334-6, Oct. 23.

[9] *C.J.* ix. 358-61, 363-4, Oct. 13, 18, 20, 21, 23, 26; *Grey*, iii. 311, 317-323, Oct. 20, 21. These bills concerned catholics as members of the Commons, illegal imprisonment, illegal exactions, and abuses in collecting the Hearth Tax.

sioners and Pepys got a hearing for his figures, but found members contradicting him on technical points in a way which argued either extreme factiousness or a considered refusal to trust Charles until the latter offered to meet at least some of the Commons' demands.[1] A meagre promise of money was made, but it would have been too little to achieve any useful result;[2] the Commons would no doubt have protested bitterly in the next session if the ships had not been built, despite having given less than half of what was required. As in the summer the court had lost control over the session and it was almost a relief when the inter-House dispute flared up and produced another deadlock.[3]

For all the apparent failure of 1675 there was in fact one ray of hope, though it was hope for Charles himself rather than for Danby. If the Treasurer found the Commons unhelpful, they were still too loyal for Shaftesbury and his friends of the extreme opposition. These men, roughly identifiable with those who had refused to approve Charles' peace treaty of 1674, were out less to restore the earlier pattern of co-operation between King and Commons than to impose parliamentary dictatorship on the King, and they now pressed strongly for the dissolution which one of them, Buckingham, had been advocating for nearly ten years.[4] This naturally horrified the place men but it also shocked the moderates of the centre. Further demands by this

---

[1] *Grey*, iii. 323–33, 372–417, Oct. 22, Nov. 2, 3, 4, 6. The leading opposition spokesman was Sir William Coventry, Pepys' former friend and colleague, who had stood by him when under personal attack in the previous year, supra, Chapter XII. Coventry's attitude in these debates is hard to excuse, or even explain, yet it is interesting to note that he and Pepys were still able to exchange compliments amid their wrangling, *Grey*, iii. 415–16, Nov. 6, a fact overlooked by Bryant, op. cit., pp. 150–6, who gives a very critical account of the opposition's attitude at this time. Coventry may have been embittered by the failure of his moderate Place Bill in the previous session, *C.J.* ix. 321, 326–7; *Grey*, iii. 56–7, April 22, 29, 1675. A draft of this Bill is in Coventry MSS., Longleat, 8, ff. 168–86.

[2] The sum offered was £200,000 for twenty ships, *C.J.* ix. 369, Nov. 6. W. A. Shaw, *Cal. Treasury Books 1676–79*, pp. xlvii–lii, states that in the following year £600,000 was too little to build 30 ships, and see also Bryant, op. cit., p. 156.

[3] *C.J.* ix. 377–80, Nov. 14–19, passim; *Grey*, iv. 9–53, Nov. 13–19, passim; Howell, op. cit., vi. 1170–88.

[4] Supra, Chapter VIII; Browning, op. cit., i. 182–4; Feiling, op. cit., pp. 161–2.

extreme group were in time to lead to the Exclusion crisis and to the final reaction in favour of the crown.

It has been said that this offered hope to Charles but not to Danby. By the end of 1675 it seemed clear that the latter's bid for the support of the centre had failed. However, when Parliament met again in 1677, he was able to take advantage of Shaftesbury's extremism to make another appeal to the Commons,[1] and this time supply was granted before the Commons made their requests. The requests were not, however, forgotten, and by April 1677, Charles, already promised £600,000 for ships,[2] was being pressed by both Danby and Parliament to engage actively against France, with a guarantee of full financial support.[3] Charles, however, had bitter memories of the Dutch war of 1664. He would not engage himself until Parliament had given him the necessary funds;[4] Parliament would not produce the money until Charles took some definite step to show his good faith. Sir William Coventry, by now detested by both Danby and Shaftesbury,[5] but leading those members—probably a majority—who still hoped to work with the King, attempted to organize a conditional grant which would be confirmed when Charles had made an alliance with the Dutch.[6] Charles, forgetting apparently his attitude in earlier years,[7] took offence at this invasion of his

[1] The Commons firmly rejected Shaftesbury's attempt to force a dissolution and a few days later the court were able to put their motion for supply, *C.J.* ix. 384, 386, Feb. 15–17, 21; *Grey*, iv. 64–72, 80–95, 103–30, Feb. 15, 16, 17, 20, 21; Browning, op. cit., i. 212–20.

[2] *C.J.* ix. 386, 389, Feb. 21, 27. The Commons also granted a renewal of the Additional Excise of 1671, *C.J.* ix. 398, 406, March 12, 26. See on all this Browning, op. cit., i. 220.

[3] *C.J.* ix. 393, 306, 406, 408, March 6, 10, 26, 29; *Grey*, iv. 188–204, 223–4, 241–53, 255, March 6, 7, 10, 13, 14, 15; Browning, op. cit., i. 221–2; Feiling, op. cit., pp. 162–4, 167.

[4] *C.J.* ix. 418, 422–3, 424, April 11, 16, 23; Browning, op. cit., i. 222, 227; Feiling, op. cit., p. 168.

[5] Browning, op. cit., i. 213–14, note 4. Compare an earlier example of Shaftesbury's hostility to Coventry given by W. D. Christie, *Shaftesbury*, ii. 201.

[6] *C.J.* ix. 419, 425, April 12, May 23; *Grey*, iv. 343–53, 361–88, April 12, 13, May 23, 25; Browning, op. cit., i. 228–31. Coventry summed up his views in a letter to his nephew, Thynne MSS., Longleat, 16, f. 256, May 13: '... the King may have money if he close with his people's desires ... we must either trust the King of England or the French King; ... for my part I was for trusting the King of England.'

[7] Supra, Chapters VII, VIII, XII.

prerogative[1] and the proposal failed amid mutual, and bitter, recriminations.[2]

In the autumn of 1677 Danby tried what was really his last throw. Charles was persuaded to approve a marriage between his niece, Mary, and William of Orange. Danby hoped that this would lead to a full military alliance and Charles may possibly have been prepared to give this a trial.[3] In fact the obstacles proved insuperable. The Spanish, in whose territory the fighting would take place, rejected our help.[4] The French ambassador joined forces with the extreme wing of the opposition, their common aim being to prevent Charles getting any money.[5] More important than these well-known intrigues was Danby's failure to produce an alliance which would satisfy the moderate centre, who had by now acquired a rather unrealistic faith that Louis could be pushed back to the frontiers he had held at the beginning of his reign.[6] Instead of arguing the case logically, the court, represented in the Commons by Henry Coventry, refused for three crucial months to release details of the new alliance.[7] By this time the Commons had lost all confidence in the new policy,[8] whilst Charles was again making overtures to France.[9]

[1] E. R. Turner, 'Parliament and Foreign Affairs', *Eng. Hist. Rev.* xxxiv (1919), pp. 172–97, especially 178–80; Browning, op. cit., i. 231.

[2] For Charles see supra, note 1; for the Commons, *Grey*, iv. 389–91, May 28, July 16 and also Spencer MSS., Althorp, Halifax series, File 10, letter of Thomas Thynne, May 27, 1677.

[3] Browning, op. cit., i. 232–4, 247–56; Ogg, op. cit., ii. 546.

[4] Browning, op. cit., i. 258; Bryant, *King Charles II* (1955), p. 210.

[5] Browning, op. cit., i. 260–1; Ogg, op. cit., ii. 551; Feiling, op. cit., pp. 170–2; C. L. Grose, 'French ambassador's reports on financial relations with members of Parliament, 1677–78', *Eng. Hist. Rev.* xliv (1929), pp. 625–8.

[6] *C.J.* ix. 428, 430, Jan. 29, 31; *Grey*, v. 17–32, 37–47, Jan. 29, 31; Ogg, op. cit., ii. 550; Browning, op. cit., i. 262. Many historians have made scathing reference to this demand for a 'Pyranean Peace', without allowing for the ignorance in which the Commons had been kept by the administration. For a more favourable view of this demand see my thesis on 'The Parliamentary Career of Sir William and Mr Henry Coventry', Oxford B.Litt., 1954, pp. 165–76.

[7] *Grey*, v. 22–3, Jan. 29; *C.J.* ix. 431–2, Feb. 4. The proposals were eventually released on April 29, *C.J.* ix. 464–6. See also Ogg, op. cit., ii. 553–4; Feiling, op. cit., pp. 169–70 and Browning, op. cit., i. 262–3, the last of whom fails to provide an entirely satisfactory explanation of the delay.

[8] This is made clear in numerous debates among which are *Grey*, v. 292–315, 318–58, May 2, 3, 4, 6. See also Feiling, op. cit., p. 169.

[9] Browning, op. cit., i. 271–8; Ogg, op. cit., ii. 553–6.

The net result of the sessions of spring and early summer 1678 was to provide Charles with 9,000 men, quartered expensively at Ostend,[1] to leave Louis free to make peace,[2] and to convince both King and Commons more deeply than ever that the other party was not to be trusted.[3] It is difficult to believe that even if Oates and Tongue had not produced their 'revelations' Danby could have wiped out the bitterness of 1677 and 1678. As it happened, however, the Popish Plot aroused sufficient hysteria for Danby's enemies to be able to force his dismissal.[4] With that dismissal came the end of the Cavalier Parliament;[5] the three assemblies which followed were such as no Stuart King could have worked with,[6] and for this reign parliamentary monarchy was at an end.

[1] Browning, op. cit., i. 270; Bryant, op. cit., pp. 213–14. For requests that these troops should be disbanded see *C.J.* ix. 483, May 27 and the debate on that date in *Grey*, vi. 15–26.

[2] Ogg, op. cit., ii. 554–7.

[3] Ibid., ii. 538; Feiling, op. cit., 169, 173; *C.J.* ix. 486, 499–500, June 1, 18; *Grey*, vi. 48–62, 94–105, June 1, 18.

[4] Browning, op. cit., i. 301–21; Feiling, op. cit., pp. 173–4; *Grey*, vi. 337–65, 366–87, 399–400, Dec. 19–21, 28.

[5] Browning, op. cit., i. 310–13; Feiling, op. cit., p. 175; Ogg, op. cit., ii. 576–8. A gap in the Journals at this point means that there is no official record of the prorogation.

[6] For arguments as to how far these parliaments were representative of the nation see articles by E. Lipson and Mrs George, in *Eng. Hist. Rev.* xxviii (1913), pp. 67–72 and xlv (1930), pp. 574–8. The second of these articles, arguing that the assemblies were not a true representative seems to tally best with the events of 1681–85.

CHAPTER XIV

CONCLUSION

T HE question posed at the beginning of this study was whether parliamentary monarchy could have provided a workable system for the government of Restoration England. Some answer to this must now be attempted. The session of 1663 confirmed what earlier sessions had suggested: that the strong loyalty felt by the majority of the members towards the Crown was not as great as the loyalty which they felt towards the Established Church. Charles, for his part, made it clear that he wished to extend some form of toleration to those of his subjects who remained outside the Establishment. Neither the King nor the Lower House was prepared to give way; when the former tried to achieve his aim by non-parliamentary methods he not only failed to do this but goaded the Commons into demanding new sanctions, which eventually became so severe that they conflicted with the legitimate prerogatives of the Crown. Given this conflict it appears that a breakdown of the revived constitution could only have been a matter of time. The circumstances of that breakdown were, however, governed by a number of subsidiary factors.

During the first ten years of the Cavalier Parliament's life Charles chafed, for the most part, in silence. Three times he made proposals for some form of toleration but when these were rejected he appeared to accept defeat. Religion did not, therefore, become an obvious matter of dispute between the Commons and the Crown. Far more time was given to arguments over supply and here the differences in viewpoint were never fundamental. In the Convention Parliament Charles' representatives had accepted a bad estimate, and the incompetence of the Treasurer made the effect of this still more serious. The Commons, however, continued to accept an obligation to provide for Charles' needs. They more than once increased his peacetime revenue, voted unprecedented sums to pay for the Dutch war, and, overriding a hostile minority, they refrained from holding back supply until Charles had satisfied them on all other matters. Such conflict as did arise came very largely from the inability of the court to understand the reasons for their master's insolvency, and their consequent failure to make the situation clear to the House. The Commons, as tax payers, demanded evidence of need before they made fresh grants, and if they looked also for assurances that their money would be well spent they can hardly be blamed. By 1667 both sides had lost their tempers but when, three years later, Clifford and Downing gave the Commons a few plain figures the members' response showed that their willingness to provide for *proved* needs had remained unimpaired. The grants made before 1664, the war grants of 1664 to 1666, and the final grants of 1670 to 1671 make it difficult to accept the picture of a niggardly Commons starving a patriot King.

Less serious than supply, but producing considerable heat, was the controversy over imported Irish Cattle. This was a matter less of principle than of self interest: it was exasperating for the King to see an impoverished part of his domains reduced to a still worse condition to satisfy one section of his subjects. Possibly Clarendon's advice should have been accepted and the Commons have been told that this was one topic on which the royal veto would be used. As it was Charles fell between two stools, surrendering with a bad grace and winning little gratitude from those whom he presumably hoped to placate. Despite all the interest it aroused, however, this was not a matter of the highest importance. The effect on Ireland of the embargo was considerably less than had been expected, and it could not be said that such a difference was sufficient to do permanent harm to the relationship between the Commons and the King.

Much more dangerous would have been a claim by the Commons to control Charles' choice of officials, or even to insist on the dismissal of any who had incurred their distrust. To read Pepys' diary or the letters of some court correspondents it might appear that such claims were being both made and enforced, but when looked at more closely the Commons' proceedings appear much less serious a threat. Clarendon, to take the most eminent victim, was driven from office by ministerial intrigue, and further persecuted by his ex-colleagues and a few place-hungry members. Even then he might have stood a good chance of escape if he had only kept his nerve. Pepys himself, and William Coventry, gathered 'papers' to show the House and found a rational majority who were prepared to hear and accept a systematic defence. The apparent attacks of 'the Commons' on members of the administration were certainly helped by a general mood of dissatisfaction and suspicion, but for success they required the leadership of men far more ambitious, and indeed more ruthless, than the ordinary backbenchers, and they caused little harm to men who were neither betrayed nor overcome by panic.

Religion apart, the greatest problem which Charles had to face was his lack of able speakers to 'lead' the Lower House. Clarendon, without our present knowledge of Elizabethan parliaments, thought that if a few of his friends made the King's wishes known a majority in the Commons would see these carried out. On many issues this might have proved correct, but the system was weakened by bad briefing of the interpreting committee, by the reluctance of even that committee to accept the idea of toleration, and by the alternative court 'lines' suggested by the rival court group. So far as debating was concerned the court had Finch and the two Coventrys,with possibly Charlton as a useful committee chairman, but they lacked reserves and their silent voters were irregular in attendance. On some occasions, as in the great supply debate of 1664, the court mustered its full strength and scored a resounding success, but all too often its supporters argued amongst themselves, failed to seize the initiative, or were simply absent when the time came to vote.

Into the vacant role of 'leaders of the House' stepped a group of competent debaters, half linked with Clarendon's court rivals, but purporting to speak as 'honest country gentlemen'. Honest they may have been: they were mostly loyal to the cause of toleration, none of them became involved in Charles' secret intrigues, and if they had their eyes on the perquisites of office then that was still nothing of which to be ashamed. Countrymen, however, they were not, if this term is to be taken in its usual sense. Far from being disinterested amateurs these were skilful and ambitious professionals, and as such considerably more difficult to deal with. There were, however, limits to their power: when they denounced grievances, the embezzling of prize goods, the sale of offices, the misappropriation of supply, they could carry the House easily, but when they challenged cavalier prejudice with a Triennial Bill or a proposal for toleration they received a crushing snub. They could ride, but not turn, the tide of opinion, and the desertion of a number of them to the court followed, rather than produced, the swing in true country opinion that took place in the spring of 1670.

By 1669 Charles had to face a choice. Parliament had given him a reasonably large revenue, but one not quite large enough for the administration's needs. If, moreover, he ever wanted to fight a war he would have to rely on parliamentary supply. The House of Commons had shown itself restless, irritable, and suspicious; it had thwarted his efforts to bring in toleration, forced him to discriminate against his Irish subjects, and was in the middle of a tedious, and not particularly well conducted, enquiry into the 'miscarriages' of the recent war. During the previous session it had become clear that the dominant group within the Commons was composed of 'Clarendonians' or 'old cavaliers', in other words of members loyal to the Crown but still more loyal to the Anglican church. From such a body he might hope for money but only if he was prepared to find some competent speakers, to buy over one or two of the professional 'opposition' and, most important, to respect the religious prejudices of the cavalier majority. If he was not prepared to do these things he would have to look elsewhere for supply.

It would be doing Charles scant justice to suppose him incapable of making this analysis for himself. In 1668 he had in fact told the French ambassador that the cavaliers controlled the Commons. Yet perhaps from irritation at the Commons' presumption, or perhaps from a genuine love of toleration, he chose the more dangerous course and set in motion secret negotiations with France. Having done this, he allowed his ministers to make one last bid for parliamentary support. Abandoning toleration they found in the Second Conventicle Act an offering sufficient to win back the loyalty of the cavaliers. Adroit canvassing of individuals and the offer of a place or two rounded off this enterprise, and by the time that Charles left to sign the Dover treaty the Lower House had been reduced to its most compliant state during the whole reign. Charles' treaty with Louis brought him the prospect of some £300,000 a year, balanced by the obligation to finance a new war. His second line of attack, the campaign to win back the Commons, brought him £160,000 a year, soon to be much increased by the trade boom, a lump sum of over £300,000, and no additional expenses. Charles may well have wondered, in the spring of 1671, if he had chosen wisely, but by that time he had gone too far to draw back.

The further consequences of Charles' decision will concern us shortly. Before passing to these, however, we must say a little more about the organization of the Commons at this time. Both court and opposition drew up lists of those on whom it was hoped, or feared, that the King could rely. As early as 1666 Broderick reckoned court strength at 140, though in fact the division figures gave him the lie. In that same session the court are said to have united against a proposal for electoral reform, a sign of some political sophistication, and even reports of divisions in the court ranks suggest that those ranks were, to some extent, defined. Talk of bribery again suggests cohesion; Andrew Marvell writes bitterly of the court's discipline, and if all such references were collected together the existence of a court party might well seem an established fact.

Two qualifications must, however, be made. The members on the various lists compiled by the court are usually credited with a specific allegiance to one or other of the ministers, and these ministers were often at odds among themselves. In the second place the activities of most of those on the lists cannot be known—the absence of division lists, and many members' silence in debates, makes it even uncertain whether they attended the House, and of those who left traces by no means all filled the roles ascribed to them. The divisions and vacillations of the court leaders have already been noticed; it seems that they were frequently reflected in the conduct of the rank and file.

As for the 'opposition', this was still more nebulous a term. By 1663 the existence of some members who were out to cause trouble had already been recognized, but most of these seem to have been the place hunters to whom we have already referred. Milward's 'old parliament gang' can be equated with the often mentioned 'presbyterians', but apart from supporting toleration this group does not seem to have acted with either unity or much effect. Howard's sixty malcontents, who met before the 1670 session, were probably responsible for the walk-out some weeks later, a remarkably well organized gesture for self-styled 'countrymen', but their names are unknown and their numbers may well have been exaggerated. The 'old cavaliers' during their period in the wilderness produced something like a party programme, but again this may have been the work of only a very small group. No minutes of party meetings survive, no correspondence between leaders, no lists of names, and, still lacking division lists or a full report of the debates, we can speak with little confidence of any formal opposition.

From these comments it will appear that neither the court's successes, nor its failures, can be attributed to party manœuvres. Particular debates may have been swayed by individuals, though if the diarists are to be trusted the course of a debate often failed to indicate which way the division would go. In general however the central mass followed their own line, combining loyalty to the Crown with suspicion of Crown servants, and with a determined adherence to the Anglican church. It was under these circumstances that Charles, having received the most generous supply of the reign, issued a Declaration indulging both dissenters and recusants, embarked on a war as the ally of the greatest of the catholic powers, pledged himself secretly to accept the catholic faith, and, for good measure, temporarily suspended payment on a number of the Exchequer's debts. The reluctance of ministers to face Parliament in the spring of 1673 can easily be understood.

The most striking feature of that spring session is the comparative recovery of the court. So long as Charles stuck to his Declaration nothing could be done, but once that was withdrawn the court majority at once reappeared. Delight at this reconciliation was by no means confined to courtiers, and when a new band of trouble-makers brought forward their grievances they failed to persuade the Commons to apply the most effective sanction by delaying the current bill of supply. The members' loyalty to the King was strong enough to survive the new foreign policy and the Stop of the Exchequer; this loyalty, and not the Venetian ambassador's ponderous revelation of bribery, provides the best explanation for the supply of March 1673.

This happy reprieve was not, however, destined to last for very long. Among the court all the old jealousies were reviving; by the autumn it would be each man for himself. On the other side the extreme opposition had found, in Sacheverell, not only a first rate debater but a leader who was prepared to extend his attacks from royal servants to royal policy, and perhaps to royalty itself. Even among the uncommitted centre, which had so recently rallied to the court, doubts were developing. The old aim of preserving the Established Church produced a rather changed effect when the threat to that church was thought to come not from 'fanatics' but from followers of Rome, and the recent conduct of certain ministers and even of the King himself appeared in a more sinister light. Brooding over the events of the previous two years even a loyal cavalier might ask if there could be any truth in the rumours of catholicism at court, and whether such rumours might explain our alliance with the great catholic autocracy of France.

For Charles it was vital to win back this moderate opposition. If it joined the extremists it might not only command a majority in the House but become infected by its new allies' ideals. It was thus highly unfortunate that during the summer of 1673 a whole series of events gave colour to the tale of a great catholic intrigue which du Moulin, in his pamphlet, was so eager to relate. French tactlessness, fear of war with Spain, Clifford's resignation and suicide were all serious, but worst of all was the revelation that the Heir Presumptive was no longer a member of the Anglican church. Not surprisingly a great flurry of political activity preceded the autumn session, and although information regarding the many 'party' meetings is sparse and unreliable it seems clear that a majority of members approached the session with at least two aims in mind. Firstly they wished to prevent the Duke from marrying a new catholic princess; secondly they wanted Charles to withdraw from the Dutch war. Quite possibly the extremists were already thinking further ahead, but if exclusion had already crossed their minds they kept the thought concealed.

The autumn session did little more than exacerbate feelings on the part of both the Commons and the King. Its sequel was the dismissal of Shaftesbury, the collapse of the Arlington-Buckingham alliance, and the disintegration of the party of the court. As for the opposition they had been divided over whether to refuse supply outright or to offer it on conditions, and the decision had gone against the extremists. On the other hand they had been united against the standing army and the Duke's marriage, and the debates on the war gave Charles little reason to expect any further grants.

In the 1674 session, the last to be studied in detail, the most dramatic events were the appearances of Arlington and Buckingham at the Bar of the House. Though essentially episodes in a private feud they gave the Commons a chance to repudiate the

N

new foreign policy, and Charles reluctantly faced the need to make peace. His decision to do this brought a momentary advantage in that once again the moderates rejected the extremists' lead and approved his action, but he was still no nearer getting a supply. In the meantime a long programme of bills had been brought forward, designed it seems to provide against the possible threat of a catholic King; several of these bills encroached on the prerogative but all seem to have enjoyed majority support. If Charles was to pacify this majority he would have to show that the Church was not in danger. Under Danby's guidance he made a fair attempt to do this, but James' position as Heir remained a stumbling block which no half measures could remove.

Ending in 1674 this study misses the best known period of party organization, but there is time for one last survey of the way in which the House was influenced and led. If Danby's court pensions had not yet begun it was already being alleged that French, Spanish and Dutch gold was reaching members, and the reports of the French ambassador confirm such suggestions. No names are available, and if they were the old lack of division lists would inhibit further investigation, but if we may judge from a later period we may guess that the significance of these payments was not very great. Of members who are later known to have taken money from either Danby or Barillon not one seems to have changed his attitude after receiving his bribe. Money may well have stiffened resolutions which had already been formed, but talk of members who exchanged their consciences for pensions, though common enough, lacks the support of even one authenticated example.

Not only were the court not bound by pensions in 1674; they lacked also any form of organization. The fact that only one member spoke in favour of supply during the whole session is eloquent testimony both to the court's weakness at that time, and to Danby's energy in producing even the limited success of 1675 to 1678. As for the opposition, there are many references to meetings but little to suggest the development of what we might properly call a party. If programmes were drawn up or tactics discussed the records were subsequently destroyed, and from this period at least no evidence survives to give the term 'Country Party' any precise significance.

Having sought in vain for formal parties we are left with our vague central mass, reaching its conclusions in silence and leaving evidence for its views only in the records of divisions. With these divisions as our guide we may conclude that if this cavalier Parliament stood for anything, it stood for the ultimate superiority of Parliament over the Crown. The one time when the political system worked smoothly was in 1670 and 1671, during a period in which Parliament's fundamental prejudices were respected. When, in their different ways, Clarendon and Danby demanded a loyalty overriding such prejudices, their efforts met with no success. Equally unsuccessful, however, were the efforts of the extreme opposition, who were as eager as Charles to get the whole constitution revised. Illogically, yet sensibly, the 'gross of country gentry' insisted on treating the King as the head of the administration, with the right to choose both ministers and policy, and at the same time demanded that he should not choose a policy which threatened liberty, property or religion. Theirs was perhaps a selfish aim, less inspiring than the tolerance of the King or the high republicanism of the Whigs. It was also more attainable and more likely to be permanent when attained. The rights preserved by these 'simple country gentlemen'—as Sir Richard Temple contemptuously called them—were held in trust for the nation at large, to whom in due time they were eventually transmitted. If we value these rights and are glad to enjoy them then a portion of our gratitude should be reserved for the Cavalier House of Commons.

A NOTE ON SOURCES

A complete list of my sources is given below: in this note I hope merely to indicate those which other writers may find particularly helpful. First among these I would place the official records of Parliament, the *Journals* of both Houses, the *Statutes of the Realm*, and the 7th, 8th and 9th reports of the Historical Manuscripts Commission covering the MSS. of the House of Lords. These routine summaries of the business of each session serve as a useful corrective to the highly selective accounts in letters, memoirs and parliamentary diaries.

As far as particular debates are concerned the longest and most vivid source is the diary published as Grey's *Debates*. This appears to report many speeches *verbatim* but its dates are not exact, it is not always easy to follow, and it is consistently biased against the court. The diaries kept by John Milward and Edward Dering are, for the short periods they cover, more reliable than Grey and make it easier to follow the main course of a debate. Their original MSS., unlike Grey's, are still accessible; if Grey's MS. could be found this might be very useful since it seems probable that its editing was not done with any great care. A MS. diary kept by Bullen Reymes covers only the period 1661 to 1662 and adds nothing of value to the *Journals*. The last two volumes of the *Parliamentary History* cover debates of the Convention and provide interesting information about the activities of members who became prominent in later years.

Other sources devoted entirely to Parliamentary business include several MS. accounts of Clarendon's impeachment, but none of these differs materially from the diaries kept by Milward and Grey. A particularly good collection of speeches is that made by Holland, now in Tanner MSS., Bodleian Library. Three other collections, including both draft speeches and notes on particular debates, are those made by Arthur Capel, Sir Richard Temple, and Sir William Coventry; they are in Additional and Stowe MSS., British Museum and Coventry MSS., Longleat.

References to proceedings in Parliament occur in many letters, but of those which have survived the great majority represent the views of some faction within the court. An outstanding series is that of letters written to Ormonde during his Irish service from 1662 to 1668. A few of these are calendared by the Historical Manuscripts Commission, and others are quoted in Carte's *Life* but the majority must be searched for in some thirty volumes of Carte MSS.,

Bodleian Library. Similar to these are the letters sent to Essex, also serving in Ireland, between 1673 and 1675. Although a number have been printed it is again worth going to the originals in Stowe MSS., British Museum.

Also informative, but noticeably less frank, are letters sent to ambassadors. For the period 1663 to 1665 there are letters to Fanshaw and Winchelsea, calendared by the Historical Manuscripts Commission, whilst a much larger and more varied collection has been printed in the Camden Society's *Letters to . . . Williamson*. Excellent as a court source for the period from 1666 to 1668 are the letters of Sir John Nicholas in Egerton MSS., British Museum; rather less valuable are the letter books kept by Henry Coventry between 1672 and 1678, of which there are copies both in Additional MSS., British Museum and Coventry MSS., Longleat.

As for the opposition or even the neutrals, they wrote less or destroyed more, so that it is a question of gleaning single letters, or rather single paragraphs, from boxes of volumes filled with private and family news. More helpful than most are letters between Sir William Coventry and his nephew Thomas Thynne, in either Thynne or Coventry MSS. at Longleat. John Starkey's news letters, of which there is a collection in Additional MSS., British Museum, are biased enough to count as an opposition source, but contain inside information passed on by the parliamentary diarist Anchitell Grey. Cavalier opposition can be studied in the Verney MSS., now to be seen on microfilm in Buckinghamshire County Record Office, and the less extensive Legh MSS., now being arranged in the John Rylands Library, Manchester. The handful of private letters by Andrew Marvell, edited by H. G. Margoliouth, represent an opposition more extreme than any found elsewhere.

Foreign ambassadors refer frequently to Parliamentary proceedings but their accounts should be treated with caution. The French, whose transcribed reports can be read in the Public Record Office, exaggerated their own influence and, with the exception of the elder Ruvigny, were often misinformed. The Venetians were strongly biased against the House of Commons, and the *Calendar of State Papers Venetian* includes a number of letters, cited by previous historians, which were written not from London but from Paris or Madrid and provide news at second or third hand.

Among memoirs covering the period those of Clarendon, Pepys, and Burnet have been much used in the past. Clarendon's *Life* is highly inaccurate, even about his own conduct, but does show something of the workings of his mind. Burnet writes generally at second hand, and although he may have received useful information from Littleton his unwillingness to reject an entertaining anecdote makes him unreliable. As for Pepys, he shows strong court bias but he

writes interestingly when at first hand; when relying on William
Coventry he is also to be trusted, but it would help greatly to know
more about his friend Captain Cocke, who was a mine of information but not in fact a member of the Lower House.

Party lists fall into two main categories. On the one hand there
are records of payments made by court leaders, though these may
well be accompanied by the comment that the money has not in fact
been earned. Much the best collection of these has been made by
Browning, in the third volume of his *Danby*. On the other hand there
are the libellous lists of 'court cullies', put out by opposition pamphleteers and often bearing little relation to the truth. The best collection
of these appears in the Bulletin of Historical Research for 1934, but
it is essential to make use of the editor's careful notes and to consider
both the date of each list and the reliability of its compiler. Failure
by writers to do this has produced some rather misleading party
patterns.

Last to be mentioned are three secondary accounts which I have
found particularly useful. Two articles by Dr Clayton Roberts, on
the period 1667 to 1668, apply to Restoration politics the sophisti-
cated calculations previously reserved for the eighteenth century.
Dr Roseveare's thesis on 'The King's Credit' provides a lucid guide
to a series of financial debates between 1665 and 1671. Most fundamental, Professor Chandaman's exhaustive review of the revenue
system between 1660 and 1688 has shattered the legend of Parliamentary meanness and royal poverty and so paved the way for a
complete reconsideration of the relationship between Parliament
and King.

LIST OF SOURCES

Sources of particular importance for this study are marked with an asterisk.

PRIMARY SOURCES: MANUSCRIPT

ALTHORPE   *Spencer MSS.*

Halifax Series: File 2. Letters from Sir William Coventry 1667–78.
   File 10. Letters from Thomas Thynne (later Viscount Weymouth)
   1677–8.

BRITISH MUSEUM   *Additional MSS.*

4107   Draft reply to an address from the Commons, 1663—probably in Clarendon's writing.
25116   Notes on Skinner versus the East India Company.
25122–5   Letters of Henry Coventry, 1672–8.
28051–3   Danby papers.
28091   Miscellaneous parliamentary papers, including some party lists.
32094–5*   Papers of Sir William Coventry including several memoranda on the Navy and the Second Dutch War.
35865*   Notes on parliamentary proceedings, including fragments of debates and drafts of speeches (mostly before 1670).
36830–46   Copies of the Journals of the House of Commons giving certain passages excised from the originals (as in the Skinner dispute).
36916*   News letters, mostly from John Starkey, 1667–1672, including parliamentary information supplied by Anchitell Grey.

Egerton MSS.

2043   Diary of Colonel Bullen Reymes, covering proceedings in the Commons, 1661–1662.
2508   One letter from Sir George Downing.
2539*   Letters from Sir John Nicholas to his father, 1666–9.
2717   One or two letters to William Gawdy.

Harleian MSS.

4706   Two speeches against an Irish Cattle Bill.
7020   List of alleged court pensioners.

Stowe MSS.

201–204*   Letters to Essex, 1673–4.

303–4* Parliamentary memoranda, notes of speeches, etc., collected by Sir Richard Temple.

Lansdowne MSS.

478 Parliamentary precedents, mostly before 1660.
805 List of alleged court pensioners.

BODLEIAN LIBRARY   Carte MSS.

32, 34–6,
46–7, 215, } *Letters to Ormonde, 1662–8. These represent almost
217, 220–1   every shade of 'court' opinion, during this period.

72, 75 Letters to Sandwich.
77 News letters.
79–81 Parliamentary papers collected by Lord Wharton, mostly duplicating existing records.

Clarendon MSS.

Calendar of Clarendon MSS., vol. v, 1661–1726, F. S. Routledge, typescript.

Tanner MSS.

42–3, 45 Correspondence of Sir John Hobart, including letters from Roger Pepys, 1667–8, 1673–5.
239* Speeches of Sir John Holland, 1662–8, some already printed.

CHETHAM LIBRARY   Raines MSS.

44 Transcripts of Legh MSS., now superseded by the originals.

CLAYDON   Verney MSS.

Boxes for 1661–74,* containing letters by Dr Denton, Sir Ralph Verney, and others.

JOHN RYLANDS   Legh MSS.
  LIBRARY

Boxes for 1661–73,* containing letters, chiefly from Richard Legh, many already printed.

KENT RECORD OFFICE

C2/122 One letter of Peter du Moulin.

LANCASHIRE RECORD OFFICE

DDKE Letters of Roger Kenyon, 1665–72.
DDH–V Letters to William Jessop.

LONGLEAT *Coventry MSS.*

4–5, 104–5* Letters to Henry and William Coventry, 1666–78.

82–4, 92–3 Letter books of Henry Coventry, 1672–7.

8, 16, 95,⎱Memoranda, draft bills, speeches, of Henry and William
101–2* ⎰ Coventry, 1664–78.

Longleat MSS.

67, 72, 90,⎱Parliamentary proceedings, mostly Clarendon's
120 ⎰ impeachment.

Thynne MSS.

16* Correspondence between Henry and William Coventry and Thomas Thynne, 1666–78.

PUBLIC RECORD OFFICE

PRO 31/3/111–141* Transcripts of French ambassador's reports, 1663–78.

SP 29/105 Two letters of William Coventry to Bennet, 1664.

SP 29/337 Letters to Sir Joseph Williamson, many printed.

SP 98/35 Report of committee on Foreign Trade, 1664.

SP 104/177 Minutes of committee of Foreign Affairs 1672–73, including discussion of parliamentary tactics.

SP 266/152 Pamphlet, 'The Alarum', 1669, printed.

PRIMARY SOURCES: PRINTED

HISTORICAL MANUSCRIPTS COMMISSION

The numbers in brackets are those used by many, though not all, libraries when arranging these volumes on their shelves.

4 Rep. app. pt. 1: (Bagot MSS.) p. 329, two letters, 1663.

5 Rep. app. pt. 1: (Hallerton, Strickland MSS.) pp. 298, 330–1, letters, 1660–73.

6 Rep. app. pt. 1: (Graham, Ingoldsby MSS.) pp. 337–40, letters, 1665–6; pp. 364–74, Paston letters and papers, 1664–73.

7 Rep. app. pt. 1*: (House of Lords, Verney MSS.) pp. 143–82, Parliamentary papers, 1661–5; pp. 461–70, 484–95, letters of Sir Ralph Verney, Dr Denton and others, 1660–78.

8 Rep. app. pt. 1*: (House of Lords MSS.) pp. 102–74, Parliamentary papers, 1666–71.

9 Rep. app. pt. 2*: (House of Lords MSS.) pp. 1–125, Parliamentary papers, 1671–8.

10 Rep. app. pt. 2 (11)*: (Gawdy MSS.) pp. 190–206, letters including some from Sir John Holland, 1660–9.

10 Rep. app. pt. 6 (15): (Braye MSS.) pp. 123–87, Parliamentary papers, 1669–75.

11 Rep. app. pt. 4 (19): (Townshend MSS.) pp. 26–9, letters, some from Sir John Holland, 1663–77.

12 Rep. app. pt. 5 (17): (Rutland MSS. II) pp. 8–39, letters, 1669–77.

12 Rep. app. pt. 7 (25) (Le Fleming MSS.) pp. 24–41, letters, 1660–76.

12 Rep. app. pt. 9 (27): (Beaufort MSS.) pp. 50–80, letters, 1661–78.

13 Rep. app. pt. 2 (29): (Portland MSS. II) pp. 144–50, letters 1662–75 including one on the Conventicle Bill of 1668.

13 Rep. app. pt. 4 (31): (Rye Corporation MSS.) pp. 235–45, letters, 1660–2, mostly about elections.

14 Rep. app. pt. 2 (29)*: (Portland MSS. III) pp. 217–305, letters, 1660–7.

14 Rep. app. pt. 4 (35)*: (Kenyon MSS.) pp. 67–84, letters, 1660–71, useful for 1670.

   (36)*: *Ormonde MSS., new series, III*, pp. 96–283, letters, 1663–8, useful for 1663.

   (36)*: *Ormonde MSS., new series, IV*, pp. 35–314, 375–497, letters, including many from Henry Coventry and Robert Southwell, 1677–9.

15 Rep. app. pt. 2 (39): (Hodgkin MSS.) p. 169, letter of 1667.

15 Rep. app. pt. 7 (43): (Somerset, Ailesbury MSS.) pp. 92–103, 161–77, letters 1660–73, several concerning elections.

   (50)*: *Heathcote MSS.*, pp. 73–175, letters to Fanshaw at Madrid, 1663–5.

   (55): *Various Collections II*, (Wombwell MSS.) pp. 118–46, letters to Fauconberg, 1662–70.

   (71)*: *Finch MSS. I*, pp. 94–505, letters to the Earl of Winchelsea, 1660–8.

   (71): *Finch MSS. II*, pp. 35–8, letters, 1678.

   (78)*: *Hastings MSS. II*, pp. 140–57, letters, 1660–7.

PARLIAMENTARY PROCEEDINGS

CHANDLER, R., *History of the Proceedings of the House of Lords from the Restoration*, vol. 1, 1742.

COBBETT, W.,* *Parliamentary History of England from 1066 to 1803*, vol. iv, 1808.

DERING, SIR EDWARD,* *Parliamentary Diary . . . 1670–1673*, ed. B. D. Henning, 1940.

GREY, A.,* *Debates of the House of Commons 1667–1694*, vols. i–viii, 1763/1769.

HATSELL, J., *Precedents of Proceedings in the House of Commons*, vol. iii, 1818.

HOWELL, T. B., *A complete collection of State Trials*, vol. vi, 1816.
MILWARD, J.,* *The Diary* . . . *1666–1668*, ed. Caroline Robbins, 1938.
TORBUCK, J., *A Collection of the Parliamentary Debates from 1668*, vol. i, 1741.
Journals of the House of Commons,* vols. viii, ix, 1803.
Journals of the House of Lords,* vols. xi, xii, n.d.
The Parliamentary . . . History of England . . . from the Earliest times to the Restoration of King Charles II,* vols. xxii, xxiii, 1740–3.
The Proceedings in the House of Commons touching the Impeachment of . . . Clarendon, 1700.
Return of the Names of Every Member . . . in each Parliament,* pt. 1, 1213–1702, 1878.
The Statutes of the Realm,* vol. v, 1819.

CALENDARS

Calendar of Wynn Papers 1515–1690, 1926.
Calendar of State Papers Domestic 1660–1678,* 22 vols., 1860–1911.
Calendar of State Papers Venetian 1659–1675,* 7 vols., 1931–47.
Calendar of Treasury Books 1660–1679, 7 vols., 1904–11.

DIARIES

EVELYN, J., *Diary of* . . ., ed. E. S. de Beer, vols. iii, iv, 1955.
PEPYS, S.,* *Diary of* . . ., ed. H. B. Wheatley, 8 vols., 1904–5.

LETTERS

CHARLES II, *Letters of* . . ., ed. A. Bryant, 1935.
MARVELL, A.,* *Letters and Poems of* . . ., ed. H. Margoliouth, 2 vols., 1952.
PEPYS, S., *Further correspondence of* . . . *1662–1679*, ed. J. R. Tanner, 1929.
Essex Papers 1672–75,* ed. O. Airey (Camden Society) 1890.
Essex Correspondence 1675–7, ed. C. E. Pike (Camden Society) 1913.
Hatton Correspondence 1601–1704, vol. i, ed. E. M. Thomson (Camden Society) 1878.
Savile Correspondence, ed. W. D. Cooper (Camden Society) 1858.
Williamson Correspondence,* ed. W. D. Christie, 2 vols. (Camden Society) 1874.

MEMOIRS

BAXTER, R., *Reliquiae Baxterianae*, ed. M. Sylvester, 1696.
BRAMSTON, SIR JOHN, *Autobiography* . . . *1611–1700*, ed. Lord Braybrooke (Camden Society) 1845.
BURNET, G., *History of my own Time*, ed. O. Airey, 2 vols., 1897.
Supplement to Burnet's History, ed. H. C. Foxcroft, 1902.

CLARENDON, EDWARD, EARL OF,* *The Life of . . .*, 3 vols., 1827.
RERESBY, SIR JOHN, *Memoirs of . . .*, ed. A. Browning, 1936.
TEMPLE, SIR WILLIAM, *Memoirs of the Life of . . .*, ed. T. P. Courtney, vol. i., 1836.

PAMPHLETS

State Tracts, 1693.
  includes:
DU MOULIN, P.,* 'England's Appeal', 1673.
ANON., 'A Seasonable Discourse', 1675.
MARVELL, A., 'An Account of the Growth of Popery', 1677.
Parliamentary History, ed. W. Cobbett, vol. iv, 1808.
  includes as appendices:
SHAFTESBURY, ANTHONY, EARL OF, 'Letter from a Person of Quality', 1675.
ANON., 'A Seasonable Argument', 1677.

MISCELLANEOUS

BROWNING, A., *English Historical Documents, 1660–1714*, 1953.
CHAMBERLAYNE, E., *Anglice Notitia*, 1669, 1671, 1674.
DALRYMPLE, SIR JOHN, *Memorials of Great Britain and Ireland*, vol. i, 1790.
MIGNET, A. M., *Negociations Relatives à la Succession d'Espagne*, vols. i–iv, 1835–42.
WESTERGAARD, W., *The First Triple Alliance 1668–1672*, 1947.

SECONDARY SOURCES

GENERAL HISTORIES

AYLMER, G. E., *The Struggle for the Constitution 1603–1689*, 1963.
CLARK, G. N., *The Later Stuarts*, 1940.
DAVIES, G., *Bibliography of British History: Stuart Period 1603–1714*, 1928.
DEANE JONES, I., *The English Revolution*, 1931.
EACHARD, L., *History of England*, vol. iii, 1718.
GROSE, C. L., *Select Bibliography of British History 1660–1760*, 1939.
HILL, C., *Century of Revolution*, 1961.
KEIR, D. L., *Constitutional History of Modern Britain*, 1948.
KENYON, J. P., *The Stuarts*, 1958.
KLOPP, O., *Der Fall des Hauses Stuart*, vol. i, 1875.
LINGARD, J., *History of England*, 1849.
LODGE, R., *Political History of England: From the Restoration to the death of William III*, 1910.
MACAULAY, T. B., *History of England*, ed. C. H. Firth, vol. i, 1913.

McELWEE, W., *England's Precedence*, 1956.
MAITLAND, F. W., *Constitutional History of England*, 1908.
OGG, D.,* *England in the Reign of Charles II*, 2 vols., 1955.
OLDMIXON, J., *The History of England during the reigns of the Royal House of Stuart*, 1730.
(RALPH, J.),* *History of England*, vol. i, 1744.
RANKE, L. VON, *History of England*, vols. iii, iv, 1875.
RAPIN DE THOYRAS, P., *History of England*, vol. ii, 1743.
TANNER, J. R., *English Constitutional Conflicts 1603–1683*, 1938.
TREVELYAN, G. M., *England under the Stuarts*, 1947.
WHITE KENNET, *Complete History of England*, vol. iii, 1939.

BIOGRAPHY

AIREY, O., *Charles II*, 1904.
BARBOUR, VIOLET,* *Henry Bennet, Earl of Arlington*, 1914.
BERESFORD, J.,* *The Godfather of Downing Street*, 1925.
BROWNE, LOUISE, *The First Earl of Shaftesbury*, 1933.
BROWNING, A.,* *Thomas, Earl of Danby*, 3 vols., 1944, 1951.
BRYANT, A., *King Charles II*, 1955.
—— *Samuel Pepys: The Man in the Making*, 1959.
—— *Samuel Pepys: The Years of Peril*, 1948.
BURGHCLERE, WINIFRED, LADY, *George Villiers, Second Duke of Buckingham*, 1903.
CARTE, T., *History of the Life of James, Duke of Ormonde*, vol. iv, 1851.
CARTWRIGHT, JULIA, *Madame*, 1900.
CHAPMAN, HESTER, *Great Villiers*, 1949.
CHRISTIE, W. D., *A Life of Anthony Ashley Cooper, First Earl of Shaftesbury*, 2 vols., 1871.
CLARKE, J. S., *The Life of James II*, 2 vols., 1816.
C(OKAYNE), G. E., *Complete Peerage*, 1910–59.
—— *Complete Baronetage*, vols. i–iii, 1900–04.
Dictionary of National Biography, 1908–9.
FOXCROFT, H. C., *Life and Letters of Sir George Savile, First Marquis of Halifax*, 2 vols., 1898.
HARRIS, F. S.,* *Life of Edward Montagu, First Earl of Sandwich*, 2 vols., 1912.
HARTMANN, C. H., *Clifford of the Cabal*, 1937.
—— *The King's Friend*, 1951.
—— *The King my Brother*, 1954.
LEGH, EVELYN,* *The House of Lyme*, 1917.
—— *Lyme Letters 1660–1760*, 1925.
LISTER, T. H., *Life and administration of . . . Clarendon*, 3 vols., 1837–8.
MARSHALL, G., *The Genealogist's Guide*, 1903.
NORTH, HON. ROGER, *Lives of the Norths*, vol. i, 1890.

PRIBRAM, A. F., *Franz Paul Freiheur von Lisola*, 1894.
RUSSELL, LORD JOHN, *The Life of William, Lord Russell*, 1819.
SITWELL, SIR GEORGE, *The First Whig*, 1894.
TOWNSHEND, DOROTHEA, *George Digby, Second Earl of Bristol*, 1924.
TURNER, F. C., *James II*, 1948.
WORMALD, B. H. G., *Clarendon: Politics, History and Religion 1640–1660*, 1951.

PARLIAMENT AND POLITICS

BRUNTON AND PENNINGTON, D. H., *Members of the Long Parliament*, 1954.
ELSING, H., *The Manner of Holding Parliaments in England*, 1675.
FEILING, K. G.,* *History of the Tory Party*, 1924.
HOLDSWORTH, W. S., *History of English Law*, vol. vi, 1924.
JONES, J. R., *The First Whigs*, 1961.
KEELER, MARY F., *The Long Parliament of 1640–1641*, 1954.
KEIR, D. L., *The Constitutional History of Modern Britain*, 1948.
KEMP, BETTY, *King and Commons 1660–1832*, 1957.
MAITLAND, F. W., *Constitutional History of England*, 1908.
PETYT, G., *Lex Parliamentaria*, 1690.
PORRITT, E. AND A., *The Unreformed House of Commons*, vol. i, 1903.
REDLICH, J., *The Procedure of the House of Commons*, 3 vols., 1908.
RONALDS, F. S., *The Attempted Whig Revolution of 1678*, 1937.
SCOBELL, H., *Memorials of Proceedings in Parliament in passing Bills*, 1670.
TANNER, J. R., *English Constitutional Conflicts*, 1928.
THOMSON, M. A., *Constitutional History of England 1642–1801*, 1938.

OTHER TOPICS

ABERNATHY, G. R., *The English Presbyterians and the Stuart Restoration*, 1965.
BAXTER, S. B., *The Development of the Treasury 1660–1702*, 1957.
BOSHER, R. S., *The Making of the Restoration Settlement*, 1951.
EVANS, F. G., *Principal Secretaries of State*, 1923.
FEILING, K. G., *British Foreign Policy 1660–1672*, 1930.
FIRTH, C. H., *Essays, Literary and Historical*, 1938.
HALEY, K. D.,* *William of Orange and the English Opposition*, 1953.
HERTZ, G. B., *English Public Opinion after the Restoration*, 1902.
HUGHES, E., *Studies in Administration and Finance 1558–1825*, 1934.
SHAW, W. A., *The Beginnings of the National Debt*, 1902.
TURNER, E. R., *The Privy Council of England in the Seventeenth and Eighteenth Centuries*, 1927.

ARTICLES AND THESES

The following abbreviations are used:

A.H.R.	*American Historical Review*
B.I.H.R.	*Bulletin of the Institute of Historical Research*
C.H.J.	*Cambridge Historical Journal*
Econ. Hist. Rev.	*Economic History Review*
E.H.R.	*English Historical Review*
H.L.Q.	*Huntingdon Library Quarterly*
J.E.H.	*Journal of Ecclesiastical History*
J.M.H.	*Journal of Modern History*
L.Q.R.	*Law Quarterly Review*
N.Q.	*Notes and Queries*
T.R.H.S.	*Transactions of the Royal Historical Society*

Parliament and Politics

ABBOTT, W. C.,* 'The Long Parliament of Charles II', *E.H.R.*, xxi, 1906.

—— 'The Origin of English Political Parties', *A.H.R.*, xxiv, 1919.

AYLMER, G. E., 'Office Holding as a Factor in English History, 1625–42', *History*, xliv, 1959.

—— 'Place Bills and the Separation of Powers', *T.R.H.S.*, 5th series, xv, 1965.

BROWNE, LOUISE F., 'The Religious factors in the Convention Parliament', *E.H.R.*, xxii, 1907.

BROWNING, A., 'Parties and Party Organisation in the Reign of Charles II', *T.R.H.S.*, 4th series, xxx, 1948.

BROWNING, A. AND MILNE, DOREEN J., 'An Exclusion Bill division list', *B.I.H.R.*, xxiii, 1950.

CRISSEY, M. H. AND DAVIES, G.,* 'Corruption in Parliament 1660–1677', *H.L.Q.*, vi, 1942–3.

DAVIES, G.,* 'The Political Career of Sir Richard Temple 1634–1697', *H.L.Q.*, iv, 1940–1.

—— 'The General Election of 1660', *H.L.Q.*, xv, 1952.

DE BEER, E. S., 'The Development of Political Parties during the ministry of Danby', London M.A. thesis, 1923.

——* 'Members of the Court Party in the Reign of Charles II', *B.I.H.R.*, xi, 1934.

EVANS, T. W., 'Hyde and the Convention Parliament of 1660', London M.A. thesis, 1964.

FRYER, C. E., 'The Royal Veto under Charles II 1663–1680', *E.H.R.*, xxxii, 1917.

GEORGE, DOROTHY, 'Elections and Electioneering 1679–1681', *E.H.R.*, xlv, 1930.

GROSE, C. L., 'French ambassadors' reports on financial relations with members of Parliament 1677–1678', *E.H.R.*, xliv, 1929.

HELMS, MARY E. W., 'The Convention Parliament of 1660', Bryn Mawr Ph.D. thesis, 1963.

JONES, J. R., 'Court Dependents in 1664', *B.I.H.R.*, xxxiv, 1961.

LIPSON, E., 'Elections to the Exclusion Parliaments 1679–1681', *E.H.R.*, xxviii, 1913.

MUKERJEE, H. N., 'Elections for the Convention and Cavalier Parliaments', *N.Q.*, clxvi, 1934.

ROBBINS, CAROLINE, 'A critical study of the Political Activities of Andrew Marvell', London Ph.D. thesis, 1926.

——* 'The Oxford Session of the Long Parliament of Charles II', *B.I.H.R.*, xxi, 1946–8.

——* 'The Repeal of the Triennial Act', *H.L.Q.*, xii, 1949.

ROBERTS, C.,* 'Sir Richard Temple's Discourse on the Parliament of 1667–1668', *H.L.Q.*, xx, 1956–7.

——* 'The Impeachment of the Earl of Clarendon', *C.H.J.*, xiii, 1957.

ROSKELL, J. S., 'Perspectives in English Parliamentary History', *Bulletin of the John Rylands Library*, xlvi, 1963–4.

TURBERVILLE, A. S., 'The House of Lords under Charles II', *E.H.R.*, xliv and xlv, 1929, 1930.

TURNER, E. R., 'Parliament and Foreign Affairs 1603–1760', *E.H.R.*, xxxiv, 1919.

WITCOMBE, D. T.,* 'The Parliamentary Career of Sir William and Mr. Henry Coventry 1661–1681', Oxford B.Litt. thesis, 1954.

—— 'The Cavalier House of Commons: the session of 1663', *B.I.H.R.*, xxxii, 1959.

Economics and Finance

BROWNING, A., 'The Stop of the Exchequer', *History*, xiv, 1929–30.

CHANDAMAN, C. D.,* 'The English Public Revenue 1660–1688', London Ph.D. thesis, 1954.

GILL, DORIS M., 'The Treasury 1660–1714', *E.H.R.*, xlvi, 1931.

—— 'The Relationship between the Treasury and the Excise and Customs Commissioners 1660–1714', *C.H.J.*, iv, 1932.

HABBAKKUK, H. J., 'The Long term rate of Interest and the price of Land in the Seventeenth Century', *Econ. Hist. Rev.*, 2nd series, v, 1952.

HUGHES, E., 'English Stamp Duties 1664–1764', *E.H.R.*, lvi, 1941.

JUDGES, A. V., 'The Origins of English Banking', *History*, xvi, 1931–2.

MARSHALL, LYDIA M., 'The Levying of the Hearth Tax 1662–1688', *E.H.R.*, li, 1936.

PRIESTLEY, MARGARET, 'Anglo-French Trade and the unfavourable balance controversy 1660–1685', *Econ. Hist. Rev.*, 2nd series, iv, 1951–2.

ROSEVEARE, H. G.,* 'The Advancement of the King's Credit 1660–1672', Cambridge Ph.D. thesis, 1962.

SKEEL, CAROLINE A. J., 'The Canary Company', *E.H.R.*, xxxi, 1916.

Miscellaneous

ABERNATHY, G. R., 'Clarendon and the Declaration of Indulgence', *J.E.H.*, xi, 1960.

BEHRENS, BETTY, 'The Whig theory of the Constitution in the reign of Charles II', *C.H.J.*, vii, 1941.

FEILING, K. G., 'A letter of Clarendon during the election of 1661', *E.H.R.*, xlii, 1927.

FIRTH, C. H., 'Clarendon's "History of the Rebellion" ', *E.H.R.*, xix, 1904.

—— 'The Development of the study of Seventeenth Century history', *T.R.H.S.*, 3rd series, vii, 1913.

GAY, E. F., 'Sir Richard Temple—the debt settlement and estate litigation', *H.L.Q.*, vi, 1944.

GROSE, C. L., 'The Anglo-Dutch alliance of 1678', *E.H.R.*, xxxix, 1924.

—— 'Notes and suggestions on Charles II of England', *A.H.R.*, xliii, 1937–8.

—— 'Studies of 1931–1940 on British History 1660–1760', *J.M.H.*, xii, 1940.

HIGHAM, F. AND HIGHAM, C. S., 'The reign of Charles II as a field for research', *B.I.H.R.*, ii, 1924.

KENYON, J. P., 'The Reign of Charles II' (review article) *C.H.J.*, xiii, 1957.

TANNER, J. R., 'The administration of the Navy from the Restoration to the Revolution', *E.H.R.*, xii, 1897.

TREVOR ROPER, H. R., 'The Gentry 1540–1640', *Econ. Hist. Rev.*, supplement, 1953.

VALE, V., 'Clarendon, Coventry, and the sale of naval offices 1660–1668', *C.H.J.*, xii, 1956.

BRIEF NOTES ON CERTAIN LEADING FIGURES IN THE HOUSE OF COMMONS

THE following notes may perhaps assist readers to identify members mentioned frequently in the narrative. They are based largely on the *Dictionary of National Biography* and on *preliminary* notes made by the team now working on the official *History of Parliament* for this period. Whilst I am most grateful to Professor Henning and to Mr E. L. C. Mullins for permission to use this material I must point out that much of it is, as yet, unchecked and incomplete. In due course the appearance of the official biographies will render these preliminary sketches superfluous; in the meantime I can only hope that their defects will be outweighed by the lack of any single alternative source.

Atkins (Atkyns), Sir Robert

1620–1710. East Looe, Cornwall, 1661–72. *DNB*. Civil War attitude unknown. Attended Parliament 1656 Carmarthen, 1659 Evesham. Knight of the Bath 1660. Recorder of Bristol 1661. Gave up his seat in the Commons on becoming Justice of Common Pleas 1672. Dismissed 1680. Assisted Lord Russell at his trial 1683. Lord Chief Baron of Exchequer, 1689–94. Speaker of House of Lords in Convention 1689. Moderate courtier; effective chairman of committees; drifted away from court after 1673 but by then no longer in the Commons.

Aungier, Francis

Baron, Viscount, later Earl of Longford in Irish Peerage. 1635–1700. Arundel, Sussex, 1661. Son of a prebendary of St Patrick's Cathedral. Royalist in Civil War. Succeeded his uncle in Barony 1654. Irish Privy Council 1660. Vice-Treasurer of Ireland 1670–5. Viscount 1675. Earl 1677. Not active in Commons but wrote many letters describing debates 1673–5. Hostile to Ranelagh and to Danby but still a member of the court. Supported all ministries of William III.

Barnadiston, Sir Samuel

1620–1707. Suffolk, 1673. *DNB*. City merchant opposing Charles I in 1640. No part in Civil War. Knighted 1660. Baronet 1663. Deputy Governor of East India Company 1668 and fined by House of Lords in Skinner's case. Elected for Suffolk in 1673 as an avowed opponent of the court. Moderately active speaker. Presented articles against Danby 1678. Chairman of Grand Jury that threw out indictment against Shaftesbury 1681. Fined £10,000 for a libel 1684. Verdict reversed 1690.

Birch, John

1616–91. Penryn, Cornwall, 1661. *DNB*. Bristol merchant (not, as often alleged, a carter). Active as a Captain on Parliament's side during Civil War. Bought Bishops' lands. Elected for Leominster 1646. Excluded 1648. Joined Charles II before battle of Worcester. Imprisoned. Elected for Leominster 1654, 1656, 1659 and 1660 but restrained from sitting in 1654. Excise commissioner at end of protectorate. Member of Monck's Privy Council 1660. Commissioner for Excise 1660–4 and Sole Auditor for life 1661. Though thus receiving a considerable salary from the crown remained an extremely independent, and very active, speaker often criticizing ministers. Spoke effectively for toleration of dissenters and attacking Catholics and France. Also active in debates on finance as an advocate of government economy. Elected for Weobley 1679, 1681, 1689, 1690.

Birkenhead, Sir John

1616–79. Wilton, Wiltshire, 1661. *DNB*. Son of a saddler. Servitor at Oriel College, Oxford. Secretary to Laud. Edited royalist news sheet *Mercurius Aulicus* during Civil War. Exiled 1648. Knighted 1649. Strong Anglican. Leading court spokesman after 1673 but his speeches were badly received.

Boscowen, Edward

1628–85. Truro, Cornwall. *DNB*. A rich merchant of the Levant Company. First sat in Commons 1659. Elected for Truro 1660, 1679, 1681. Spoke occasionally as a very strong critic of court. Exclusionist 1679.

Capel, Sir Henry

1638?–96. Tewkesbury, Gloucestershire, 1661. *DNB*. Second son of 1st Baron Capel who was strongly royalist in Civil War. Sat for Tewkesbury in all Parliaments from 1660 to 1681 and in 1690; sat for Cockermouth 1689; no seat 1685. Knight of the Bath 1661. Irish Privy Council 1673–85. English Privy Council 1679–80. Despite his official position often an opponent of the court. Supported Exclusion and attacked Halifax. Created Baron Capel in 1692 and became Lord Deputy for Ireland 1695.

Carew, Sir Nicholas

1635–88. Gatton, Surrey, 1664. Father a member of an old Surrey family, and heavily fined by Parliament. Son joined Booth's royalist rising 1659 but passed over at Restoration. Bitter opponent of court speaking frequently after 1667. Attacked Clarendon, Arlington and Danby. Exclusionist 1679. Sat for Gatton 1679 (2) and 1681.

Carr, Sir Robert

1638–82. Lincolnshire, 1665. Son of Sir Robert Carr, Bart., leading Lincolnshire family. St John's College Cambridge. Sat for Lincolnshire 1661 to 1681. Succeeded as 3rd bart. 1667. Called to the bar 1672. Chancellor of Duchy of Lancaster. Married Elizabeth Bennett, sister of Henry, 1st Earl of Arlington. Moderate court supporter, capable of criticism.

Carteret, Sir George

1609?–80. Portsmouth, Hampshire, 1661. *DNB*. Captain in Navy 1633. Active royalist in Civil War holding Jersey for the King. Knight and Baronet 1646. Treasurer of Navy 1660. Claimed to have spent his own fortune on Navy but bitterly attacked in Commons 1667–8. Exchanged offices with Anglesey and became Vice-Treasurer of Ireland 1667. Further attacked 1669 and suspended from the Commons. Resigned office 1670 but appointed Admiralty Commissioner 1674. Spoke seldom in Commons except in self-defence. Son created Baron in 1681.

Cavendish, William, Lord

1641–1707. Derbyshire, 1661. *DNB*. Eldest son of 1st Earl of Devonshire. Father active royalist. Named to many committees in 1660, but no evidence of activity as a speaker until 1673. Strong critic of court and especially of Danby but opposed Exclusion. Welcomed William in 1688 and was raised to be 1st Duke of Devonshire 1691.

Charlton, Sir Job

1614–97. Ludlow, Shropshire, 1661. *DNB*. Son of a goldsmith. Elected for Ludlow as a royalist 1659. King's Sergeant 1660. Knight and Chief Justice of Chester 1662. Chairman of many committees 1661–73 as a supporter of the court. Court nominee as Speaker 1673 but withdrew almost at once on plea of illness. Chief Justice Common Pleas 1680–6 but removed for questioning dispensing power.

Churchill, Sir Winston

1620?–88. Weymouth and Melcombe, Dorset. 1661. *DNB*. Royalist in Civil War. Knight and member of Board of Green Cloth 1664 as compensation for losses in war. Courtier but strong opponent of toleration. Less active after 1673. Re-elected to 1st Parliament of 1679 and elected for Lyme Regis 1685. Father of 1st Duke of Marlborough.

Clarges, Sir Thomas

1618–93. Southwark, Surrey, 1666. *DNB*. Said to have been son of a blacksmith. Doctor in Parliamentary army. Sister married Monck. Member for Ross and Cromarty 1656. Took messages from Monck to Charles II. Knighted 1660. Commissary General 1661. Sat for a Cornish borough 1660, for Christchurch, Hampshire, 1679 (2), 1681, 1685 and for Oxford University 1689, 1690. Spoke frequently. No strong party links; opposed Danby but also opposed Exclusion. Welcomed William 1688. Opposed William's ministers. Genuine country member despite official post.

Clifford, Thomas

1630–73. Totnes, Devon, 1661. *DNB*. Father a royalist. Very poor. Sat for Totnes 1660. Opposed court but supported toleration 1663. Arlington helped him to minor offices. Commissioner of Treasury 1667. Active in council advocating secret catholic policy. Also effective in Commons appealing for supply 1670–1. Lord Treasurer and 1st Baron Clifford 1672. Resigned after Test Act 1673 and died, or committed suicide, in same year.

Coventry, Henry

1619–86. Droitwich, Worcestershire, 1661. *DNB*. Son of Charles I's Lord Keeper. Strong royalist. In exile after Civil War. Close friend of Clarendon. Gentleman of Bedchamber 1662. Strong supporter of court but opposed toleration. Strongly defended Clarendon and showed signs of opposition 1669. Returned to court 1670, Secretary of State 1672. Very vigorous speaker for the court 1673–81 but lukewarm in defence of Danby. Always popular. Sat for Droitwich 1679 (2) and 1681. Resigned as Secretary 1680.

Coventry, Sir John

Weymouth and Melcombe, Dorset, 1667. *DNB*. Nephew of Henry, Sir William and Shaftesbury. Strong royalist. Knight of the Bath 1661. Minor office 1667. Made jest against King 1670 and was assaulted by royal guards. Turned to opposition joining Shaftesbury and speaking seldom but strongly. Exclusionist. Reconciled to court 1683. Said to have died a catholic 168–.

Coventry, Sir William

1627–86. Great Yarmouth, Norfolk, 1661. *DNB*. Brother to Henry. Brief exile after Civil War but returned to England during Protectorate. Helped to organize Restoration though mistrusted by Clarendon. Secretary to Duke of York 1660. Active in Commons by 1663 as one of rival court group to Clarendon's. Knight 1665. Commissioner of Treasury 1667 but quarrelled with Buckingham and Arlington and dismissed from all offices 1668. Strong court speaker to 1668; then strong opposition speaker, but consistent supporter of toleration for dissenters. Attacked Danby and French alliance after 1673 but opposed Exclusion and was attacked by Shaftesbury. Closely linked with Halifax who was his nephew. Elected 1679 first parliament but refused to stand again.

Crouch, Thomas

1607–79. Cambridge University, 1661. Fellow of King's College. Sent college plate to King but deprived of his fellowship 1650. Restored in 1660. Strong enemy of dissenters and of catholics. Spoke little on other topics.

Denham, Sir John

1615–69. Old Sarum, Wiltshire, 1661. *DNB*. Royalist in war. Surveyor General 1660; Knight of the Bath 1661. Reasonably active court speaker to 1667 when withdrew, probably because of quarrel with Duke of York.

Dering, Sir Edward

1625–84. East Retford, Nottingham, 1661. Father, 1st Baronet, active royalist. Son married daughter of wealthy merchant. Member for Kent 1660. Reasonably active supporter of court. Valuable diary 1669–73 presenting anglican court view. By 1680 tending towards Exclusion.

Downing, Sir George

1623–84. Morpeth, Northumberland, 1661. *DNB*. Son of a lawyer. Brought up in New England; graduate of Harvard. Scoutmaster-General for Cromwell 1650. Sat for Edinburgh 1654, Carlisle 1656. Teller in Exchequer 1656. Ambassador to the Hague 1657. Elected for Morpeth 1660. Teller of the Exchequer 1661. Baronet 1663. Ambassador to the Hague 1657–64; Secretary to the Commissioner of the Treasury 1667; Ambassador to the Hague 1671. Strong court speaker, effective on need for taxation 1670–1. Not active after 1673.

Finch, Heneage

1st Earl of Nottingham, 1621–82. Oxford University, 1661–73. *DNB*. Son of Charles I's Speaker. Private practice during Civil War. Knight and Baronet 1660. Solicitor-General 1660. Attorney-General 1670. Lord Keeper of the Great Seal 1673 and Speaker of the House of Lords. Lord Chancellor 1675. 1st Earl of Nottingham 1681. Active and effective court speaker in the Commons. Opponent of toleration. As Lord Keeper lost touch with the Commons and his opening orations were badly received.

Ford, Sir Richard

1613?–78. Southampton, Hampshire, 1661. Royalist merchant. Helped Charles II in exile. Knighted 1660. Governor of East India and Royal African Companies. Lord Mayor 1670. Though himself a convert from Presbyterianism was active in prosecuting dissenters. Considered a courtier but spoke generally for the mercantile interest. Seems to have been confused by Grey with Sir Henry Ford of Tiverton (*DNB*) who took little part in debates.

Garraway, William

1616–1701. Chichester, Sussex, 1661. Royalist Captain in Civil War, heavily fined. Neglected in 1660. Very active in Commons becoming a strong critic of Clarendon, and of royal policy, but supporting toleration for dissenters. Appointed Commissioner of Customs 1671 and appeared temporarily as an advocate of supply but opposed 1672 Declaration and soon turned against the French alliance. Dismissed from office 1674. At first supported Exclusion but opposed Monmouth's claim in 1681. Welcomed William but remained a strong country critic of taxation and of government blunders. One of the outstanding speakers in the Commons. Thought by some to be self-seeking but seems to have retained strong principles.

Goodrick, Sir John

1617–70. Yorkshire, 1661. Royalist Captain of Horse, imprisoned by Parliament. Baronet. Opposed toleration and was reluctant to grant supply for Dutch War. His son warmly welcomed William.

Grey, Anchitell

1624–1702. Derby, Derbyshire, 1665. *DNB*. Second son of 1st Earl of Stamford. Sheriff under Protectorate. Father, as a leading presbyterian, helped Booth's royalist rising. Deputy Lieutenant 1660. Soon after his election, in 1665, began to keep a Parliamentary Diary which runs from 1667 to 1694 and is the main source for the debates of this period. Though not apparently an active speaker, Grey shows strong opposition sentiments in his Diary. Associate of William Sacheverell, member for the county, and of John Starkey, an opposition newswriter.

Hampden, Richard

1631–95. Wendover, Buckinghamshire, 1661. *DNB*. Eldest surviving son of John Hampden of the Long Parliament. Elected for Buckinghamshire 1656. Supported Cromwell and was one of his Upper House. Elected for Wendover from 1660 to 1690 and for Buckinghamshire 1690–5. Not active until 1678 when he became a strong Exclusionist. Welcomed William. Chancellor of the Exchequer 1690–4.

Harbord, Sir Charles

1595–1679. Launceston, Cornwall, 1661. Surveyor General 1632. Civil War record uncertain. Surveyor General of Woods and Forests 1666–79. Critic of Clarendon. Moderate Anglican. Not very active.

Harbord, William

1632–92. Clifton, Dartmouth and Hardness, Devon, 1661. Son of Sir Charles. Auditor of Duchy of Cornwall 1661. Secretary to Robartes 1668 and Essex 1673 when each was Lord Lieutenant of Ireland. Critic of Clarendon and of Danby. Moderately active speaker and very active letter writer in period 1673–5. Opposed Exclusion Bill though said to have received a pension from Barillon. Elected for Thetford 1679 (2) and 1681; Launceston 1685–92. Paymaster General 1689–90; ambassador to Turkey 1691.

Holland, Sir John

1603–1701. Aldeburgh, Suffolk, 1661. Member of old Norfolk family; created baronet without paying a fee 1629. Presbyterian but steward to catholic Howards and himself married to a catholic. At first supported Parliament in Civil War but excluded in 1648; retired abroad and helped Restoration in 1660, as a member of Monck's Council of State. Spoke often in Commons for toleration and against taxation, especially of Norfolk. Defended Arlington in 1674 but generally moved into stronger opposition; helped opponents of the court in Norfolk elections and was dismissed from post as Deputy Lieutenant 1675. Brought back as a J.P. in 1685 but dismissed in 1688. Brought back again 1689. Kept drafts of a number of speeches.

Howard, Sir Robert

1626–98. Stockbridge, Hampshire, 1661. *DNB*. 6th son of Earl of Berkshire. Knighted on battlefield 1644. Made his peace after the war and received farms of customs from Cromwell 1657. Active opposition speaker until Clarendon's fall and thought by many to be a client of Buckingham. Supported the court, especially over supply 1670–1 and became Auditor of the Exchequer 1673. Reverted to opposition by 1674 but retained his post to 1677. Sat for Castle Rising in all parliaments 1678–98 except that of 1685. Privy Council and Commander of the Horse 1690.

Ingoldsby, Sir Richard

1617–85. Aylesbury, Buckinghamshire, 1661. Sat for Wendover 1647–53; for Buckinghamshire in Protectorate Parliaments. Had been a signatory of Charles I's death warrant and was on the Protectorate Council of State but helped Booth's royalist rising, 1659, and arrested Lambert. Knight of the Bath 1661. Moderate supporter of the court but spoke little. Some influence over his very active stepson, Sir Thomas Lee. Retained his Irish lands despite his activities before 1660 and despite close links with Hampden and Cromwell.

Jones, John

1610–92. London, 1661. London Grocer. Parliamentarian in Civil War. Though a presbyterian sat in Protectorate Parliaments. Spoke frequently in finance debates as a constant critic of taxation.

Knight, Sir John

1612–83. Bristol, Gloucestershire, 1661. Merchant. Ardent royalist. Knighted 1663 and given pension from the excise. Persecuted nonconformists. Sat for Bristol 1660 to 1681. Spoke chiefly on religion.

Lee, Sir Thomas

1635–91. Aylesbury, Buckinghamshire, 1661. Helped Ingoldsby secure Buckinghamshire for the King in 1660. Baronet 1660. Long career in Commons sitting for Aylesbury 1660–81 and 1690–1 and Buckinghamshire 1689–90. Very active speaker for the country opposition, opposing supply but supporting toleration for dissenters. Gradually stiffened in opposition until supported exclusion 1679. Served as commissioner of Admiralty 1679–80 and 1689–91 but seems to have been genuinely disinterested in his choice of sides.

Legh, Richard

1634–87. Newton, Lancashire, 1661. Inherited Lyme Hall, Cheshire, in 1643. Sat in Cromwell's parliaments and is said to have supported

P

the proposal to make him King. Later helped Booth and in his correspondence shows himself a bitter enemy of presbyterians and a strong anglican supporter of the court. Spoke little but took a keen interest in debates, especially those on religion.

Littleton, Sir Thomas

1620–81. Much Wenlock, Shropshire, 1661. Second Baronet. Sat for Much Wenlock 1640 but expelled in 1644 as a royalist. Fined heavily by parliament. After his election in 1661 attached himself to Arlington and strongly criticized Clarendon. Brought in as Commissioner of the Navy 1668 and became an effective supporter of the court but was driven from office by Osborne in 1671. By 1673 had reverted to opposition but remained moderate and opposed exclusion, preferring regency. Sat for Much Wenlock 1679 (1) and for Great Yarmouth 1679 (2) and 1681. A very prominent speaker, often associated with Garraway and a friend of Burnet to whom he gave information about Parliament. His son (*DNB*) was also a leading member of the Commons.

Love, Alderman William

1620–89. London, 1661. Civil War record unknown but strong presbyterian. Sheriff of London 1659 and Commissioner of Customs 1659–60. Sat for London 1661–89, except for 1685. Expelled from office of Alderman 1662 for refusing to take the oaths; often ordered to take the oaths by the Commons but does not seem to have done so. Spoke regularly for toleration, gaining support for this by 1673. Supported exclusion.

Mallet, Sir John

1622–86. Minehead, Somerset, 1666. Father an active royalist. Knighted 1667. Recorder of Bridgwater 1669–85. Began as a courtier and supporter of toleration. Moved to opposition by 1673 and supported exclusion. Dismissed from office as J.P. 1680. Confused by Grey with the less active Michael Mallet, member for Milbourne Port, who spoke seldom but who launched a violent attack on Clifford in 1673.

Marvell, Andrew

1621–78. Kingston upon Hull, Yorkshire, 1661. *DNB*. Father an anglican clergyman. Abroad during war. Fairfax became his patron in 1650 and he was appointed to be Latin secretary as a colleague of Milton 1657. Supported Richard Cromwell. Sent on a Baltic embassy 1663. Defended Clarendon 1667. Spoke occasionally in Commons, usually in support of toleration for dissenters. Wrote colourless letters to constituents but violent opposition letters to private friends and still more violent anonymous pamphlets attacking the Cabal and Danby.

Maynard, Sir John

1601–90. Bere Alston, Devon, 1661. *DNB*. Sat for Devon and Somerset boroughs from 1624 to 1690. Presbyterian. Led prosecution of Strafford 1641. At first opposed Cromwell but was Solicitor General for Richard and a member of Monck's Council of State. Knight and King's Counsel 1660. Defended Clarendon but moved to moderate opposition criticizing both Danby and Shaftesbury. Commissioner of the Great Seal 1689. Spoke frequently, showing moderation and good sense and was heard with respect as 'father of the House'.

Meres, Sir Thomas

1634–1715. Lincoln, Lincolnshire, 1661. Son of the Chancellor of Lincoln Cathedral. Anglican royalist but sat for Lincoln 1659 and continued there to 1685 and from 1701 to 1708. A very active member, speaking for the anglican opposition in the '60s but almost made court candidate for Speaker in 1673. Despite continuing criticism of the court was proposed as a court alternative to Seymour in 1679 but rejected by Commons. Supported exclusion shortly afterwards.

Milward, John

1599–1670. Derbyshire, 1665–70. Sheriff of Derbyshire 1635. Royalist Colonel, fined by parliament. Not active as a speaker but kept a useful diary showing support for anglicanism, some criticism of taxation but general desire to support the King.

O'Neill, Daniel

1612–64. St Ives, Cornwall, 1662–4. *DNB*. Anglican royalist from a catholic family. Very active royalist in civil war. Captain of Horse Guards 1660; Postmaster General 1663. Not an active speaker but wrote many letters in 1663 giving court viewpoint on Commons' proceedings.

Osborne, Sir Thomas

1st Duke of Leeds, 1631–1712. York, Yorkshire, 1665. *DNB*. Father Vice-President of Council of the North. Active royalist. Entered Commons as a client of Buckingham and opposed Clarendon. Treasurer of the Navy 1668. Effective as a court spokesman for supply 1669–73. Raised to peerage 1673 and made Lord Treasurer. Earl of Danby

1674. Chief minister to 1678 when articles of impeachment were drafted against him and though not put on trial was in the Tower from 1679 to 1684. Emerged as Marquis of Carmarthen and worked actively in support of William's landing. Active in politics after 1689, Duke of Leeds 1694 but again threatened with impeachment 1695 and finally driven from office 1699. Less important for his relatively brief career as a speaker in the Commons than for his largely unsuccessful efforts to organize a court party 1674–8 and after 1690.

Paston, Sir Robert

1631–83. Castle Rising, Norfolk, 1661–73. *DNB*. Father an active royalist. Knighted 1660 and succeeded as 2nd baronet 1663. Chosen by Clarendon to move the supply vote of 1664 but otherwise spoke little before being rewarded with a barony in 1673. Created 1st Earl of Yarmouth 1679. Helped court candidates in elections in the '70s.

Penn, Sir William

1621–70. Weymouth and Melcombe, Dorset, 1661–70. *DNB*. Son of a sea captain. Active for Parliament in Navy during Civil War. Active in Navy against Dutch and Spanish during Interregnum but maintained links with Charles II. Knight 1660. Naval command 1665. Violently attacked in Commons 1667–8 and articles of impeachment drafted against him. Spoke only to defend himself.

Pepys, Roger

1617–88. Cambridge, Cambridgeshire, 1661. Lawyer. Recorder of Cambridge 1660. Royalist later moving to criticism of court. Removed from office as J.P. 1680. Cousin of Samuel. Not an active speaker but wrote letters on Commons activities in the '60s.

Pepys, Samuel

1633–1703. Castle Rising, Norfolk, 1673. *DNB*. Son of a tailor. Served Montagu in the Navy Office during the Protectorate and transferred with him to support Charles II in 1660. Clerk of the Acts in the Navy Office 1660. Treasurer of Tangier 1664. Secretary of the Admiralty 1673. Defended naval estimates and conduct of the war as a witness before the Commons committees 1667–8 and strongly criticized Commons Commissioners of Accounts 1670. Spoke strongly for the court 1673–8 but incurred great unpopularity and had to fight off attempts to have his election quashed. Attacked during Popish Plot and expelled from his seat for Harwich in 1679, suffering a short imprisonment. Restored to the Admiralty but removed again 1689, after which out of office.

Powle, Henry

1630–92. Cirencester, Gloucestershire, 1671. *DNB*. Lawyer. Strong
opposition speaker from the time of his election. Said to have received
money from Barillon but opposed exclusion. Privy Council 1678.
Welcomed William and took the Chair of the Convention 1689.
Master of the Rolls 1690. Sat for Cirencester from 1660 to 1681 and
for New Windsor 1689–90.

Prynne, William

1600–69. Bath, Somerset, 1661. *DNB*. Son of a farmer. Oriel College, Oxford. Lawyer. Attacked Charles I and Laud and was
severely punished in 1630's. Elected for Newport 1644 but expelled
as a presbyterian 1648. Imprisoned. Sat for Bath 1660. Spoke
strongly against regicides and was made Keeper of the Rolls. Quite
active, speaking for toleration and generally for the court but unpopular in the Commons.

Russell, William

1639–83. Tavistock, Devon, 1661. *DNB*. 3rd son of Earl of Bedford,
who had supported Parliament. Married French ambassador
Ruvigny's niece. Took little part in debates until 1673 but then
became a leading opposition speaker. Strong supporter of exclusion.
Succeeded to courtesy title of Lord Russell 1678. Implicated, probably unfairly, in Rye House Plot 1683 and executed for treason.

Sacheverell, William

1638–91. Derbyshire, 1670. *DNB*. Entered parliament as a declared
opponent of the court. Though Danby tried to win him over in 1674
remained the most violent and effective of the extreme opposition.
Strong supporter of exclusion. Possibly took money from Barillon.
Heavily fined 1682. Admiralty Commissioner 1689 but continued
to criticize ministry. Sat for Derbyshire 1670 to 1681, then for
Heytesbury 1689–90 and Nottinghamshire 1690–1.

Seymour, Sir Edward

1633–1708. Hindon, Wiltshire, 1661. *DNB*. Fourth Baronet. Father
royalist, fined by parliament. Sat for Gloucester 1660. Early opposition. Commissioner of Prizes 1665. Critic of Clarendon. Constant
supporter of toleration. Joined court 1670. Speaker 1673. Very skilful tactician and debater. Survived violent attacks 1673 and 1680.
Opposed Exclusion. Succeeded as Baronet 1685. Opposed supply.
Welcomed William 1688. A Lord of the Treasury 1692–4. Opposed
Whig ministry. Comptroller of Household 1702. Dismissed 1704.
Sat for Devon, Totnes or Exeter 1679–1705.

Strangeways, Colonel Giles

1615–75. Dorset, 1661. Sat for Bridport in 1640 but ejected in 1644 as an active royalist. Imprisoned, fined, and had his house burnt by Ashley Cooper (Shaftesbury) during Civil War. Normally a court supporter but the most violent opponent of toleration for dissenters and attacked Shaftesbury strongly in 1673. Privy Council 1675.

Swale, Sir Solomon

1609–78. Aldeburgh, Suffolk, 1661–78. Lawyer. Disbarred 1664, having already spoken in favour of toleration for catholics. Reckoned a court voter but spoke seldom and was expelled as a catholic in February 1678.

Swinfen, John

1613–94. Tamworth, Staffordshire, 1661. *DNB*. Sat for Stafford 1645 but expelled as a presbyterian 1648. Sat in 1658 and in the Convention of 1660. Spoke often and effectively for toleration of dissenters and as a moderate critic of the court. Became steadily more violent and supported exclusion. Sat for Tamworth in 1679 (1) and for Bere Alston 1690–4. Reckoned a supporter of the ministry 1690–2.

Temple, Sir Richard

1634–97. Buckingham, Buckinghamshire, 1661. *DNB*. Father supported Parliament in Civil War but opposed the execution of Charles I. First entered Parliament in 1654 and sat again 1659. Succeeded as 3rd Baronet 1653. Helped Restoration. Heavily in debt and although Knight of the Bath 1661 passed over for office. Very active in opposition 1661–70 but made several offers to come over as a court manager. Council of Foreign Plantations 1671 and Commissioner of Customs 1672. May have used salary to clear his debts and certainly became, and remained, a leading court spokesman. Speeches read well but were badly received. Seems to have opposed exclusion. Remained in Commons until 1695. In and out of office 1683 to 1694 but not employed by James II. Supported ministry under William. Though his attitude on supply changed when given office he remained a firm supporter of toleration for dissenters.

Titus, Colonel Silas

1623?–1704. Lostwithiel, Cornwall, 1670. *DNB*. Parliament side in Civil War but for Charles by 1648 as a presbyterian. With Charles II in 1653 and joined Sexby in plotting to kill Cromwell. Joined Booth's rising 1659 and sat in the Convention speaking strongly against regicides. Keeper of Deal Castle and Groom of the Bedchamber. By 1670 turning against the court and strongly attacked Danby. Became a strong supporter of exclusion. Sat in the Commons 1679 (2), 1681 and 1690. Member of James II's Privy Council 1688 and opposed the ministry in 1690. An active, unpredictable speaker.

Tomkins, Sir Thomas

1608?–74. Weobley, Herefordshire, 1661–74. Sat in 1640 but expelled in 1644 as a strong royalist. Heavily fined by parliament. Sat in 1660. Granted a pension 1660 and Knighted 1662 but by 1666 had become a violent critic of Clarendon. Little trace of activity after 1669. Strong anglican.

Trevor, Sir John

1626–72. Great Bedwyn, Wiltshire, 1663. *DNB*. Moderate parliamentarian during Civil War. Sat in 1646 but ejected 1648. Committee of Forests 1654 and sat in all protectorate parliaments. Member of Monck's Council of State and of the Convention. Supported toleration and opposed Clarendon. Bought Secretaryship from Morrice in 1668 and was knighted. Not a leading debater and not to be confused with his namesake who became Speaker under William III.

Vaughan, Francis, Lord Vaughan

1638–67. Carmarthenshire, 1661–7. Son of the Earl of Carberry. Only active moment seems to have been his attack on Clarendon 1667.

Vaughan, John, Lord Vaughan

1639–1713. Carmarthen Borough, 1661. Son of the Earl of Carberry. Governor of Jamaica 1675–8. Lord of the Admiralty 1693–4. No known activity in the Commons.

Vaughan, Sir John

1603–74. Cardiganshire, 1661. *DNB*. Lawyer with a Star Chamber practice before Civil War. Sat in Commons 1628 and 1640 but excluded as a royalist 1642. Defended Strafford but approved Triennial Act. Strong anglican. Imprisoned during Interregnum. Offered a seat on the bench by Clarendon but refused. Moderate opposition during '60s winning much respect from the Commons. Knighted and made Chief Justice of Common Pleas 1668. Delivered the well known judgement in Bushell's case 1670.

Waller, Edmund

1606–87. Hastings, Sussex, 1666. *DNB*. Sat in Parliament 1624 to 1685. Friend of royalists in 1630's and defended Strafford. Remained in London during Civil War, was arrested for plotting against Parliament and betrayed his associates. Fined, imprisoned and exiled. Returned to the Commons in 1651 and became a Commissioner for Trade 1655. Strong supporter of toleration for Dissenters and a frequent and effective speaker on numerous topics, showing moderation and good sense. Well received by the Commons. After opposing Clarendon came to be considered a courtier and opposed exclusion.

Walpole, Sir Edward

1621–68. Kings Lynn, Norfolk, 1661. Civil War record unknown but sat in Convention for Lyme Regis and was made Knight of the Bath 1661. Became Surveyor General to Henrietta Maria but opposed supply grant in 1664. Supported Clarendon, otherwise not very active. Grandfather of Sir Robert.

Wheeler, Sir Charles

1620?–83. Cambridge University, 1667. Colonel in royalist army. Gentleman of Privy Chamber 1660. Baronet 1666. Opposed Clarendon but supported the Cabal. Was Governor of the Leeward Islands 1671–2 and returned to speak for the court. Unpopular in the house; later drifted towards opposition and may have supported exclusion.

Whorwood, Brome

1615–84. Oxford, Oxfordshire, 1661. *DNB*. Active royalist in war; fined by Parliament. J.P. 1660 but passed over for office. Active in opposition as a follower of Buckingham in 1666–7. Spoke little after 1670 but is said to have supported exclusion. Involved in much litigation over his attempt to obtain a divorce.

Williams, (alias Cromwell) Henry

1625–73, Huntingdonshire, 1661–73. Father an active royalist and fined by Parliament. Son sat in protectorate parliaments but favoured Restoration. Spoke seldom but reckoned a supporter of the court.

Williams, Sir Trevor

1623–92. Monmouthshire, 1667. Royalist until 1643; then changed to support Parliament. Returned to royalist side 1648 and supported Restoration. Moderately active speaker, supporting the court but against toleration. Veered round in 1679 to support exclusion. Sat in all parliaments from 1660 to 1690 except that of 1685.

CLARENDON AND TOLERATION

IN 1662 Clarendon tried, unsuccessfully, to make the Act of Uniformity less strict. In 1665 however he urged the Commons to make the Five Mile Act severe. Within a few months of his fall a group known as 'the Clarendonians' took the lead in opposing toleration, and such members of this group as Henry Coventry and Finch remained strong for persecution until at least 1673. So far as the 1663 attempt at Indulgence is concerned Clarendon criticized the way in which it was made and quarrelled with Henry Bennet, who was one of its main supporters. On this, and on the more detailed evidence cited in the relevant chapters, I have credited Clarendon with deciding, by 1663, that no kind of toleration would be acceptable to the cavalier majority in the Commons.

Since I constructed this argument my attention has been drawn to two studies by Dr G. R. Abernathy in which he presents an important new piece of evidence.[1] This consists of a defence of toleration, written by Clarendon himself, and clearly dating from the spring of 1663.[2] From this, and other evidence, Dr Abernathy deduces that Clarendon was a supporter of Charles' proposal, and that friction between him and Bennet has been greatly exaggerated.

It is true that Clarendon's own account gives no support to Dr Abernathy, but this account is known to be unreliable, whilst continued tolerance by Clarendon might explain his defence by many presbyterians in 1667. Yet there remains the fact that with the single exception of Southampton Clarendon's friends were firm for persecution; his enemies were generally, though not universally, for toleration. In the absence of any evidence for Clarendon's attitude towards the Conventicle Act of 1664 I still think it probable that, perhaps because of the views expressed by the Commons in the 1663 session, Clarendon had become a 'Clarendonian' in religion before the end of 1663.

[1] G. R. Abernathy, 'Clarendon and the Declaration of Indulgence', *Journal of Ecclesiastical History*, xi (1960), pp. 55–73; 'The English Presbyterians and the Stuart Restoration', *Transactions of the American Philosophical Society*, new series, lv, part 2, 1965, pp. 84–93.

[2] B.M. (Sloane) Add. MSS. 4107, ff. 260–4.

INDEX

942.066
W81
C.1.